CASINO ACCOUNTING AND
FINANCIAL MANAGEMENT

Casino Accounting and Financial Management

E. Malcolm Greenlees

UNIVERSITY OF NEVADA PRESS
RENO AND LAS VEGAS

Library of Congress Cataloging-in-Publication Data

Greenlees, E. Malcolm, 1944–
    Casino accounting and financial management.

    Bibliography: p.
    Includes index.
    1. Casinos—Accounting.   2. Casinos—Finance.
I. Title.
HF5686.G23G74   1988   657'.84   87-25542
ISBN 0-87417-125-3

The paper used in this book meets the requirements of American
National Standard for Information Sciences—Permanence of
Paper for Printed Library Materials, ANSI Z39.48-1984. Binding
materials are chosen for strength and durability.

University of Nevada Press, Reno, Nevada 89557 USA
Copyright © E. Malcolm Greenlees 1988. All rights reserved
Printed in the United States of America
Book design by Dave Comstock

08 07 06

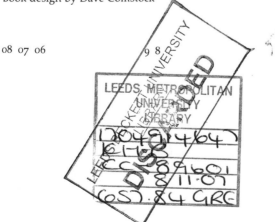

To my wife Sue, my family, and my many friends in the casino industry.

Without all of their help, this book would not have been possible.

Contents

Preface

This book is an attempt to bring a higher level of understanding of America's newest industry, casino gaming, to a broad segment of the American business public, including attorneys, accountants, and governmental officials.

Casino gaming is an emerging industry, which was limited to the state of Nevada until 1976. With the legalization of casino gaming in New Jersey, the visibility of the industry has expanded greatly. Many members of the business and investment community have become more interested in casinos and the different aspects of their operations. There is, however, a significant lack of information about the casino business and, most importantly, a lack of comprehensive reference materials dealing with the operations of the industry.

One factor that is indicative of the adolescent nature of the industry is that, while its accounting operations and controls have been in existence in various forms for over fifty years, they have not been compiled, analyzed, or presented in any coherent form until now.

The purpose of this book is to bring about a systematic examination of the vital features of casino accounting practice. A good presentation of casino accounting should not be merely a presentation of sterile accounting practices and procedures, but should also include a discussion of casino operations as they affect the accountability, controls, and financial presentation of the results of casino operation.

The material contained in this book outlines existing casino accounting practices. The practices described are generalized to some degree, and the description does not attempt to provide for every possible alternative accounting or control method. This attitude coincides with the regulatory attitude of the state of Nevada, where the nature of mandated controls provides only for basic minimum control procedures.

The text is organized into twelve chapters and presents accounting for casino operations in an organized sequence. Part I gives background information on casino gaming. Chapter 1 presents a history and overview of casino operations and their environment. Chapter 2 examines the licensing and regulation required for legalized casino operations. Chapter 3 discusses the taxation of casino operations, which constitutes the primary governmental interest in the operation of licensed casinos.

Part II presents casino accounting in detail. Chapter 4 is an overall discussion of casino accounting concepts and organization. Chapter 5 deals with slot machine accounting; chapter 6, with games accounting; and chapter 7, with keno, bingo, and other casino games. Chapter 8 examines the role of central cashiering. Chapter 9 discusses credit accounting and control.

Part III is a discussion of public accounting for casinos. Chapter 10 treats in considerable detail the topics of casino auditing, financial reporting, and internal controls. Chapter 11 examines the principal issues of federal income taxation of casino operations. Chapter 12 discusses various cost and managerial accounting applications in a casino operation.

Acknowledgments

Many individuals have contributed to this book. It would be impossible to acknowledge their contributions individually. They are the multitude of managers, accountants, and casino employees whose daily work is what has been documented within these chapters. Without their sharing of talent and experience, I would never have been able to compile the material for this book.

A special thanks is due to my former employer, the CPA firm of Kafoury, Armstrong & Co. in Reno, Nevada, for enthusiastic support and assistance in the project. Special thanks are due to Don McGhie and Clyde Turner for sparking my interest in this most fascinating accounting topic.

I also wish to acknowledge the many contributions of sample forms, documents and assistance with preparation of procedures from persons in the casino industry. These include Lowell Chichester, Tim Cope, and Earl Howsely. Stu Curtis at the Economic Research Division of the Nevada Gaming Control Board has helped immeasurably in providing statistics and industry information.

Thanks also goes to Bonnie Briscoe for her help in proofing and editing the manuscript. Special thanks goes to my daughter Janey for her exceptional help in proofreading and editing in the face of tight deadlines and a demanding author.

♠ ♡ ♣ ◇ I

Background and Environment of Casino Gaming

♠ ♡ ♣ ◇ CHAPTER 1

Casino History and Operating Environment

Introduction

In order to understand the details of casino accounting, it is helpful to appreciate the overall environment in which the accounting takes place. It is also beneficial to realize historical development and structure of the casino industry, as well as the typical organization and operation of an individual casino.

The History of Gambling

In examining the history of casino gaming, one must first secure an understanding of gambling of all types.[1] Gambling is as old as human culture. Ancient Egyptian artifacts have indicated gambling as a sport or pastime as early as 2000 B.C. Gambling was practiced in India and Greece long before the birth of Christ. American Indians had been enthusiastic gamblers for centuries before the discovery of the New World.[2]

Gambling of various forms was widespread in western European civilizations, and card games were extremely popular in Europe during the thirteenth century. Around 1360, the French contributed the style of cards that has become the world standard.[3]

The modern word *gambling* has its roots in the Anglo-Saxon word *gamnian*, which means to sport or play. The term *gaming* is both a corruption of the word *gambling* and a deliberate attempt to differentiate legalized casino gambling from its illegal predecessors. The word *gaming* also focuses on the air of sport and minimizes the negative emotional aspects of excessive risk sometimes associated with gambling.[4]

Attitudes Toward Gambling

The history of gambling is the history of public acceptance of various games of chance. Gambling has been allowed, encouraged, and banned. The first recorded banning of card games was in 1387, when John I, the king of Castile, prohibited card playing because of heavy financial losses by members of his court.[5]

Europe and America have had alternate periods of encouragement and repression of various forms of gambling. In the United States, there were frequent lotteries when the new country was struggling for survival and the need for government funds was acute. As a rule, economic pressure for increased government revenues has often brought greater tolerance for gambling, as illustrated by the practices in many states, both in the past and at present.[6]

The Gaming Industry

In about one-half of the states, pari-mutuel wagering on horse racing is legal. In addition, since 1963, twenty-eight states have adopted a state lottery. In 1971, off-track betting was legalized in New York. The most recent addition to legalized casino gambling is the state of New Jersey, which in 1976 allowed gambling in Atlantic City. Proposals are currently under consideration to allow legal casino gambling in New York, Pennsylvania, Massachusetts, Florida, Louisiana, and Michigan, with state lotteries being actively considered in many other states.

Gambling today is a business, a very big business. The final report of the President's Commission on the Review of the National Policy toward Gambling conducted in 1974–1976, entitled *Gambling in America*,[7] estimated that $17.7 billion was wagered legally every year, and some 14 million people gambled annually in casinos alone. The survey also found that two-thirds of Americans indulged in some form of gambling, and 80% approved of legalized gambling. Clearly, gaming is an integral part of American society today, almost as much as it was 100 years ago.

There are numerous international locations for casino gaming as well. Casino gambling is legal in thirty-eight countries around the world. It is also interesting to note that national lotteries and pari-mutuel wagering are far more popular than casinos.[8]

Casinos are only one aspect of the gambling industry. The most widespread type of gambling activity is pari-mutuel betting on horse racing. Other forms of pari-mutuel betting are also important, most commonly involving sporting events such as soccer, football, or jai alai. Games such as bingo have achieved widespread popularity in the United States, Canada, and England. In Australia and on some foreign U.S. military bases, slot machines are very popular and generate significant revenues.

Recognizing the importance of other forms of gambling will enable the reader to appreciate that casino gambling is just one form of a multitude of legal gambling activities. Casino gambling, in terms of overall revenue generation, often lags far behind pari-mutuel betting. For many years, the revenues in California from pari-mutuel horse race betting have exceeded the revenues in Nevada from all casino gaming by a factor of 2 to 1.[9]

The History of Casino Gaming in the United States

The first casinos in the United States were undoubtedly the early taverns of New England, where card games and other activities were accepted as a regular part of the social fabric of the day. Following the Civil War, the southern states instituted state lotteries to assist in rebuilding depleted state treasuries.[10] At this same time, gambling developed on the frontier, where it was tied less to governmental revenues and more to recreation. As thousands of people poured westward, many early boomtowns had only two industries, saloons and casinos.[11] The more flamboyant aspects of the American gambling scene developed on steamboats, which slowly plied the Mississippi and other midwestern and southern rivers for transportation and communication. Louisiana became the center of all gaming activity in the United States and underwent various periods of legalization and prohibition, depending on the mood of local politics.[12]

This scenario was repeated on a similar basis in most developing population centers of the country. As the United States grew, frontier laissez-faire attitudes eventually gave way to the acceptance of widespread actions to eliminate public gambling. During the latter part of the century, this drove the remaining professional gamblers even further west with the new settlers. The west had fostered many places originally designed for the rough-and-ready entertainment that gambling provided. These institutions survived the modernization of the frontier, and various forms of legal gambling were widespread in New Mexico, Arizona, Colorado, Minnesota, Idaho, Montana, and Nevada.

Although neither formally legalized nor declared illegal, gambling continued to be common in the mountain and western states until the early 1900s. Eventually, increasingly widespread objection to gambling developed throughout the west following the periods of initial settlement and development. In Nevada, the first law to ban gambling was passed in 1910.[13] This law, rather than shutting down the gambling business, merely forced it underground for a period of time. As the years passed, these back-room establishments became more and more visible.

The modern era of casino gambling (gaming, as it is known today) began in 1931, when the bill to legalize gaming in Nevada was passed by the State Legislature. This bill was based on a dual wish to legalize an activity that was already widespread (thereby eliminating the undesirable aspects of political corruption) and to create additional revenue for the state and counties during the Depression.[14]

The conduct of gaming in Nevada was not significantly changed by the mere legalization of the activity. In fact, it was decried in many circles as an experiment doomed to failure. The years from 1931 to 1937 were marked by a period of inconspicuous operation for most of the casinos, with the emphasis continuing to be on the local trade. Two significant changes occurred in 1935 and 1937. In 1935, Pappy Smith and his son, Harold Smith, Sr., opened Harolds Club in Reno, with a $500 investment.[15] In 1937, Bill Harrah opened his first Bingo Club.[16]

These two owners built casino operations that attracted a larger clientele, primarily from outside Nevada. Prior to World War II, each casino exhibited only modest growth, but the period during the war and immediately following led to enormous success for both operations and substantial enlargement of their casinos. There were also significant developments of additional casino operations in the northern Nevada area. From 1935 to 1946, the center of the Nevada gaming industry was clearly located in Reno.

A second major event that was quietly occurring in southern Nevada was the construction of the El Rancho Las Vegas in 1941. This was the first major casino in southern Nevada. By the later 1940s, three additional hotels were completed: the Last Frontier, the Flamingo, and the El Cortez. The El Cortez was located in downtown Las Vegas. With the huge financial success of these new hotels, additional enterprises were attracted, which created a building boom in Las Vegas that continued unabated until the late 1970s.[17]

As the number of hotel-casinos grew throughout the state, so did the revenues and the extent of their operations. Casino gambling had become a big business. The development of the casino industry in Nevada was an evolutionary one. The process was slow and took place throughout the state, from the massive structures of the MGM Grand (now Bally's Grand) in Las Vegas and the scenic beauty of Harrah's at Lake Tahoe, to the frontier ambience of the El Capitan in Hawthorne and the Stockman's Hotel in Elko. Along with the development of the large variety of casinos in differing locations, a very substantial support or secondary service industry was created to meet the needs of the casinos.

The modern casino industry in Nevada is a business that has an impact on every aspect of life there. It is the principal employer group in the state, and various economic studies have estimated that between 50 and 65% of the work force in Nevada either directly or indirectly depends upon this industry for a livelihood.[18] The industry in Nevada is characterized by a variety of sizes of operations, ranging from small slot machine locations to the massive football field–sized casinos of Reno and Las Vegas. In addition, the industry is dispersed throughout the entire state.

Until 1976, Nevada was the only state with legalized casino gaming. In that year, however, New Jersey began to allow this type of activity.[19] The development of the casino gaming industry in New Jersey was initiated in 1976 with the passage of a referendum allowing legalized casino gambling in Atlantic City and was accomplished virtually overnight. The nature of the casino industry in Atlantic City is radically different from that in Nevada.

The casino industry in New Jersey consists of a highly homogeneous group of large casinos, all similar in methods of operation. Even the types of games allowed are specified. The industry is also highly geographically concentrated in Atlantic City.[20] The differences between the Nevada and New Jersey gaming industries are also reflected in substantial differences in the nature of mandatory accounting procedures, internal controls, and regulatory attitudes toward the casino operations.[21]

Financial Aspects of Casino Operation

The casino industry itself can be characterized by its financial success. In the thirty-nine years from 1946 to 1985, there was a history of steady growth in the casino revenues in the state of Nevada. In 1946, the first year that Nevada levied a gaming tax, the total gaming revenues were $24.5 million.[22] Today, that figure has exceeded $3 billion.[23] During this period, Nevada gaming has experienced an overall average annual growth rate in excess of 15% per year. In addition, casino revenues appear to be very resistant to changes and downturns in the national economic trends. There has not been a year when gaming revenues in Nevada have not increased over prior years. These gaming revenues have been characterized as being generally recession proof or at least recession resistant.[24]

However, as with all generalizations, there are exceptions. It was not until the late 1970s and early 1980s that the first forced financial closures of casinos took place. It appeared that a radical overexpansion of casinos in Nevada, competition from New Jersey, and a substantial national economic recession all conspired to cause these first celebrated changes in the casino industry.

The advent of the New Jersey branch of casino gaming has focused attention on the tremendous casino market potential of the eastern United States.[25] Operating results have confirmed that initial potential. For example, in 1977, with only one casino operating during the first year of legalized gaming, that one location (Resorts International) generated a gross revenue of $228 million. This was more than the gross revenue for the same period for the two locations of Harrah's Hotels and Casinos in Reno and Lake Tahoe— and Harrah's had a successful operating history spanning thirty years![26] With only three locations operating in 1980, the casino industry in New Jersey took in approximately $560 million dollars. These three locations did about 25% of the total business for the state of Nevada—which at the time had approximately 1,200 licensed gaming locations. New Jersey's first $2-billion-dollar year occurred in 1985, and with the total Nevada gaming revenue running about $3 billion per year, the New Jersey market is clearly a significant element in the national casino business.[27]

One factor that is of considerable importance to the development of future casino gaming in New Jersey is the attitude of the state policymakers regarding the continued expansion of the casino industry. Government officials have indicated that there is to be a switch from "quick to quality," away from the emphasis on casino building during the hectic early days. This was a clear signal to the casino industry in New Jersey that the total number of casino locations was not going to be allowed to proliferate without limit. Currently, the official position is that the state will allow approximately ten to fifteen first-class hotel-casino locations in Atlantic City and will discourage further development in order not to saturate the market.[28]

Given this spectacular growth performance in Atlantic City, along with national trends toward increasing social acceptability and legalization of gaming, many analysts expect that casino gaming will become a major growth industry of the country through the 1980s.[29] This prospect for growth is dependent upon the achievement of widespread legalization of casinos, which in turn depends on the social acceptance of the legitimacy of casino gaming.

Characteristics of the Nevada Gaming Industry

Nevada gaming, as previously described, is extremely diverse, ranging from the very smallest locations with one or two table games and a limited number of slot machines to the football field–sized casinos containing hundreds of games and thousands of slot machines. In Nevada, there are approximately 1,200 gaming licenses. Of this number, 145 of the licensees accounted for over 95% of the gross gaming revenue. Of these 145 casinos, the largest 60 casinos accounted for 78.9% of the total gross gaming revenue.[30] Clearly, size is an important differentiating characteristic for casinos in Nevada. Larger casinos tend to be more financially stable, with better profitability, and have more resistance to economic downturns than smaller casinos. One factor given as a reason for this resistance to downturn in the larger casinos is their ability to provide a full array of services to their patrons and therefore to remain more attractive to gaming customers over a period of time.

Corporate Ownership

Another factor that has emerged in the Nevada gaming industry has been the growth of the hotel-casino operations owned and operated by corporations. These corporations are usually publicly owned, and their shares are traded on various stock exchanges. These thirteen corporations and their twenty-five operating units are indicated in table 1-1. Prior to 1969, public corporations were effectively prohibited from entering the casino industry because of the strict licensing standards that required all owners (that is, all stockholders of the corporation) to be individually licensed. Changes in Nevada state laws in 1965, which are discussed in detail in chapter 2, modified and limited the licensing requirements for stockholders and corporate management. Since the start of publicly traded corporate gaming, its impact has grown

Table 1-1. Publicly Owned Casino Operations.

BALLY GRAND RESORTS, INC.
Bally's Grand–Las Vegas
Bally's Grand–Reno

CAESARS WORLD
Caesars Palace
Caesars Tahoe

CIRCUS CIRCUS ENTERPRISES, INC.
Circus Circus Hotel and Casino
Circus Circus Hotel and Casino–Reno
Edgewater Hotel and Casino
Silver City Casino
Slots-A-Fun

DUNES HOTELS AND CASINOS, INC.
Dunes

ELSINORE
Four Queens
Hyatt Lake Tahoe

GOLDEN NUGGET, INC.
Golden Nugget

HILTON HOTELS CORPORATION
Flamingo Hilton
Las Vegas Hilton
Reno Hilton

HOLIDAY INNS, INC.
Harrah's Club–Reno
Harrah's Club–Tahoe
Holiday Casino

RAMADA INNS, INC.
Tropicana Hotel and Country Club

SAHARA RESORTS
Hacienda Resort Hotel and Casino
Sahara Las Vegas Hotel and Casino

SCOTT CORPORATION
Union Plaza

SHOWBOAT, INC.
Showboat

DEL E. WEBB CORPORATION
Del Webb's High Sierra

significantly. In 1984, according to the *Nevada Gaming Abstract*, these twenty-six publicly owned casinos generated 50.8% of the state's gaming revenues, had 65% of the operating income, and employed over 50% of all persons in the gaming industry. These statistics support the role of the public corporation as being particularly significant in the Nevada casino industry.[31]

Geographic Location

In Nevada, the casino industry is divided into seven main geographic locations described in the *Nevada Gaming Abstract*. Each of these separate geographic areas has a different operating style, revenue pattern, and profitability results. The principal geographic locations are the Las Vegas Strip, Downtown Las Vegas, Laughlin, Reno-Sparks in Washoe County, Douglas County (South Lake Tahoe), Elko County, Wendover, Boulder Strip, and the balance of the state.

The largest casinos are clustered on the Las Vegas Strip. The Downtown Las Vegas operations are very different from the Strip operations, and the southern Nevada operations are different from the northern Nevada locations of Reno and Lake Tahoe. Lake Tahoe is operated in a style characterized as midway between the lavishness of the Las Vegas Strip and the simplicity or even austerity of the Reno-Sparks area. Wendover and Laughlin, although at different ends of the state, are unique in that they are remote, isolated, and located at ports of entry into Nevada. They are generally more cosmopolitan than the balance of the state, which represents many of the small towns scattered throughout Nevada.

Game Mix

Another way to characterize the differences in casino operations beyond their mere geographic location is to look at the game mix in casinos in each area. Game mix generally refers to the ratio of slot machines to table games and the ratio of various games, such as 21 games to crap games. These ratios are surrogates for the analysis of the type of customers who frequent each geographic area. Table 1-2 indicates the game mix in each of the geographic locations. These figures are based on averages for the entire area. If individual locations are analyzed, the game mix for most of the casinos in a certain geographic area follows that area average very closely. In several instances, initial proposals for new casinos may have suggested different game mixes than standard for the area,

Table 1-2. Game Mix by Geographic Location.

1979:

Location	SLOT TO GAMES			21 TO CRAP		
	Slots	Games	Mix	21	Crap	Mix
Las Vegas Strip	16,860	1,069	15.8	795	139	5.7
Downtown Las Vegas	10,557	500	21.1	388	60	6.5
South Lake Tahoe	7,374	442	16.7	362	39	9.3
Reno-Sparks	17,722	875	20.3	708	89	8.0
Elko County	1,348	87	15.5	75	9	8.3
Balance of State	7,067	349	20.2	269	30	9.0

1984:

Location	SLOT TO GAMES			21 TO CRAP		
	Slots	Games	Mix	21	Crap	Mix
Las Vegas Strip	23,154	1,378	16.8	1,041	151	6.9
Downtown Las Vegas	12,661	500	25.3	378	62	6.1
South Lake Tahoe	6,817	453	15.0	371	35	10.6
Reno-Sparks	18,627	783	23.8	644	73	8.8
Elko County	2,515	167	15.1	148	13	11.4
Balance of State	10,157	426	23.8	353	39	9.1
Laughlin	1,555	96	16.2	76	9	8.4

1985:

Location	SLOT TO GAMES			21 TO CRAP		
	Slots	Games	Mix	21	Crap	Mix
Las Vegas Strip	22,132	1,150	19.2	938	131	7.2
Downtown Las Vegas	11,388	424	26.9	338	59	5.7
South Lake Tahoe	6,683	416	16.1	362	32	11.3
Reno-Sparks	19,409	746	26.0	642	63	10.2
Elko County	2,087	171	12.2	147	15	9.8
Balance of State	n/r	n/r		n/r	n/r	
Laughlin	2,571	87	29.6	76	7	10.9

n/r: not reported in 1985.

but when they were eventually opened and in operation, the game mixes were quickly adjusted to reflect the game mix appropriate for the market they were operating in. This was the case for the MGM–Reno (now Bally's Grand–Reno), which when first proposed had a game mix appropriate for the Las Vegas Strip. However, the management found out very quickly that the number of table games had to be reduced and the number of slot machines expanded to approximate more closely the game mix for the Reno-Sparks market.

Game mix is presented in two ways. The first is the ratio of slot machines to total number of table games. The second is the ratio of 21 tables to crap tables. The differences in these game mixes are apparent in table 1-3. The Las Vegas Strip and Downtown Las Vegas are differentiated largely on the basis of their slot to game mix. In the Downtown area, there are more slots to each table game. This difference indicates that Lake Tahoe was similar to Downtown Las Vegas with regard to its slot to game mix in 1979. By 1983, the South Lake Tahoe area had changed its profile to appeal to a premium player,[32] and had a game mix more typical of a Las Vegas Strip operation. The Reno-Sparks area is different from the South Lake Tahoe market, indicating that as slot machines become more popular, the slot to game mix ratio increases. The balance of the state ratio indicates the importance of slot machines for entertainment of the local population. This same pattern is found in the tourist-oriented slot machine trade typical of Reno and Downtown Las Vegas.

The table further shows the second differentiating factor, the ratio of 21 games to crap games. A definite pattern emerges, with

Table 1-3. Game Mix by Casino Revenue.

1979:

Revenue Range	SLOT TO GAMES			21 TO CRAP		
	Slots	Games	Mix	21	Crap	Mix
$2 M–$5 M	2,633	142	18.5	116	14	8.3
$5 M–$20 M	9,441	506	18.7	399	51	7.8
Over $20 M	24,655	1,607	15.3	1,241	191	6.5
Public Traded	20,157	1,382	14.6	1,074	153	7.0

1984:

Revenue Range	SLOT TO GAMES			21 TO CRAP		
	Slots	Games	Mix	21	Crap	Mix
$2 M–$5 M	3,786	206	18.4	164	22	7.5
$5 M–$20 M	9,889	462	21.4	388	40	9.7
Over $20 M	35,198	2,124	16.6	1,639	228	7.2
Public Traded	20,826	1,346	15.5	1,025	149	6.9

1985:

Revenue Range	SLOT TO GAMES			21 TO CRAP		
	Slots	Games	Mix	21	Crap	Mix
$2 M–$5 M	n/r	n/r		n/r	n/r	
$5 M–$20 M	4,746	197	24.1	164	18	9.1
Over $20 M	34,391	1,843	18.7	1,532	197	7.8
Public Traded	27,072	1,526	17.7	1,268	161	7.8

n/r: not reported in 1985.

the Las Vegas area having the highest number of crap tables and the highest ratio, indicating the popularity of craps in that area. The ratios slowly diminish as the number of 21 games is expanded in other areas of the state relative to a fairly stable number of crap games in other locations.

The variance in the ratios is significant enough to indicate that there are indeed several different markets in Nevada, with each geographic location having its own unique game mix and slot to game mix. As these game mixes are examined over time, several observations can be made. The first is that game mixes change as the overall marketing strategy of the casino or location changes. This is reflected in the increasing emphasis of the Las Vegas Strip on slot machine business, a change that has taken place over the past three–four years. This change downplays the importance of the high roller or premium business that traditionally emphasized table games over slot machines. Also, an increasing sophistication of the Lake Tahoe market has led to more 21 game tables, with accompanying changes in the game to slot ratios for this area. Elko County has been fairly stable, while both Downtown Las Vegas and the Reno-Sparks area have reemphasized the number of slots, and thus the ratio has increased.

There are significant differences in the slot to game mix ratio according to the revenue range or size of the casino. In 1979, there appeared to be little difference in the mix ratio between the casinos of the $2–$5 million and $5–$20 million revenue range. By 1983, there appeared to be some differences in the game mix between casinos in these two ranges. However, there is significant variation in the slot to game mix for the very largest casinos (including the publicly owned casinos) when compared to the smaller casinos in both 1979 and 1983. The same pattern exists when the ratio of 21 to crap games is compared among the various size categories. Generally, the larger casinos tend to have more crap tables, both absolutely and when compared to the number of 21 tables.

Revenue Sources

Another method of distinguishing casino operations is based on the revenue sources of the casino. Tables 1-4 and 1-5 indicate the revenue sources as percentages of gaming revenue for different revenue ranges and for different locations. The percentage of revenue that is derived from table games when compared to slot ma-

Table 1-4. Gaming Revenue by Casino Revenue Range (percent of total).

1979:

Revenue Range	Games	Slots	Other	Total
$2 M–$5 M	37.9	52.2	9.9	100
$5 M–$20 M	43.5	46.9	9.6	100
Over $20 M	61.5	31.6	6.9	100
Public Traded	60.1	32.5	7.4	100

1984:

Revenue Range	Games	Slots	Other	Total
$2 M–$5 M	33.0	58.2	8.8	100
$5 M–$20 M	31.8	58.3	9.9	100
Over $20 M	49.9	42.5	7.6	100
Public Traded	53.8	39.4	6.8	100

1985:

Revenue Range	Games	Slots	Other	Total
$2 M–$5 M	n/r	n/r	n/r	n/r
$5 M–$20 M	31.2	60.4	8.4	100
Over $20 M	41.2	45.4	13.4	100
Public Traded	42.0	43.8	14.2	100

n/r: not reported in 1985.

chines tends to vary considerably with the size of the casino and the location. In general, as the size of the casino increases, the percentage of revenue derived from table games also increases. From a geographic perspective, the Las Vegas Strip has a very high percentage of total revenue from games, with a division of approximately 55% games to 40% slots. Lake Tahoe shows a 30% games, 60% slots revenue division, while the lowest games revenue contribution is in the Laughlin area, where only 22% of the revenue comes from games, and 72% comes from slots. Elko County and the balance of the state markets are very similar, with 32% and 24% for games and 62% and 65% for slot machines, respectively. The Reno-Sparks area derives 47% of its revenue from games and 44% from slot machines.

These numeric classifications yield several clear indications that there are important structural differences in the gaming markets throughout Nevada and that these differences are very pronounced with respect to the geographic location and the size of the casino operation.

Table 1-5. Gaming Revenue by Location (percentage of total).

1979:

Location	Games	Slots	Other	Total
Las Vegas Strip	64.5	29.9	5.6	100
Downtown Las Vegas	37.4	52.2	10.4	100
South Lake Tahoe	49.6	41.7	8.7	100
Reno-Sparks	38.5	49.7	11.8	100
Elko County	37.7	56.9	5.4	100
Balance of State	33.0	56.3	10.7	100

1984:

Location	Games	Slots	Other	Total
Las Vegas Strip	53.8	40.0	6.2	100
Downtown Las Vegas	31.8	57.6	10.6	100
South Lake Tahoe	29.0	60.1	10.9	100
Reno-Sparks	47.9	44.3	7.8	100
Elko County	32.2	62.2	5.6	100
Balance of State	24.8	64.8	10.4	100
Laughlin	22.0	72.6	5.4	100

1985:

Location	Games	Slots	Other	Total
Las Vegas Strip	44.0	42.1	13.9	100
Downtown Las Vegas	33.9	53.8	12.3	100
South Lake Tahoe	39.2	47.9	12.9	100
Reno-Sparks	27.1	61.5	11.4	100
Elko County	29.5	63.4	7.1	100
Balance of State	n/r	n/r	n/r	100
Laughlin	18.2	75.2	6.6	100

n/r: not reported in 1985.

Characteristics of the New Jersey Gaming Industry

The casino industry in New Jersey is a very homogeneous group of twelve extremely large hotel-casinos, similar in size and in methods of operation. The industry is also highly geographically concentrated in Atlantic City. The casinos currently operating in New Jersey and their characteristics are indicated in table 1-6. All of the casinos are operated by publicly owned corporations. These New Jersey locations are virtually identical in nature, with specific minimums in casino size and number of rooms mandated by the New Jersey regulatory authorities. The casino industry is highly localized, with ten of the twelve operating locations being on the ocean front boardwalk; only Trump's operations are located in the Marina district. The geographic distribution amounts to less than two miles between the furthest casinos on the boardwalk and less than five miles overall.[33] Because the New Jersey casinos operate in such close geographic proximity, there is little difference attributable to the location or type of customer, such as exists in the Nevada casino market.

Financial Structure and Ownership of a Casino

On a national basis, the ownership of a casino is numerically most popular under the proprietorship or partnership form of organization. However, when the dollar magnitude of the casino operations is considered, the largest proportion of the total gaming revenue is generated by the publicly owned corporate casino operations. There is a close relation between the size of the casino and the form of ownership. In addition, it is generally felt that there is also a high correlation between the size of the casino and its rates of profitability. Table 1-7 indicates the profitability of Nevada casinos by revenue size and location for 1984.

Impact of Corporate Ownership

The impact of corporate ownership on the casino industry has been particularly significant in Nevada. First, the corporate operations tend to be larger, are consistently more profitable, and have succeeded in projecting an image of corporate respectability that has benefited all casino operations. The addition of corporate

Table 1-6. New Jersey Casino Operations.

Property	Table Games	Slot Machines
Resorts International	121	1,663
Caesars Atlantic City	114	1,600
Bally's Park Place	118	1,596
Sands	99	1,420
Harrah's Marina	121	1,710
Golden Nugget	93	1,288
Elsinore Atlantis	107	1,395
Claridge	84	1,283
Tropicana	117	1,545
Trump Plaza	118	1,665
Trump's Castle	117	1,675
Showboat	114	1,628
Total	1,323	18,408

Table 1-7. Casino Profitability by Size and Location
(Nevada 1979, 1984, 1985).

	SIZE OF CASINO					
	Net Operating Income (%)			Number of Locations		
Revenue Range	1979	1984	1985	1979	1984	1985
$2 M–$5 M	1.1	−4.5	n/r	5	9	n/r
$5 M–$20 M	1.0	2.5	2.0	18	21	8
Over $20 M	14.1	7.7	10.2	27	39	33
Public Traded	14.5	8.0	11.1	21	28	26

	LOCATION OF CASINO					
	Net Operating Income (%)			Number of Locations		
Location	1979	1984	1985	1979	1984	1985
Las Vegas Strip	14.7	8.3	11.4	34	38	38
Downtown Las Vegas	19.4	2.9	4.7	21	22	21
Lake Tahoe	0.2	0.0	3.5	7	7	6
Reno-Sparks	7.7	8.1	6.0	34	30	29
Elko County	17.2	3.6	3.1	7	11	11
Balance of State	9.4	8.0	7.4	22	32	28
Laughlin	n/r	18.7	18.8	n/r	5	5
Statewide	n/r	7.0	8.6	n/r	145	145

n/r: not reported in *Gaming Abstract*.

gaming in New Jersey has also resulted in bringing the casino gaming industry to the attention of the major financial centers. This in turn has resulted in two significant actions. The first is widespread acceptance of the casino securities in the public market with improved access to the stock market as a source of financing for casino development.[34] Second, the process of informing major institutional investors regarding the profitability, operations, and controls existing in the casinos has resulted in the recognition of the legitimacy of the industry. This has in turn resulted in institutional mortgage and other long-term financing sources becoming available.

The impact of corporate operations in the gaming area has also resulted in several important changes in the nature of accounting, auditing, and financial report services rendered by accountants and others to the casino industry. These changes range from increased corporate accountability to the involvement of accounting firms in the design and implementation of internal control systems. There are also expanded needs for financial reporting and disclosure for public investors under the requirements of the Securities and Exchange Commission.

Casino Financing

A brief overview of the current structure and the trends in casino financing will assist the reader in understanding the financial environment within which casinos operate.[35]

The history of casino financing in Nevada was closely tied to the public perceptions of legality and organized crime involvement in the casino industry. The early investment capital for most of the casinos in Nevada was provided by families, individuals, or small groups of investors. These investors included people in Reno such as the Smith family and Bill Harrah. In the case of southern Nevada, individuals who had earned their fortunes in unusual or unconventional methods (such as illegal gambling or bootlegging) supplied the initial venture capital. The early casino financing was entirely risk capital. Funds were difficult to obtain, and the lack of substantial sums made the rapid expansion of the gaming facilities very difficult, if not impossible.[36]

During the 1950s, the negative image of Nevada gaming, particularly in southern Nevada, discouraged investors and traditional lenders.[37] However, the high profitability of the casino operations did not escape the notice of knowledgeable financiers. One such person was Jimmy Hoffa. Hoffa had a strong interest in the casino business and moved slowly and consistently to promote long-term loans to Nevada casinos from the Teamsters pension funds. During the period from 1962 to 1977, the Teamsters Central and South West Pension Fund investment in casinos grew from $5.5 million to $240 million. This represented a growth from 3% of the total investment portfolio in 1962 to 24% of the portfolio in 1977.

During this time, several Nevada-based banks were expanding their involvement in the financing of the casino industry. Valley Bank of Nevada played a prominent role in the financial development of the Las Vegas Strip under the direction of its chairman, Perry Thomas.[38] However, lending by Nevada banks was constrained by the Controller of the Currency regulations, which prohibit loans in excess of 10% of the capital of the bank to any one business. Thus, the loan demand by Nevada casinos for expansion capital could not be fully met by the relatively small Nevada banks. Several innovative mechanisms were therefore used, with consortiums of banks from many states being established to lend to the casinos with the Nevada banks taking the lead role in these offerings.

Another significant development in the field of casino financing came in the early 1970s with the widespread adoption of equipment leasing (particularly slot machine leasing) as a method of capital acquisition for the casinos. This segment of casino financing continues to be strong even today, with substantial amounts of leasing being done through both third-party and manufacturer-related leasing companies.

Early public stock sales by corporations that owned and operated casino facilities met with only moderate success. Harrah's Hotels and Casinos made one of the first casino public stock offerings in 1973, but the industry lacked the stature and widespread reputation for profitability necessary to create a very active and favorable stock market reception.[39]

Three significant financing events have taken place that may hold some promise for the future. The first was the issuance of first mortgage bonds by Golden Nugget, Inc., the parent corporation of the Golden Nugget Casino in Las Vegas and Atlantic City. Although offered at the price of 9%, unheard of at the time, the bonds were well accepted by the market and, in light of the market interest rates over the past few years, turned out to be a very inexpensive source of expansion capital for that casino.

The second event was the financing of a major casino operation by more traditional institutional investors. The first of these was the investment by the state of Nevada through its Public Employees Retirement System in the long-term mortgage of the Riviera Hotel and Casino in Las Vegas. Another financing arrangement was concluded between Aetna Life and Casualty and Caesars Palace for a long-term mortgage commitment on its Las Vegas property in the amount of $40 million. This marked the first time that a life insurance company made an investment in a Nevada casino gaming property. Operating problems at the Riviera, as well as New Jersey licensing difficulties at Caesars, have created an aura of uncertainty about these investments, and the initial optimism regarding the use of institutional financing for other casino projects in Nevada has become somewhat subdued since that time.

The third significant financing event was the increasingly widespread use of equity financing through publicly traded stock issues as a source of financing for casinos. This mechanism was

utilized extensively for the development of Atlantic City proper-
ties. After a period of broad enthusiasm for casino industry stocks
in the market following the legalization of casino gaming in Atlantic City, a recent trend toward conservatism has been evident and
few new issues of casino stocks have been made. Recent smaller
public offerings of casino stocks have actually been rejected by the
market.

Casino Organization Structure

Casino operations are often characterized by a very substantial physical plant, which provides anywhere from 500 to 3,000
hotel rooms as well as a broad variety of support facilities. Despite
the appearance, however, the principal source of revenue in the
hotel-casino is the gaming revenue, which constitutes about 60%
of the total revenue. The rooms, food and beverage, and other
areas are relatively minor. Table 1-8 indicates the percentage distribution of revenues among the principal activities of the hotel-
casinos in Nevada for 1984 and 1985.

In general, all the facilities of the hotel exist to serve the casino patron, either directly or indirectly. It is vitally important that
all of the hotel-casino facilities be established in such a manner as
to balance and complement the overall casino operation. When the
organization charts are examined, the importance of the role of the
casino executives in the overall operation is clearly indicated.

Figure 1-1 indicates a typical organization chart used in a casino in Nevada. Figure 1-2 indicates the organization chart used
for a casino operating in New Jersey. The most important observation in the Nevada organization chart is the relatively important
positions that the casino executives occupy in relation to the overall
organization. Recently there has been a trend away from the almost absolute power position of the casino executives as more tra-

Table 1-8. Distribution of Casino Revenues, Statewide Hotel Casinos.

Department	1979	REVENUE PERCENTAGE 1984	1985
Casino	58.2	62.0	61.5
Rooms	12.5	11.9	12.5
Food	14.1	12.2	12.2
Beverage	9.5	7.6	7.3
Other	5.7	6.3	6.5
Total	100.0	100.0	100.0

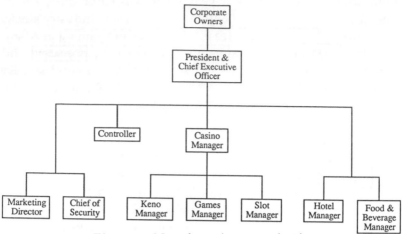

Fig. 1-1. Nevada casino organization.

ditional corporate organizations are developed. Still, casino personnel who are responsible for the lion's share of the revenue have a substantial amount of informal power in the organization.

Another important observation is the relatively senior position that accounting, financial, and control personnel have in the organizations. There is a widespread acknowledgment that the maintenance of a high degree of internal control over all aspects of

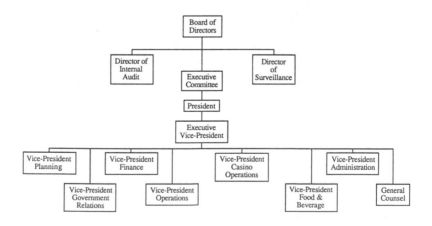

Fig. 1-2. New Jersey casino organization.

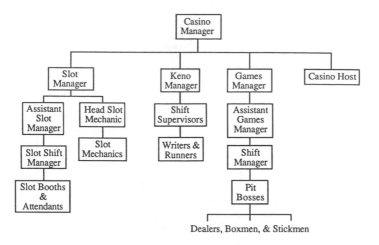

Fig. 1-3. Casino manager responsibilities.

the hotel and casino operations is mandatory if the casino is to continue to be licensed, as well as to operate in an effective and efficient manner.

When the organization chart for the New Jersey casino is examined, the importance of the control functions (as specifically legislated by the state) and the role of regulatory compliance (which typically is a major part of the accounting and finance functions) are evident: these responsibilities are assigned to positions with senior vice-president status. Typically, the financial and control functions in a Nevada casino are considered less important.

When the casino organization is examined in detail, two additional issues come to light. The first is that although the casino manager has extensive responsibility for all aspects of casino operations, as well as the supervision of the various shift personnel, the manager does not control or supervise any of the revenue accounting in the casino. An important separation of duties is the supervision of the casino cage and vault operation by the controller or financial personnel. This division of responsibilities is indicated in figure 1-3, which shows those areas that report to the casino manager, and figure 1-4, which shows the areas that report to the controller. This supervision by the controller also includes direct responsibility for both the operational supervision of the casino and supervision of the recording of the financial transactions originating in the casino.

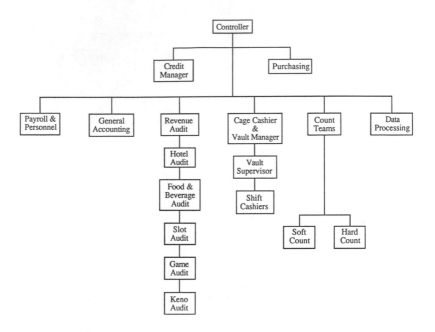

Fig. 1-4. Controller responsibilities.

Conclusion

This chapter has very briefly described the history of casinos and some of their more important operating characteristics in order to build an understanding of the casino operating environment before discussing some of the more detailed aspects of casino operations and accounting.

CHAPTER 2

Casino Licensing and Regulation

Introduction

This chapter discusses the licensing and continuing regulation of casino operations. It begins with a brief discussion of the historical development of gaming regulation in the state of Nevada. The differences in regulatory philosophy between Nevada and New Jersey are examined, including a detailed look at the respective gaming control agencies and their operations. The chapter concludes with a discussion of a number of special problems associated with casino licensing and regulation.

The Function of Licensing and Regulation

It must be recognized from the beginning that in order to operate casino gaming in a legal and publicly supported manner, there must be an effective system of controls over that gaming activity. Not only must the gaming regulation be effective, but the operation of the gaming regulation groups must be such that public confidence in the agencies remains at a very high level. This confidence in the regulatory mechanisms is an important factor in the continuing success of casino gaming.

Casino gaming is an industry that is considered to be only marginally accepted by many people in the United States. There is a very thin line between the social acceptance of casino gaming and the rejection of other types of social behavior as undesirable. Even where casino gaming is accepted, there is always some danger of movements to prohibit or otherwise significantly limit it. Unforeseen shifts in public opinion arising from new social attitudes or, more importantly, from an erosion of confidence in the regulatory controls over casino operations could have a negative impact on the industry.[1]

In 1976, the President's Commission on the Review of the National Policy toward Gambling issued its final report entitled *Gambling in America*, which stated the following: "In the past 45 years since gambling in Nevada was legalized, the state's role in licensed gaming has evolved from a simple tax collection scheme into a sophisticated regulatory system covering every facet of the gaming industry."[2]

The tone of the report was generally favorable and seemed to support the widely held belief that gaming control has long been effective in Nevada and that its operations will serve as a good model for other states that are considering the adoption of legalized gaming. The report concluded by saying: "Nevada has used its 45 years of experience in the gaming field to develop a regulatory system that is sophisticated, efficient, and, on the whole, capable of maintaining the integrity of the gaming industry at an acceptable level."[3]

History of Gaming Regulation

Although the formal process of gaming regulation in Nevada did not start until 1955, there were many historical antecedents in earlier years that have had an impact on gaming regulation. The development and changes in the gaming regulation laws are the result of a mixture of needs for enforcement and needs for economic revenue. The basic economic need is raising tax revenues for both state and local governments. The enforcement component has been constantly modified to accomplish certain public policy objectives, which most commonly correct deficiencies in the licensing and operating procedures as they are discovered. A second enforcement emphasis is to make changes that react to the perceived threat of federal government intrusion into the regulation of casinos and to maintain strong state control of the gaming regulatory process.

Gaming had its legal inception in Nevada in 1931 with the passage of the so-called wide open gaming act, more formally known as the 1931 Gambling Act.[4] The passage of the 1931 act ended a period from 1910 to 1931 when all forms of casino gaming had been outlawed in the state of Nevada, but were still widely carried out in a variety of clandestine locations.

From 1931 until 1945, gaming licensing and taxation were completely in the hands of the sheriff of the local county in which the gaming was taking place. The original taxation levels for these casinos included a tax of $25 per month per table game, $50 per month per machine for coin-operated games, and $10 per month per slot machine. This revenue was then distributed, with 25% going to the state and 75% going to the county. The only license required was that issued by the local county or sheriff.[5]

In 1945, the need for state revenue again prompted a major change in taxation of gaming activities. The original legislative intent was to levy a percentage tax on casino revenues. The first casino revenue tax was 1% of the quarterly gross gaming revenue in excess of $3,000. The responsibility for the collection of the tax was assigned to the Nevada Tax Commission. The gross revenue tax was subsequently increased to 2% by the 1947 State Legislature, and a sliding scale of fees or taxes on the number of games, slots, and card games was adopted. In order to facilitate the collection of the tax, the Legislature required the gaming establishments to obtain a gaming license from the Tax Commission. Prior to this time, the acquisition of a gaming license was a mere administrative formality. There was, however, no formal investigation or determination of an establishment's suitability for licensing.

During this period, the licensing procedure and the accompanying tax collections were quite lax, primarily due to a lack of manpower to enforce the tax laws. Some casinos continued to operate with just the county license. Over the next five years, there was considerable expansion of the powers of the state concerning the enforcement of these new tax and license laws.[6]

The first major expansion was the determination that the issuance of a gaming license was not a constitutionally guaranteed right, but rather a privileged class of license that could be strictly controlled by the issuing body. The second major step was the requirement that local county licenses could not be issued until the state license was issued. This gave the Nevada Tax Commission a strong basic set of rules by which to regulate the industry and the individuals involved in it.[7]

The 1954 state election marked a major turning point in gaming control in Nevada. During this election, the strength of state control over casino licensing was a pivotal issue and resulted in the re-election of Governor Charles Russell, who had previously supported strong gaming control and licensing investigations.

In 1955, in recognition of the limitations under which the Nevada Tax Commission was operating, a full-time gaming control division was created. This division was headed by a three-member board with backgrounds in accounting, administration, investigation, law enforcement, and gaming. The group operated under the Tax Commission until 1959, when it became autonomous. The Gaming Control Board has continued until the present time and bears the primary responsibility for enforcement of the gaming laws and collection of the proper amount of taxes.[8]

The 1959 legislation that created the independent Gaming Control Board also created a senior organization called the Nevada Gaming Commission, consisting of five part-time members appointed by the governor for staggered four-year terms. No more than two can come from the same occupation, no more than three can have the same major political affiliation, and none can have a financial interest in any gaming establishment. The primary function of this group is the licensing of applicants.[9]

The operations of the Gaming Control Board and the senior Gaming Commission are generally complementary. The Gaming Commission is formally empowered to issue all licenses upon the recommendation of the Gaming Control Board. The Control Board is the body empowered to investigate the background and qualifications of each candidate. It exercises all enforcement activities in the name of the Gaming Commission. In addition to these responsibilities, the Gaming Commission is responsible for all action involving the collection of fees and taxes from gaming establishments. The Gaming Control Board makes all recommendations to the Gaming Commission on the licensing of individuals based on its investigations. In the case of a recommendation for denial by the Control Board, the Gaming Commission may take one of three actions: deny the license, refer the matter for further investigation by the Control Board, or overrule the Control Board and grant the license. This overruling is only allowed with the unanimous vote of all members present.

The final body that forms the gaming control structure in Nevada is the Gaming Policy Committee. This committee was authorized and established by the 1961 State Legislature in order to hold public hearings and recommend changes in gaming policy to the Nevada Gaming Commission. The recommendations are advisory and can be ignored by the Gaming Commission. The governor chairs the policy committee, which consists of eight other members representing the public, the legislative bodies, the gaming industry, and the gaming regulatory agencies.[10]

The next significant changes in the process of gaming regulation occurred in 1967 and 1969. In 1967, largely in response to the purchase of several major Las Vegas casinos by Howard Hughes, the State Legislature passed the first corporate licensing law. Prior to this time, only individuals could be licensed. In 1969, the corporate licensing laws were modified and extended so that all publicly traded corporations could be licensed, providing that all major stockholders, corporate officers, directors, and key employees were investigated and licensed.[11]

The 1977 Legislature enacted another key element of gaming control legislation—permission for foreign gaming. This allowed licensees of the state of Nevada to operate gaming establishments in other states or jurisdictions, providing there was a clear and effective program of gaming control in these other jurisdictions.[12]

Gaming Litigation and Court Decisions

In addition to the development of administrative rules for gaming control, there have also been a number of related steps taken by the courts to support the continuation of the actions of the gaming regulators. The general trend of all these administrative and legal actions has been to support the state's absolute power to regulate, enforce, and tax the gaming industry.

A series of important administrative and judicial actions has served to form the foundation of gaming control in the state of Nevada. These judicial and administrative determinations have occurred in two significant areas. The first is the power of the Gaming Commission and the Gaming Control Board to regulate the operation of the casinos.

This issue relates to the power of the state to enforce the "Black Book" regulations, which provide for the mechanism by which certain individuals must be excluded from gaming casinos. If they are not excluded, then the licensee can be called before the Gaming Commission and may possibly be subjected to disciplinary action. One significant confrontation over the Black Book was the 1963 incident when Sam Giancana (then listed in the Black Book) visited the Cal-Neva Lodge at Lake Tahoe, which was partially owned by Frank Sinatra. Before any disciplinary hearing could be conducted, Sinatra voluntarily surrendered his gaming license, thus avoiding a direct confrontation on the issue of the state's power to exclude persons.[13]

There was a formal test of the Black Book regulations in 1967 by Frank Marshall, who was ejected from a Las Vegas Strip hotel. The Nevada Supreme Court affirmed in that case that the state did possess the authority to prohibit undesirable persons from entering licensed gaming establishments. Following the Supreme Court decision, the State Legislature adopted formal procedures to govern the process by which persons are included in the Black Book, in response to criticisms included in the Supreme Court's affirmative judgment.[14]

The second major area of gaming litigation that has formed the basis for the operations of gaming regulation of the casino industry has been the original license granting procedures. In this area, there have been four significant cases. The first, in 1970, was *George* v. *Nevada Gaming Commission*,[15] in which the Supreme Court ruled that the District Court was without jurisdiction over the state regulatory authorities and that the state constitution precluded the court's intrusion into the administration, licensing, and control of gaming.

In 1977, *State of Nevada* v. *Rosenthal* tested the validity of the state's rules, procedures, and powers regarding licensing of individuals.[16] The Supreme Court of Nevada (with the U.S. Supreme Court refusing to review or reconsider the case) stated that the statutory licensing standards were adequate and that only reasonable action was required by the Gaming Commission in licensing procedures. It also specified that there were no federally protected constitutional property rights inherent in the gaming licenses, and that the procedures then in place for the denial of a license were proper.

Further cases involving *Jacobson* v. *Hannifin* and *Rosenthal* v. *State of Nevada* have both reinforced the earlier State Court finding that there are no federally guaranteed rights of property involved in a gaming license, particularly in the case of a first-time applicant (Jacobson).[17] Furthermore, any property rights that might have existed in a license could be terminated with a proper administrative review.[18]

New Jersey Gaming Regulation

The development of casino gaming regulation in the state of New Jersey has only a recent history. The original enabling legislation to establish the control agencies, the licensing, and the taxation policies was enacted in 1976 by the New Jersey Legislature following approval of a public referendum permitting casino gaming in Atlantic City. Since that time, there have been three major developments that have resulted in changes to the New Jersey regulatory environment.

The first major development was the alteration of the basic mechanism for licensing casinos in the state of New Jersey. Due to the extensive original requirements for casino licensing not only of the casino workers but also of all workers in support industries, it was virtually impossible to complete the licensing evaluation before the dates when the casinos were scheduled to open. To avoid a considerable financial problem resulting from the delay in opening, the Casino Control Commission provided for the granting of six-month temporary licenses, which would become permanent upon subsequent approval. At the present time, there are eleven casinos operating, and all have been granted permanent licenses. Many licensees have had very restrictive conditions attached to their licenses.[19]

The second major development in the regulation of New Jersey gaming is the change in the composition of the five-member Casino Control Commission that resulted from the ABSCAM scandals. One of New Jersey's part-time commissioners was implicated in taking a bribe to secure a casino license for an undesirable person. When this was disclosed, the governor immediately pressed for a change in the status of the Casino Control Commission from part-time to full-time. It was felt that a full-time commission would be more insulated from this type of influence buying. This change was accomplished in 1980.[20]

The third major development was in connection with the licensing of Caesars Boardwalk Regency Hotel and Casino. A temporary license was granted to the company. During the hearing for the permanent license, it was brought to the attention of the Casino Control Commission that the major shareholders of Caesars World, the Pearlman brothers, had previously had business and social dealings with known members of organized crime. The permanent license of Caesars Boardwalk Regency was granted only after the Pearlmans agreed to step down from the management of the hotel and casino operations and to sell their stock in the corporation. This condition was partially met when the brothers stepped down and the stock was assigned to a voting trust. In the meantime, the validity of the action of the Casino Control Commission was affirmed by the courts. In the absence of a major failure to follow reasonable procedural rules, the validity of the conditions set by the New Jersey authorities was upheld by the New Jersey courts.[21]

Types of Gaming Regulation

Gaming regulation has evolved in two principal phases.[22] The first and most critical is the original or entry licensing. The second is the process of ongoing enforcement of the gaming laws, with the accompanying review of suitability for continuing operation.

Entry Licensing

In both Nevada and New Jersey, the greatest regulatory emphasis is on the process of entry licensing. In Nevada, original licensing focuses on the licensees: the individuals operating the business, the members of a partnership, or the principals of an operating corporation. Key employees in the casino are also licensed.

In addition to the licensing of the owners and key employees, there are also procedures associated with the licensing of various games manufactured or distributed. These various forms of licensing and the procedures associated with the securing of a license are discussed in detail later in the chapter.

The entry level licensing in New Jersey is much broader than in Nevada. Original licensing includes all casino employees, all hotel-casino employees, and, most significantly, all industries that support or supply goods and services to the casinos. This casino service industry licensing is a significant broadening of the scope of licensing authority of the state gaming agencies. In both Nevada and New Jersey, labor organizations are subject to registration requirements (but not strict licensing), and there are suitability requirements associated with this registration procedure.

Ongoing Regulation

Ongoing control and regulation in the state of Nevada is the primary responsibility of the enforcement division of the Gaming Control Board. The principal area of activity is surveillance and audit. The surveillance group is to assure that the games are being conducted in a fair and honest manner. This group also has responsibility for the gathering of intelligence regarding the conduct of the business activities of the casinos. The audit division is most commonly associated with the process of tax collection, but it also forms an important link in the process of continuing enforcement by its review of the financial results of the casino's operations and investigation of financial or operating improprieties.

Ongoing regulation of casino activities in New Jersey is much more highly structured. There are two separate regulatory bodies concerned with this type of regulation: the Division of Gaming Enforcement and the Casino Control Commission. Both of these groups are responsible for casino regulation. The Division of Gaming Enforcement has an enforcement unit and a compliance unit, both of which provide surveillance activities of the casino operations. The Casino Control Commission has divisions working on financial and internal control evaluations, as well as evaluating overall compliance of operating procedures at all times that the casino is in operation.

Philosophy of Gaming Regulation

With the advent of casino gaming regulation in New Jersey in 1976, there was for the first time an opportunity to compare the style of gaming control in Nevada to another model. That comparison has been most informative. There are both many similarities and many differences between the gaming regulation procedures of these two states.

The differences and similarities can be analyzed in several ways. The first is the overall state policy toward regulation. In Nevada, gaming is considered to be an industry, with significant importance to the overall economic health of the state. In New Jersey, casino gaming is only one small part of a program of economic revitalization of a specific resort location. Other regulatory differences are a result of basic differences in the casino industries in Nevada and New Jersey. The Nevada casino industry has great diversity in location, size, and style of operation. In New Jersey, the operation of casinos is limited to one specific geographic area, with all the casino operations being highly constrained by statute and regulation in the type of operations, games offered, and even the physical facility layout, design, and colors permitted.

A second major difference is in the attitude and philosophy of gaming control. In Nevada, gaming, which is an activity that is half a century old, enjoys a good reputation in the local community for its honesty, integrity, and contribution to the state. In New Jersey, the industry is ten years old, has had a long association (prior to its legalization) with undesirable and illegal elements of the population, and does not enjoy a high standing in the community. Under these circumstances, one would expect the degree of gaming control to be much more rigorous in New Jersey than in Nevada.

A third difference lies in the philosophies of how gaming control is accomplished. The New Jersey regulations are highly specific, with little room for interpretation, innovation, or change in the method of doing business in a casino. This could be expected in a highly structured system of regulation, where the industry itself is highly structured, geographically limited, and under considerable suspicion. The Nevada situation is much more flexible, with almost any style or size of operation being accommodated in the regulations. Most of the Nevada regulations dealing with control items are expressed in general terms, with specific implementation left up to the individual casino. A good example of the difference lies in the systems of casino internal controls. In Nevada, the individual casino presents its system of casino internal controls to the state. These individual systems are evaluated against a set of basic minimum standards of operation and control. If these minimum standards are met, then the casino is allowed to operate using its own methods and style of internal control. Each Nevada casino has a different way of operating, even though the basic minimum operational standards are common to all. In New Jersey, the nature of the system of internal controls is prescribed and leaves little room for change by the individual casinos. This required uniformity does not allow for innovation or changes by the individual casinos. The Nevada approach is typical of a widespread industry, where the differences between the large clubs and the small clubs must be recognized.

The final difference between the Nevada and New Jersey regulatory attitudes is found in the background of the development of the processes of gaming control. Nevada gaming control has grown up slowly over the past fifty years. The New Jersey gaming control environment, on the other hand, was created instantly in 1976. The basic attitude in Nevada was somewhat casual, recognizing that changes can be implemented at any time to assure proper gaming control. This led to a high degree of flexibility in Nevada gaming controls. New Jersey, on the other hand, felt that the legalization of this industry demanded rigorous and rigid con-

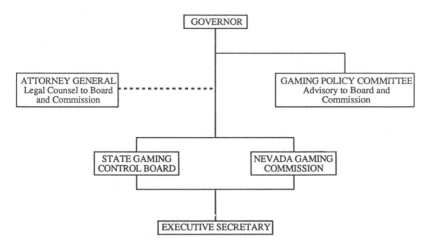

Fig. 2-1. Organization of gaming control agencies and staff.

trols. If necessary, authorities believed, these controls could be revised later to accommodate different operating requirements. This process has already taken place in a number of areas where controls were modified after original procedures were determined to be too rigid.

The Structure of Gaming Regulation in Nevada

There are three basic state organizations concerned with the regulation of gaming in Nevada: the Gaming Policy Committee, the Gaming Control Board, and the Gaming Commission. The organizational structure of these agencies is indicated in figure 2-1. Each of these groups is discussed in some detail below.[23]

Gaming Policy Committee

This group is unique to the state of Nevada. As previously noted, it was created by legislation in 1961, and its primary purpose is to make recommendations on matters of gaming policy to the executive branch of government and to the State Legislature. It can only make recommendations, which are not binding on either the Gaming Control Board or the Gaming Commission. The Policy Committee can hold public hearings and has the force of persuasion through its members. The membership of the group includes the chairperson, who is always the governor; gaming industry representatives—one from the northern part of the state and one from the south; general public representatives—one from the north and one from the south; one member from the State Senate; and one member from the State Assembly.

The Gaming Policy Committee has made two very important contributions to the process of gaming regulation in Nevada during the last decade. On two separate occasions, it was the body that initiated discussions of major policy changes that were subsequently adopted in revised gaming legislation. The first issue was that of allowing corporate (including publicly traded corporate) ownership of gaming enterprises. The second was the investigation of whether or not to allow Nevada casino licensees to conduct operations in foreign jurisdictions. Both of these issues were recommended for adoption, and the discussions of many aspects of each topic were instrumental in securing widespread understanding of the issues, together with a large degree of support from the public, the gaming industry, and the State Legislature for the eventual modification of the gaming legislation.

Nevada Gaming Commission

The Nevada Gaming Commission is the senior governing body of gaming regulation in the state of Nevada. It was created in 1959, with the primary responsibility for the licensing of all gaming activities. This group can grant or deny new licenses, can determine the suitability of current licensees to continue to hold licenses, and can revoke, suspend, or otherwise condition gaming licenses. This action can be taken on any basis or for any cause that the Gaming Commission deems reasonable. Its powers also include the ability to adopt various regulations that govern the conduct of the Gaming Control Board or the licensees.

Another important function of the Gaming Commission is the ability to call any previously unlicensed person forward for licensing. That person is then evaluated for suitability to hold a gaming license. This allows the Gaming Commission very broad investigatory powers with respect to all casino personnel. In cases of problem operations, the Gaming Commission can also conduct a disciplinary hearing and, if necessary, recommend to the county district attorneys or to the attorney general that either civil or criminal actions be initiated against licensees. The Gaming Commission can, on its own, initiate civil actions to collect gaming fees and taxes, including interest and penalties.

Although the Gaming Commission acts on the recommendations of the Gaming Control Board, that action is independent.

On licensing matters, the recommendation of the Control Board must be overruled by a unanimous vote of the members of the Gaming Commission present. In the absence of this unanimous vote, the recommendation of the Gaming Control Board is upheld.

The Gaming Commission consists of five lay members, appointed by the governor for staggered four-year terms. The members can only be removed for cause, except with the concurrence of a majority of the legislative commission. The members of the Gaming Commission are part-time, with no more than three members allowed from the same political party and no more than two from the same occupational area. None of the members can have a financial interest in any gaming establishment.

The members of the Gaming Commission are paid only the state per diem allowance for the periods during which it meets. The chairperson receives a small annual stipend in addition to the per diem. Based on this financial compensation, it is obvious that the Gaming Commission is made up of public-spirited individuals who customarily make a significant personal sacrifice to help regulate the gaming industry in Nevada.

Nevada Gaming Control Board

The Gaming Control Board was initially created in 1955, as part of the State Tax Commission. This group became administratively independent in 1959, together with the creation of the senior governing body, the Gaming Commission.

The Control Board has three governing members. They are appointed by the governor to full-time, compensated positions for four-year staggered terms. The appointees can be removed for cause, but cannot be removed without cause. Each of the members must have a specific background. This is required in order to allow the members of the Gaming Control Board properly to supervise the internal day-to-day operations of the Control Board.

The chairperson of the Gaming Control Board, who also serves as the executive director, must have at least five years of responsible administrative experience in public or business administration and should have broad management skills. This person is responsible for the overall administration of the Gaming Board's operations. The second member and fiscal director must be a CPA or a public accountant with five years of experience or be an expert in corporate finance and auditing, general finance, gaming, or economics. The third board member, the surveillance director, must have training and experience in the fields of investigation, law enforcement, law, or gaming.

As full-time state employees, the members of the Gaming Control Board may not pursue any other business or occupation or hold any other office or profit from any other business transactions. Of course, the members must not have any financial interest in a gaming establishment or other business relating to the gaming industry.

The powers and duties of the Gaming Control Board are very broad. It has virtually unlimited powers with respect to the enforcement of the gaming laws of the state:[24]

1. The Control Board investigates the background of all applicants for gaming licenses and makes recommendations to the Gaming Commission to grant or deny the license.

2. The Control Board also has the responsibility of enforcing the gaming laws and regulations promulgated by the Gaming Commission, including filing complaints against licensees who are felt to be violating the gaming laws and regulations.

3. The Control Board assures that revenue collection and taxing functions are being properly carried out. It also conducts audits in order to verify that the correct taxes are being collected.

4. The Control Board has the responsibility for surveillance of all gaming activity and can inspect and examine all premises where gaming is conducted or gaming devices are manufactured, sold, or distributed.

5. Finally, the Control Board has the right of access to all books and records of a licensee or any other documents necessary for its investigations.

The responsibilities of the Gaming Control Board staff are indicated in figure 2-2. The organization consists of four main divisions:

1. Investigations: this group is in charge of investigating the background of all new applicants for licenses. The investigations division is frequently augmented by persons with specific audit or enforcement skills. This division also includes the corporate securities department, which maintains information files on publicly traded corporations and reviews all documents filed with the Securities and Exchange Commission and processes the applications for public offerings of gaming securities.

2. Enforcement: this division is in charge of the enforcement of the gaming rules and regulations, to ensure proper game con-

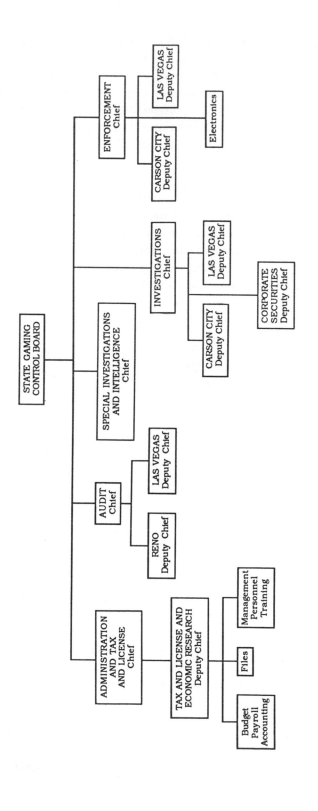

Fig. 2-2. Nevada State Gaming Control Board organization.

duct and the honesty of the games. The enforcement division protects the casino from dishonest players or employees and also investigates player complaints.

3. Audit: this division is in charge of assuring that the state receives all revenues that are properly due it. The audit division also functions to enforce accounting and internal control regulations. From time to time, the audit division provides financial expertise to the other divisions.

4. Administration, Tax, and Licensing: this division is responsible for the administrative functions of issuing licenses and amending licenses when new games or slot machines are added or when new individuals are licensed or are added to corporate licenses. It also includes the economic research division, which is responsible for the collection, analysis, and publication of financial information and statistics regarding the gaming industry.

The Structure of Gaming Regulation in New Jersey

The two agencies involved in the regulation of the New Jersey casino industry are the Casino Control Commission and the Division of Gaming Enforcement. Their functions are dramatically different than those of the control agencies in Nevada.

Division of Gaming Enforcement

This agency is a part of the State Attorney General's Office. Its responsibilities include the investigation of all applications for casino licenses and the enforcement of all criminal provisions of the Casino Control Act. The division is organized in four departments, with the investigations section being the most important. The other three departments are intelligence and research, legal, and administration.

The investigations section is divided into four areas. The first is the enforcement unit, which focuses on the proper conduct of casino operations, including investigation of cheating as well as player complaints. The second is the compliance unit, which has the responsibility for supervision and security within the individual casinos. The third and fourth are the license investigating units, whose primary activity is the background investigation and licensing of employees, casinos, and the casino service industry. Figure 2-3 indicates the organization of the Division of Gaming Enforcement.

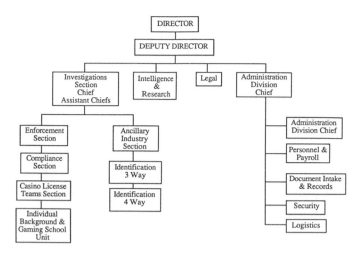

Fig. 2-3. State of New Jersey Division of Gaming Enforcement.

The licensing unit of the Division of Gaming Enforcement is an investigative body only. It gathers information and provides it to the Casino Control Commission for action or approval. Similarly, the compliance and enforcement units have supervisory roles, but cannot initiate actions against a casino. The only allowable action is the filing of criminal charges in the case of violation of the gaming statutes. In general, the Division of Gaming Enforcement is a support or advisory unit and must rely on the Casino Control Commission for the final action on issues of casino control.

Casino Control Commission

The New Jersey Casino Control Commission is a full-time five-member board. Members are appointed for four-year terms by the governor and are drawn from a broad range of business backgrounds. There are no specific background requirements such as exist in Nevada. The Control Commission maintains its own legal staff, which can and often does function independently of the legal staff of the Division of Gaming Enforcement and the state attorney general.

The Casino Control Commission has the ultimate responsibility for licensing, including new licensing, revocation, and conditioning. It is also responsible for setting rules and regulations to implement the gaming statutes and for collection of all gaming taxes and license fees.

The principal operating divisions of the Control Commission are the Licensing Division and the Financial Evaluation and Control Division. Minor administrative groups within the Control Commission include the administration and legal divisions. Its overall structure is shown in figure 2-4. The Licensing Division is charged with the responsibility for licensing of three main groups:

1. Casinos.

2. Casino employees, including all working permits and licenses.

3. Casino service industries.

The third area, the licensing of casino service industries, considerably expands the licensing and background investigation responsibilities of the regulatory authorities. Under New Jersey rules, if the business providing service to a casino is unlicensed, then each contract must be individually approved by the Control Commission. After the service entity has been licensed, then individual contract or transaction approval is not required.

The second major control function of the Casino Control Commission is performance of financial evaluation and internal control review. This group has responsibility for the evaluation of the financial strength and suitability of the casino prior to opening, as well as its financial strength and performance after licensing and during operation. The group is also responsible for approval of the submitted systems of internal control, which must be filed prior to opening the casino and must be in conformity with the specification contained in the gaming regulations of the state.

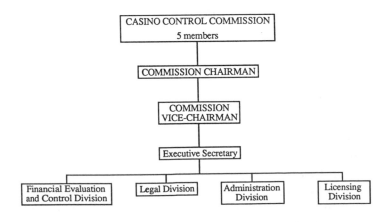

Fig. 2-4. State of New Jersey Casino Control Commission.

In addition to overseeing correct operating procedures, the financial evaluation and control group maintains oversight over the system of internal controls in place in the casino. Not only must the internal control system meet the initial state criteria before opening, but it must also be kept up to date, with appropriate documentation amended as the changes in casino operations take place and are approved by the Control Commission.

This group also has considerable responsibility for the actual inspection and review of daily operations, as well as regulatory oversight of the counting rooms. An additional area of responsibility is the monitoring of various Securities and Exchange Commission reports, including initial stock offerings. The group also reviews all periodic SEC reporting documents and subsequent stock offerings.

The administrative division of the Control Commission is responsible for collection of casino taxes on a monthly basis and for public reporting of the operating results. In addition to these support responsibilities, the Casino Control Commission also functions as an administrative hearing board and, in the process, performs much like any other administrative body, with formal rules of subpoena, adjudication, evidence, and other administrative procedures. It functions under these administrative procedures for hearings as well as when considering adoption of the various operating rules and regulations.

A final unique area of concern for the Gaming Control Commission is the formal responsibility to keep up to date on all legislative developments in gaming laws in other jurisdictions that may have an impact on New Jersey law.

Entry Licensing Procedures

This section discusses the procedures that are used to investigate the granting of licenses for gaming activities in both Nevada and New Jersey. While the licensing procedure has developed over many years in Nevada, it has only recently been put in place in New Jersey.

In general, for both states, the process of casino licensing is considered to be a privilege granted by the state to an individual or corporation, and this privilege can be revoked at any time for cause, including the general finding of unsuitability, provided that certain minimum administrative due process procedures are followed.

The overall focus on original licensing of the casinos and the persons who operate them is the key to effective gaming control. The most stringent controls are implemented at the point of entry. The entry controls focus on three main criteria: personal suitability and character, financial capability, and management capability.

Who Can Be Licensed

The general conditions that determine who must be licensed cover all individuals, partnerships, and corporations that operate a casino, have a financial interest in the casino, or share profits from the operations.[25] This general criterion is quite broad and has been modified in a variety of ways.

Individuals Generally, all individuals who have an interest based on gaming revenues or profits must be licensed. Licenses are usually granted to individual owners of a casino.

Partnerships All partners must be licensed, including both general and limited partners. Partnerships where one or more of the partners is a corporation must have the corporation approved and licensed. Exceptions to partner licensing are provided for limited partners, who are passive investors only.

Corporations Corporations, including both closely held corporations and publicly traded corporations, must be licensed.[26] A difference arises between the two types of corporations. In closely held corporations, all officers, directors, and shareholders must be licensed. In publicly traded corporations, all owners or stockholders must be registered but need not be formally licensed. All officers, directors, and key employees of a publicly traded corporation determined by the Gaming Control Board and Gaming Commission to be engaged in the administration or supervision of gaming must be licensed. In addition, shareholders who hold either directly or indirectly between 5% and 10% of the voting stock may be required to be licensed.

Key Employees In all ownership situations, the key employees of the casino must be licensed. The definition of a key employee is left strictly to the Gaming Control Board and the Gaming Commission, and any employee may be called forward for determination of suitability for licensing if so requested. In general, key employees include all direct casino employees from the supervisory level upward, all major operating department heads, and department heads in various administrative departments of the casino, such as personnel managers, controllers, and security supervisors.

In addition to owners and key management employees, the Gaming Control Board and Gaming Commission can require licensing of any individual or business entity exercising effective control over a casino through loans or other financial arrangements.[27] Specific licensing exemptions exist for national banks that may from time to time loan money to casinos or have leasing arrangements with casinos. Other financial institutions may be required to be licensed.[28]

Other Licensing Requirements

In addition to the licensing of the owners and the key employees of the casino, there are numerous other licensing requirements. First, each casino location must be licensed after the suitability of the location has been determined. Once the basic location license has been granted, it is not customarily subjected to extensive reviews in the future. New Jersey requires annual licensing review and licenses. However, one exception does occur when a Nevada casino operation requests the approval of the Gaming Control Board and Gaming Commission for the extension of its gaming into a "foreign jurisdiction." In this case, detailed justification of the financial and managerial resources must be presented to allow the licensee to venture into new casino locations.

Labor organizations and the individuals within those organizations must also be approved and licensed.[29] In addition, various support and service industries related to the casino business must be licensed. In Nevada, this is restricted to manufacturers and distributors of games and other gaming equipment, while the New Jersey licensing extends to virtually all casino industry suppliers. The more wide-ranging concern of the New Jersey authorities has been based on the belief that undesirable infiltration of the casino industry may be achieved by indirect means, rather than direct involvement. By licensing the suppliers of the casinos, control can be achieved over these undesirable elements. This departure from previous Nevada experience may prove to be a worthwhile additional step in casino regulation.

In Nevada, there is a procedure to allow the approval of new games or coin-operated gaming devices. The licensing and investigatory procedures involved in a new game are particularly lengthy. The review includes detailed technical, electronic, and engineering investigation of the design and operation of the game and the controls over the game. In addition, market acceptance is often tested by the granting of short-term licenses for test marketing of the new game. The recent proliferation of various electronic games has given rise to an entirely new division within the Nevada Gaming Control Board that specifically investigates these new machines and recommends approval or licensing of the games.

Finally, one additional area of regulatory concern in New Jersey is the licensing of the various schools that train employees for the casino industry.

Other Related Licenses

In addition to the state licenses for the operation of the casinos, a license must also be granted by the county and the individual city or town where the casino is located. The application for these licenses is made only after the state license has been granted. Also, as in any other business, liquor, cabaret, food, and general business licenses must also be secured prior to opening a casino.

License Application Procedures

The license applicant must furnish the gaming control authorities with a comprehensive and detailed personal history, as well as many items of background information to document the various items of personal history. In addition, the applicant must furnish detailed financial statements and supporting information. The general process is that the applicant first supplies the information to the gaming authorities. The regulatory group then begins an investigation of the information in various questionnaires and endeavors to determine the suitability of the applicant. The investigation, although conducted by the Gaming Control Board, is paid for by the applicant. (As a matter of fact, the estimated investigation fee must be prepaid by the applicant.) After the Gaming Control Board staff has completed its investigation, the results are presented to the Control Board and the Gaming Commission, which make the final determination on the license approval or denial. Table 2-1 indicates the various types of forms and information that customarily must be supplied by a casino license applicant in New Jersey and Nevada. Not only must the required forms be completed, but all subsidiary documents must be supplied with the

Table 2-1. Gaming Licensing Documents.

NEVADA

Individual application for State Gaming License
- Key Employees
- Change of Existing License
- Regular Application

Personal History Form

Invested Capital Questionnaire

NEW JERSEY

Individuals—Casino
  Personal History Disclosure—Form 1 (Includes application, personal
    history and financial data)
Individuals—Noncasino
  Personal History Disclosure—Form 2
Corporate Applicant
  Business Entity Disclosure Form
Other Forms
  Ancillary Services Industry Form
  Personal History Disclosure—Form 4 for service industry
  Labor Organization Registration Statement

application. Examples of this information include items such as permissions to release information and documents suspending mandatory time limits, together with releases of claims against the investigating body. All these items must accompany the application in order to have the investigatory process begin.

Appendix 2-1 contains a copy of the instructions to applicants for the state of Nevada gaming license application and describes in considerable detail the information that should be submitted in connection with a gaming application. The requirements for the New Jersey application are similar but more exhaustive. Since the New Jersey application is much longer, the volume of documentation is much greater. Finally, the materials in appendix 2-2 indicate the criteria used by the Gaming Control Board in evaluating the suitability of a particular licensee. These criteria are in addition to the three criteria described in the beginning of this section, covering personal suitability, financial capability, and management capability. Other criteria for licensing are formalized in Gaming Control Board Regulation 3.070, which is reproduced in appendix 2-3. This appendix also spells out the criteria for allowing Nevada licensees to operate in other locations. This document for the first time enumerated the concerns of the Gaming Control Board in the area of management capability in casino licensing.

Classification of Licenses Granted

The state of Nevada grants the following types of gaming licenses:

1. Gaming Licenses: restricted, nonrestricted, and nonrestricted slot machine.
2. Manufacturer's Licenses.
3. Distributor's Licenses.

Gaming licenses are divided into three subgroups. Restricted gaming licenses are for less than fifteen slot machines, where the principal business is not gaming and no table games are present. Nonrestricted licenses are for more than fifteen slot machines or any number of slot machines operated in conjunction with table games. Nonrestricted slot machine licenses apply to large-scale (more than fifteen) operators of slot machines.

Depending upon the volume of business and annual revenue, all gaming licenses are classified as either Group 1 or Group 2 licenses. If the annual revenue is under $1,000,000, then the casino is a Group 2 licensee; if the annual revenue is over $1,000,000 per year, then the casino is a Group 1 licensee. The Gaming Control Board regulations concerning the types of internal controls necessary in a casino are slightly less rigorous for a Group 2 licensee.

The state of New Jersey issues gaming licenses for the various types of persons, corporations, and support personnel and businesses involved in the casino industry. However, no distinctions are made between licenses based on the number of games and slots operated or on the amount of casino revenue.

Regulation Through Auditing and Continuing Enforcement

This section of the chapter discusses the role of ongoing control and regulation by the various gaming control agencies and the impact that these functions have on gaming control. It also considers the detailed reporting that is required of gaming licensees and the role that this reporting plays in the regulation and continuing enforcement of gaming laws and regulations.

Regulatory Audit Objectives

The basic audit objective of the Nevada Gaming Control Board is outlined in Regulation 6.110. This section grants broad powers to the Control Board to conduct audits of all gaming licensees. The objective is quite detailed and forms the basis for all audit procedures. The purpose of the audit is to assure the compliance of the licensee and its accounting system with the minimum standards set by the Control Board and to ensure that the proper amount of gaming revenue has been reported and the appropriate amount of taxes paid on that revenue. Given the significant size of gaming tax collections in the funding of the state of Nevada, the determination of the proper amount of taxes is a crucial role for the audit division of the Gaming Control Board.

It should be noted that this is strict compliance auditing and should not be confused with the audits required of all licensees to be performed by independent Certified Public Accountants.

In addition to the tax assessment objectives of the audit procedure, the audit division from time to time conducts special studies in connection with special investigations. These investigations typically involve complex financial applications that require sophisticated financial analysis or special enforcement situations where complex financial transactions or significant problems of diversion of funds or hidden ownership interests are suspected.

Other audit objectives are directed toward evaluating the systems of internal control. This process begins by evaluating the system of internal controls in place in the casino to assure that the system is operating as described. In addition, there is an important responsibility to ensure that the internal control system continues to be effective and adequate so that all transactions (particularly revenue transactions) are properly reported. In addition, the system of internal control is examined to verify that the operating procedures meet the minimum standards spelled out in the regulations and laws. A final audit objective is to make sure that all applicable gaming regulations and laws have been followed by the licensee.

New Jersey shares these same broad control objectives through its ongoing audit and compliance reviews. A modest difference exists due to the two-agency control model used in New Jersey. The Casino Control Commission has the principal responsibility for the integrity of the revenue reporting and tax collection process, while the second agency, the Division of Gaming Enforcement, has the primary responsibility for the integrity of the ongoing gaming operations. This gives the auditors different outlooks when performing the compliance audits of the New Jersey casinos.

The Role of Public Accounting in Gaming Control

In addition to the regulatory audits performed by the gaming control agencies, the public accounting profession also serves a vitally important role in the ongoing regulation of the casino industry. In Nevada, Regulations 6.040 and 6.050 require the submission of annual audited financial statements for each licensee, and there must also be an annual evaluation of the casino internal control system by an independent accountant. The results of this evaluation must be reported to the gaming control authorities. This report must include all instances where deviations from the specified internal control procedures occurred.

A similar regulation in New Jersey (Regulation 19:45.7) requires the filing of annual independently audited financial statements and evaluations of internal control systems.

Reporting Requirements for Casino Operations

There are many types of mandatory reporting by a casino operation. This reporting allows the regulatory bodies to track performance to identify problem situations and to maintain proper control of the gaming operations.

The most comprehensive set of regulations regarding record keeping and reporting is contained in Nevada Gaming Control Board Regulation #6. This regulation is comprehensive, requiring the following reporting:

1. Record retention for five years—to allow the GCB auditors to perform audits on a rotating basis.

2. Specific minimum elements of the accounting and record-keeping system that must be present in a casino accounting system. These requirements include:

  a. General accounting records.
  b. Records of all revenue and costs of operation.
  c. Maintenance of casino credit records.
  d. Complete documentation of all loans to the casino.
  e. Statistical data on individual games, including detailed revenue figures on each game.
  f. Records necessary to allow the system of internal control to operate as specified.

3. Annual reporting of data on Standard Financial Statement Forms. This requirement specifies that the licensee must submit information on various aspects of casino financial operations on a

standardized form, with amounts determined in accordance with the standard chart of accounts specified by the state. This reporting allows a statistical compilation and analysis of industry and casino operating data.

4. Annual audited financial statements, as previously described, provided by the licensee to the Gaming Control Board.

5. Internal control reporting. This reporting is quite complex and must include the following elements and meet the following conditions:

    a. All letters or comments received by a licensee from the independent auditor regarding internal control matters must be forwarded to the audit division within thirty days of receipt of the letter.

    b. A system of internal control, together with the independent accountant's report on the adequacy of these internal and administrative controls, must be submitted to the Gaming Control Board before a license can be granted.

    c. All changes that are made to the internal control system must be submitted in writing to the Gaming Control Board.

    d. The independent public accountant must perform an annual evaluation of the internal control system and the compliance of the licensee with the system as reported to the Gaming Control Board. In addition, the continuing effectiveness and adequacy of the system must be evaluated and reported upon.

6. Time of day of the drop, the count, and other related activities must be communicated to the Gaming Control Board. The casino must not only report the time of these events, but must adhere to the time schedule.

Gaming Control Board Regulations #3, 8, and 16 govern other reporting aspects of casino operation.

Regulation #3 specifies the reporting of all leases entered into by the licensee. The regulation requires that notices of changes in leases or new leases entered into be reported to the Gaming Control Board within thirty days of the inception of the lease. This action allows the Gaming Control Board time to evaluate the terms of the lease and the suitability of the lessor or to note any other problems that may arise.

Regulation #8 deals with the transfer of ownership interests in the casino. It is divided into four main types of transactions that must be reported:

1. Transfer of interest among existing licensees requires written notice of the proposed transfer of interest, and the transfer is reviewed and approved by the Control Board and Gaming Commission before becoming effective.

2. Transfer of interest to new licensee requires the same notification and review procedure as above. The length of time to approve the new licensee may vary depending upon the complexity of license investigation.

3. Permission to participate in the casino operations and profits prior to actual completion of a transfer of interest requires notification as above. This procedure allows a person to participate in the casino operation and/or profits while a transfer is pending.

4. Loans to licensees require reporting within thirty days of the effective date of the loan. This is a procedure similar to the lease disclosure noted above, again allowing the Gaming Control Board to review the loan for suitability of the lender, as well as for any potential problems.

Regulation #16 specifies the reporting requirements that must be met by publicly owned and traded corporations in the casino business. In general, the reporting requirements parallel those of the Securities and Exchange Commission. In practice, the SEC forms are merely duplicated and sent to the respective gaming authorities in order to meet the reporting responsibility.

Significant Problems of Gaming Regulation and Enforcement

Several significant problems relating to casino regulation have arisen over the years in Nevada. While these problems may be unique to Nevada, they undoubtedly could be used as signposts for other jurisdictions in pointing to problems that can arise and ways they may be guarded against. Each of these problems is outlined briefly below.

Competent Staff

The state of Nevada has had a constant battle in securing competent and adequately trained staff at all levels. The assurance of high-quality staff is the number one priority of effective gaming control. The problems of attracting and maintaining good staff arise from several causes:

1. Poor perception of the role of compliance auditing by young accounting graduates.

2. Somewhat lower levels of compensation and slower salary progression within the civil service employment environment.

3. Lack of progression within the agency due to frequent top-level changes in policy emphasis arising from the political nature of the agency.

4. The inability of the state to compete with private industry on salary and benefits at intermediate skill levels. This has resulted in the widespread exodus of supervisory personnel.

5. Poor working conditions, including extensive travel throughout the state, as well as long duration of audit assignments.

Conflicts of Interest

In 1978, the Gaming Policy Committee recommended that the regulatory agencies in Nevada adopt some form of conflict of interest regulations. This recommendation was brought about by the widespread practice of having members of both the Gaming Control Board and the Gaming Commission move from their respective regulatory positions directly into positions in the gaming industry.

New Jersey has addressed this problem and requires a specific waiting period of two years before any members of the regulatory agencies can assume a position with a firm that they are charged with regulating. Several important differences exist between Nevada and New Jersey. First, the pay for various regulatory agencies in New Jersey is much higher than in Nevada. This results in a higher degree of career commitment. In Nevada, individuals tend to leave for the higher salaries that the casinos there have traditionally offered.

Complimentaries to Officials

There has been a long-standing tradition within the gaming industry of providing free services of various types to gaming customers. These same complimentary services are provided as a matter of course to the members of the Gaming Control Board, their staff, and the members of the Gaming Commission. This has even extended to the provision of complimentaries to various elected state officials. In these circumstances, the appearance of independence on the part of the regulatory and decision-making bodies can be severely compromised. Nevada has implemented regulations against acceptance of complimentaries by gaming control employees that may help to eliminate or minimize this problem. Another solution suggested is to allow more liberal expense allowances for the gaming regulatory agencies. However, this liberalization has to be implemented in the State Legislature, which has traditionally held to a position of fiscal conservatism.

Enforcement Powers

The Gaming Control Board has requested specific powers such as the use of polygraphs and wiretaps in order to improve enforcement efforts. This authority has been consistently denied by the State Legislature, which has limited the effectiveness of some investigations.

Hidden Ownership

There is a continual problem of hidden ownership in casinos. In these situations, the real owners are not subjected to regulatory scrutiny or investigation. In this way, the effectiveness of gaming regulation is severely limited. Hidden interests are one of the main reasons cited for the request for wiretap authority by the gaming regulatory authorities. The Control Board maintains that this is a vital tool in determining the real ownership of the casino.

Nevada–New Jersey Conflicts

As mentioned earlier, the development of an aggressive enforcement and investigation policy in New Jersey has resulted in several well-publicized situations where individuals who have been licensed for many years in Nevada were found to be unsuitable to hold licenses in New Jersey. There appear to be two sets of standards operating with regard to the suitability to hold a gaming license, with Nevada being viewed as having inferior standards. This is clearly hurting the public perception of effective gaming control in Nevada. However, whenever new information regarding the licensees has become available, the Nevada regulatory agencies have promptly examined the information and, if necessary, have reviewed the status of the license.

Appendix 2-1. Instructions to Applicants for a
Nonrestricted Gaming License

AN APPLICANT FOR A STATE GAMING LICENSE IS SEEKING THE GRANTING OF A PRIVILEGE AND THE BURDEN OF PROVING HIS QUALIFICATIONS TO RECEIVE SUCH A LICENSE IS AT ALL TIMES ON THE APPLICANT. AN APPLICANT MUST ACCEPT ANY RISK OF ADVERSE PUBLIC NOTICE, EMBARRASSMENT, CRITICISM, OR OTHER ACTION, OR FINANCIAL LOSS WHICH MAY RESULT FROM ACTION WITH RESPECT TO AN APPLICATION, AND EXPRESSLY WAIVES ANY CLAIM FOR DAMAGE AS A RESULT THEREOF.

NONRESTRICTED LICENSE: A license which permits the operation of any gaming other than 15 or less slot machines.

The following forms and items must be submitted to the State Gaming Control Board in conjunction with your application for a Nonrestricted Gaming License:

1. Form GCB-3, Application for State Gaming License: To be filed in duplicate on behalf of the business entity seeking to be licensed, for example, individual proprietorship, partnership, trust, corporation, etc.

    a. Form GCB-3KE is to be submitted by applicants for key employee;

    b. Form GCB-3EL is to submitted by applicants seeking an interest in an existing licensed operation or by presently licensed applicants of licensed corporation who are changing officer and/or director positions.

2. Form GCB-4, Personal History Record: To be filed in duplicate by every person who has a financial interest, direct or indirect, in the business entity, including all officers, directors, and stockholders of a closed corporation. Certain officers, directors, and stockholders in a publicly-traded corporation must be found suitable for licensing. The Gaming Control Board has the right to require any individual who has a financial interest of any nature to be licensed or found suitable for licensing.

3. Form GCB-5, Invested Capital Questionnaire: To be filed in duplicate by each individual who has any financial interest, direct or indirect, in the business entity, and for all corporate officers, directors, and key employees. The applicant agrees to provide any additional financial information, i.e., tax returns, stock certificates, notes, passbooks, cancelled checks, etc., the Board may require.

4. Fingerprint Cards: Two completed fingerprint cards for each individual applicant must be submitted. Fingerprinting may be completed at any law enforcement facility. Each applicant must sign the fingerprint cards.

5. Form 10, Affidavit of Full Disclosure: To be filed by each individual required to be licensed or to be found suitable.

6. "Applicant's Request to Release Information" Form: To be filed in duplicate by each individual required to be licensed or found suitable.

7. "Release of All Claims" Form: To be filed by each individual required to be licensed or found suitable.

8. A check, money order, or cash in the amount of $250.00 per applicant, to cover the initial investigative fee. Checks are to be made payable to the State Gaming Control Board. Any additional costs of investigation will be charged as provided by statute and regulation.

9. Two copies of each of the following:
   a. Partnership Agreement
   b. Trust Agreement
   c. Joint Venture Agreement
   d. Articles of Incorporation and Amendments thereto; a Nevada corporation is required to file an Amendment to the Articles of Incorporation, adding the mandatory language as provided for in Regulation 15.500.1. The filing fee is $20.00 and certified copies may be obtained at $5.00 each. Checks should be made payable to the Secretary of the State of Nevada and should accompany the Amendment. The Amendment must be submitted to the State Gaming Control Board for approval and filing.
   e. Lease Agreement
   f. Purchase/Sale Agreement
   g. Management Agreement
   h. Employment Contract
   i. Stock bonus or profit sharing plans

10. A general description of the nature of the business of the applicant.

11. A complete list of all stockholders and/or partners showing the number of shares and/or interest held of record by each.

12. If the applicant has been a corporation in business for three or more fiscal years, balance sheets and profit and loss statements for the past 3 fiscal years, certified by independent certified public accountants certified or registered in the State of Nevada, must be submitted to the Board. If the corporate applicant has not been in existence for the past 3 fiscal years, such statements covering the period from the creation of the business to the present must be submitted.

13. If the business entity is seeking initial licensing, a one year Casino Cash Flow Projection and a statement of Pre-opening Cash must be submitted (See the Sample Format for further directions).

14. An internal controls procedure, as required by Regulation 6 (See the separate instructional material provided).

NOTICE

AN APPLICATION MAY NOT BE WITHDRAWN
WITHOUT THE PERMISSION OF THE STATE
GAMING CONTROL BOARD OR THE NEVADA
GAMING COMMISSION.

Appendix 2-2. Licensing Guidelines.
January 1, 1977 (Second Revision)

Pursuant to NRS 463.210, the Gaming Control Board may recommend denial of an application "for any cause deemed reasonable by the board."

In making its recommendation, the board gives due consideration for the proper protection of the public health, safety, morals, good order and general welfare of the inhabitants of the State of Nevada and the preservation of the competitive economy and the policies of free competition of the State of Nevada.

The board takes official notice that public confidence in the honesty of gambling in Nevada is essential to a viable gaming industry. It follows, therefore, that good character, honesty and integrity are qualities that any person must possess to be found suitable to receive a license.

With respect to licensing guidelines, the applicant must bear in mind Reg. 4.010 of the Regulations of the Nevada Gaming Commission and State Gaming Control Board, which reads:

4.010 Application general.

1. It is the declared policy of Nevada that all establishments, where gambling games are conducted or operated are licensed and controlled so as to better protect the public health, safety, morals, good order and welfare of inhabitants and to preserve the competitive economy and the policies of free competition of the State of Nevada. Any gaming license which is issued or registration, or finding of suitability, or approval by the commission shall be deemed to be a revocable privilege and no person holding such a license or registration or finding of suitability or approval by the commission is deemed to have acquired any vested rights therein.

2. An applicant for a state gaming license is seeking the granting of a privilege, and the burden of proving his qualification to receive any license is at all times on the applicant. An applicant must accept any risk of adverse public notice, embarrassment, criticism, or other action of financial loss which may result from action with respect to an application and expressly waive any claim for damages as a result thereof.

3. An application for a license, determination of suitability, or registration, besides any other factor attaching to such an application by virtue of the Nevada Gaming Control Act and the regulations thereunder, shall constitute a request to the board and commission for a decision upon the applicants' general suitability, character, integrity, and ability to participate or engage in, or be associated with, the gaming industry in the manner or position sought by the application, or the manner or position generally similar thereto; and, by filing an application with the board, the applicant specifically consents to the making of such a decision by the board and commission at their election when the application, after filing, becomes moot for any reason other than death.

(Amended: 6/67;4/73;9/73)

The board may, in its discretion, recommend denial for any of the following reasons, or for any other reason consistent with the general policy set forth in the second paragraph above:

1. Conviction of any crime of violence, any crime involving fraud, any crime involving gambling, any crime involving thievery, any crime involving moral turpitude, or any crime involving evasion of taxes, or any other offense indicating a lack of business integrity or business honesty, whether committed in this State or elsewhere, and whether denominated a felony or a misdemeanor.

2. Failure to satisfactorily explain arrests which suggest applicant has exhibited lack of due regard for constituted laws or authority.

3. Failure to satisfy the board as to the applicant's good character, honesty or integrity.

4. Identification as a member of, or an associate of, organized criminal elements by any law enforcement agency, legislative body or crime commission.

5. Association with, either socially or in business affairs, persons of notorious or unsavory reputation where the repute of the State of Nevada or the gaming industry is liable to be damaged by such association.

6. Failure to satisfy the board as to the source of funds to be invested in the proposed or existing venture.

7. Prior unsuitable operation as a gaming licensee without regard to whether disciplinary action was taken at that time or whether the acts were sufficient to justify revocation of a gaming license.

8. Applicant is a person whose ownership of, or presence in, a licensed casino is found by the board, on the basis of the facts and evidence before it, to constitute a threat to the public health, safety, morals, good order and general welfare of inhabitants of the State of Nevada or to the competitive economy and policies of free competition of the State of Nevada.

9. Applicant is a person whose licensing by the State of Nevada would reflect or tend to reflect discredit upon the State of Nevada or the gaming industry.

10. The proposed financial arrangements are inadequate for the proposed operation.

11. The source of any or all of the applicant's proposed investment is unsuitable to be connected with a licensed gaming operation.

12. Applicant is presently under indictment or the subject of a criminal complaint for any of the crimes described in paragraph 1 above.

13. The location is a business catering to persons under 21 years of age, or a high proportion of the persons frequenting the premises are under 21 years of age.

14. Making or causing to be made any statement in an application or document provided to the board or its agents or orally to a board member or agent in connection with an application, which statement was at the time and in the light of the circumstances under which it was made, false or misleading.

15. Lack of a satisfactory record of business competence and business ethics and integrity.

These guidelines are in addition to those which are contained in the Regulations of the Nevada Gaming Commission and State Gaming Control Board and are set forth below:

3.010 Unsuitable locations. The board may recommend that an application for a state gaming license be denied, and the commission may deny the same, if the board or the commission deems that the place or location for which the license is sought is unsuitable for the conduct of gaming operations. Without limiting the generality of the foregoing, the following places or locations may be deemed unsuitable:

1. Premises located within the immediate vicinity of churches, hospitals, schools and children's public playgrounds.

2. Premises located within the immediate vicinity of a military or naval reservation or camp.

3. Premises located in a place where gaming is contrary to a valid zoning ordinance of any county or city, unless the premises had been used for gaming at a time prior to the effective date of the zoning ordinance.

4. Premises difficult to police.

5. Areas where gaming operations would not be conducive to good relations with neighboring states.

Appendix 2-3. Multiple Licensing Criteria

3.070 Multiple licensing criteria. In every instance in which a person, entity, or persons involved in an entity, holding a gaming license in the State of Nevada, makes application for an additional license, the board and commission shall consider whether such multiple licensing is in the best interests of the State of Nevada, having due regard for the protection of the safety, morals, good order and general welfare of the inhabitants of the State of Nevada. In making this determination, the following are some factors which may be considered:

1. Has there been an adequate period of performance by the applicant upon which the board and commission could base a conclusion as to the effectiveness of the existing operations warranting further extension?

2. Does the applicant have sufficient key employees to operate an additional location so that multiple licensing would not result in dilution of effective managerial capacity and control of existing operations?

3. Has the applicant applied for an existing operation or for a facility which is to be constructed?

4. What are the plans of the applicant for the development and expansion of existing operations?

5. What are the plans of the applicant for a continuity of operation in the event of the death or disability of the applicant?

6. Does the applicant have ownership interests of any kind or nature in any of the competitor companies in the gaming industry?

7. What would the result of the multiple licensing be of the percentage of interest of the applicant to similarly situated competitors on a statewide, countywide and geographical location basis in each of the following categories:

> (a) Total number of slot machines.
> (b) Total number of games.
> (c) Total number of tables
> (d) Gross revenue.
> (e) Percentage tax.
> (f) Casino entertainment tax.
> (g) Number of rooms available for the public.
> (h) Number of employees hired.
> (i) Total payroll.

8. Would acquisition pose problems or create a monopoly?

9. Would acquisition pose problems in any of the following categories:

> (a) Becoming so large as to become its own supplier of goods and services required by the licensee at all establishments.
> (b) Establishing employment practices inimical to the welfare of the gaming industry.
> (c) Establishment of control in method of play or percentage realized from play that would be inimical to the welfare of the gaming industry.
> (d) Without cause, the establishment of a seasonal operation or reduced number of shifts per day, inimical to the economy of the area.

10. Interlocking corporation directorships within licensed or unlicensed operations which might contribute to any of the foregoing factors.

11. Any other index or criteria deemed by the board and commission to be relevant to the effect of multiple licensing upon the public health, safety, morals, good order and general welfare of the public of the State of Nevada.

(Adopted: 11/68.)

♠ ♡ ♣ ◇   CHAPTER 3

Taxation of Casino Operations

Introduction

This chapter presents and discusses the various types of taxes levied on casino operations. The discussion is limited to taxes applied on gross revenue, together with various license fees. Income taxation is dealt with in chapter 11.

These taxes are not only significant costs of operation in a casino, but they are also of great importance in the accounting and financial reporting of casino operations.

Local Government Interest in Casino Taxation

The major casinos of Nevada and New Jersey represent significant sources of taxation revenue for all levels of government. The local governments have a very real interest in the amounts of taxes generated by these operations.[1]

It has been suggested that one of the major forces behind the proliferation of various forms of gambling has been the need for local governments to generate additional tax revenues from nontraditional sources.

Proposals for legalized gaming in Atlantic City, Miami Beach, New York City, and other areas are all being or have been actively promoted on the basis of the additional revenues that would flow into the local economy for support industries and employment and into local government coffers through increased tax revenues.

Gaming taxes are also of considerable significance as an operating cost for a casino. Based on the 1984 *Nevada Gaming Abstract*, the gaming taxes and licenses, at all levels, averaged 7.8% of gross gaming revenue for 145 casinos with gaming revenue over $1 million per year.[2] This tax bill was second only to payroll as an expense item in the casino.

Definition of Gaming Taxes

This discussion of gaming taxes does not include a consideration of income taxation that may be levied at the local, state, or federal level. Income taxation is discussed separately in chapter 11. Gaming taxes in the present context could more aptly be described as license fees or excise taxes. These taxes are traditionally based either on gross revenue or on the number and type of games in the casino.

Types of Gaming Taxation

Taxation of gaming and casino activities takes place at all levels of government. Table 3-1 outlines the present major gaming taxes. There are levies at the federal, state, and local government levels in Nevada, and at the federal and state level in New Jersey. Each of these taxes is discussed below.

Federal Taxation

The federal government has for many years viewed casino taxation not as revenue generation, but as a punitive measure designed to assist various law enforcement agencies and attorneys in

Table 3-1. Gaming Taxes.

FEDERAL TAXES:
- Slot Tax (repealed 7/1/80)
- Wagering Excise Tax
- Occupation Stamp Tax

STATE TAXES—NEVADA:
- Percentage Fees—quarterly
- License Fees—annual and quarterly
- Annual Slot Tax
- Entertainment Tax
- Miscellaneous Fees

LOCAL TAXES—NEVADA:
- County quarterly license fees
- Other local ordinances as specified

STATE TAXES—NEW JERSEY:
- State License Fee
- Annual Slot Tax
- Gross Revenue Tax
- Casino Reinvestment Tax

identifying illegal gaming operations or to provide statutory avenues for punishment for not paying the various fees and taxes due, when other criminal sanctions could not be imposed or sustained. With the growing number of legal gaming establishments, there have been frequent calls for the repeal and elimination of all of these federal taxes.

Federal Slot Tax

The first federal tax, which was the most significant but was repealed effective July 1, 1980, was the coin-operated gaming device tax. This tax was imposed at the rate of $250 per year for each device. This so-called slot tax applied to all types of coin-operated devices, including automatic poker, keno, and 21 games. The tax was substantially rebated to the state in which it was collected. The rebate was 80% in 1978 and rose to 100% in 1980. At that time, the tax was eliminated at the federal level. However, both Nevada and New Jersey continued the tax as a state tax.

During the period when the tax was being applied, it had several provisions of accounting importance. First, the amount of tax was due and payable on or before June 20, for the coming year. This created substantial year-end accounting accruals on the June 30 accounts of any casino operation using the accrual method of accounting. Also, the tax was nonrefundable; if the casino closed, no refund was forthcoming. However, in case of a transfer of ownership, then the new owners would receive credit for the tax payments, since the tax was considered to be attached to the machines. When the machines were transferred, the taxes paid were also assumed to be transferred during the change.

Federal Wagering Excise Tax

This tax is known as the wagering excise tax (26 USC 4401). It is levied at the rate of .25% (1/4 of 1%) on all wagers placed on a sports event or contest with a bookmaker, any wagers placed in a wagering pool (such as a pari-mutuel pool in dog racing or jai alai), or the wagers made on a lottery. (Of course, the wagers made on a state-conducted lottery are tax exempt under traditional constitutional prohibitions on the taxation of governments.) The amount of the wagering excise tax was reduced in 1975 from the rate of 10% to 2% and in 1984 from 2% to the present .25%. There have been persistent calls for the complete elimination of the excise tax. The present rate represents virtual elimination.

From an accounting standpoint, it must be realized that this tax is levied on the gross amount of the wager and can amount to a very significant amount of money. The excise tax is due and payable on a monthly basis. The tax return used to report these tax payments is IRS Form #730, which must be filed monthly by the end of the month following the reporting period. For accounting purposes, these taxes due are accrued at the end of the accounting period.

The significance of this tax is reflected in the following comment taken from a news article:

SPARKS SPORTS BOOK CLOSES

A federal wagering tax which "bled us dry" was blamed Tuesday for prompting the closure of the Winners Circle, a Sparks race and sports book facility which opened 2½ years ago.

Co-owner Tony Maccioli conceded that generally poor economic conditions and increased sports book competition in the area contributed to the firm's problems. But he said the business was "really buried" by the special tax.

"The federal (two percent) tax was a killer for us. The government took $250,000 from our winnings during the time we were in business and that's too much for a small operation like ours to absorb," Maccioli said. "To make matters worse, the tax is assessed on the total handle rather than the net. It's a devastating, unconstitutional tax."[3]

Federal Wagering Occupational Stamp Tax

This tax, known as the wagering occupational stamp tax (26 UCS 4411), is a special occupational stamp that is required of both the principals and agents or—in legal parlance—"any person" who is liable for or who is engaged in receiving wagers for or on behalf of any person. For example, this not only makes the casino operating a sports and race book responsible for the occupational stamp, but also makes all the employees who are engaged in taking wagers liable for having the occupational stamps. The stamp amount is $50, and in 1984 there were approximately 900 stamps sold in Nevada. This stamp applies only to wagers and wagering and only to sports and race books, pari-mutuel pools, and lotteries. Again, the state-operated lotteries and their employees are exempt from the licensing requirements. The occupational stamps are nontransferable from person to person and are nonrefundable. They

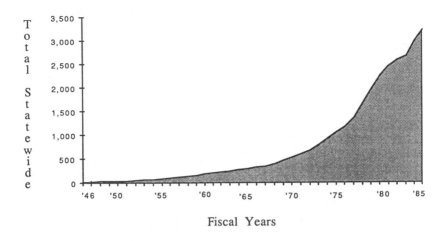

Fiscal Years

Fig. 3-1. Statewide gross gaming revenue.

must be purchased by June 30 for the next year. Application and payment are made on IRS Form 11-C; if stamps are purchased during the year, the amount due is prorated from the date of application to the end of the following year.

Nevada State Taxation

The taxes at the state level are discussed with particular regard to the present structure in Nevada and New Jersey. The number and amount of state taxes are very significant. The importance of the gaming taxes to Nevada is overwhelming. Figure 3-1 indicates the growth of the total amount of gross gaming revenue on a statewide basis in Nevada from 1946 to 1984. During 1984, the state realized $185.7 million from state tax and license fees on gaming. This amounted to 48% of the total revenues collected by the State of Nevada General Fund.[4]

The amount collected in New Jersey is similar in magnitude to the amount collected in Nevada. However, the percentage that gaming fees represent to the total New Jersey state budget is significantly less.[5]

State-level taxation in Nevada is broken into four broad categories. The first is percentage fees, which constitute a percentage tax on the gross gaming revenue of the casino. The second category is various license fees. In this category are so-called state fees, levied by and for the benefit of the state, as well as county fees, levied by the state but for the benefit of the counties. The third category is a special fee called the casino entertainment tax, which is a percentage fee on revenues arising in nongaming areas when the casino is in "entertainment status." The fourth and final category is a variety of miscellaneous fees applied to other gaming activities.

State-level taxation in New Jersey is somewhat simpler, but with a structure similar to Nevada's. The first category is a tax as a percentage fee based on the gross gaming revenue. The second category is a percentage fee for reinvestment of casino profits in redevelopment projects in New Jersey. The third category consists of various license fees for the games and slot machines. At the present time, there are no other fees applied to gaming activities.

Nevada State Percentage Fees

The monthly percentage fees in Nevada are levied under the authority of Nevada Revised Statutes (NRS 463.370). These fees are a percentage on a sliding scale based on the total amount of gross revenue. The rates in effect are indicated in table 3-2. During the 1981 legislative session, the rate of tax on the top revenue category was increased by ¼ of 1%.[6] The tax increase had a "sunset" provision and was due to be reduced to 5.5% from 5.75% as of July 1, 1985. However, actions taken in the 1984 Legislature kept the top rate at 5.75%. It is important to note that the tax rate breaks are specified in terms of the amount of gross gaming revenue on a monthly basis. The tax is due on or before the twenty-fourth of the month following the month for which the return applied. Penalties of late payment, which are mandatory, not optional, are 25% of the amount due—with a $25 minimum and a $1,000 maximum penalty. The tax is reported on form NGC-1.

There has been an extensive amount of debate, both informally and in courts of law, regarding the definition of what con-

Table 3-2. State of Nevada. Monthly Percentage Fees on
Gross Gaming Revenue.

Percentage Amount	Gross Revenue per Month
3%	of the first $50,000
plus 4%	of the next $84,000 (i.e., $50,000 to $134,000)
plus 5.75%	of revenue over $134,000

stitutes gross gaming revenue. The current statutory definition takes gross gaming revenue to mean all winnings, less only the total of all sums paid out as losses and with no deductions for general operating expenses, but allowing the deduction of certain give-away prizes added to gaming winnings.[7]

Two areas of dispute have arisen in the computation of gross gaming revenue. The first dispute centers around the definition of items such as the rake-off, time buy-in, or commissions for poker games, where the income is not really casino "win" in the traditional sense but is revenue to the casino. The second involves the timing of the receipt of gaming revenue, where the winning may be in the form of credit instruments known as *markers*, but the real cash collection may take place sometime in the future.

Poker Rake-off, Time Buy-In, and Commissions   The definition of gross gaming revenue in the statute is "total winnings minus all sums paid out as losses." A Gaming Control Board regulation further defines the gross revenue as including "all sums received by the licensee as a percentage rake-off, a time buy-in, or other compensation charged for the privilege of playing." A lawsuit challenged this expanded definition and asked that amounts paid under the poker winnings category not be subjected to gross revenue taxation. Without waiting for the judicial outcome, the 1981 Legislature acted to redefine gross revenue in order to eliminate any misunderstanding, ambiguity, or debate over what was intended to constitute gross revenue.[8] This action now requires including poker rake-off and similar items in gross gaming revenue.

Markers and Credit Instruments   The second issue of the nature of gross revenue is the practice of not requiring casinos to report winnings based on casino credit advanced to customers but not yet paid. According to Gaming Control Board Regulation 6.080, credit play winnings (receivables or markers) are not included in gross gaming revenue until they are collected. The current practice in computing the adjustment to gross gaming revenue to account for credit play is shown below.

Net win from operations: Cash and Credit	$6,854,358
Less: Adjustment for Credit Play	
1. Subtract outstanding credit issued during the period	(385,000)

2. Add credit instruments collected during the period	173,000
Net Credit Play Adjustment	(212,000)
Gross Gaming Revenue for Taxation Purpose	$6,642,358

In subsequent periods, when the balance of the $385,000 in markers was collected, the casino would then include the amounts in gross gaming revenue at the time collected.

This cash method of accounting for gross gaming revenue is allowed under Regulation 6.020 of the Gaming Control Board for revenue reporting purposes, even if the financial statements of the entity may be presented on a full accrual basis.

Another issue is that the Gaming Control Board is very concerned with the abuse of markers, where money may be transferred out of the casino by advancing money on credit and never collecting or even making an effort to collect the funds. Under revised rules passed during the 1981 legislative session, gross revenue for state taxation purposes will include certain uncollected markers if the Gaming Control Board determines that:

1. The marker is improperly executed or does not have enough information to make it reasonably collectible.

2. There was no verification of the credit-worthiness prior to issuance of the credit.

3. There was no evidence of reasonable effort to collect the marker.[9]

The state's basic position is that if the credit was not extended properly, then the amount extended should be subject to gross revenue taxation, regardless of whether or not it was collected.

The action is clearly a move both to reduce the issuance of substandard markers by putting the casino on notice that the tax is due on those amounts and to impose a small penalty on poor credit administration in order to encourage upgrading of the quality of marker credit issuance.

Nevada State License Fees

There are a multitude of Nevada state license fees, which vary according to the type of gaming license and the number of machines and table games in operation. The fees are payable both annually and quarterly, with some rates computed on an annual basis and some on a quarterly basis.

Annual Slot Tax The first state annual fee is the annual state slot machine tax that is authorized by NRS 463.385. This is the tax that has replaced the federal slot tax. The amount of this tax is $250 per year, due and payable—in advance, as of June 20, for the ensuing year of operation. There is a provision for the prorating of the fees on a monthly basis on new machines put into operation. There is a penalty of 25% of the amount due for late payment. In addition, under changes of ownership, there are limited provisions under NRS 463.386 for the transferability of the tax due. However, if the operation is under substantially new ownership, then the fees must be paid again by the new owners.

The federal slot tax was payable on the basis of $250 per mechanism. This often resulted in confusion regarding the number of slot machines or other coin-operated devices in a casino. Specialty slot machines, consisting of multiple reels, or totem pole slots, or banks of three or four machines in a row with a single handle are taxed on the number of sets of reels in the machine.

This is in direct contrast with the state of Nevada, which regards the number of slot machines or coin-operated devices as the number of machines with a separate handle to play. In simple terms, the old federal rules counted the machines on a "mechanism basis," while the state counts on a "handle" basis. This often resulted in minor but troublesome differences in the counts of the number of slot machines in the casino.

Annual State License Fee The annual state license fee is levied under NRS 463.380 and is computed according to the total number of games that the casino operates. The number of games is computed by excluding card games that are not "banking" games, such as keno and bingo. Games such as 21, craps, and roulette are included. The fees are set on a sliding scale, which is indicated in table 3-3.

The tax amount generally increases as the number of games goes up, but there appears to be a somewhat heavier per game tax burden for those clubs that operate five to sixteen games. For example, a casino with five games would pay a fee of $350 per game for a total of $1,750. A sixteen-game casino would pay $1,000 per game for a total of $16,000. However, a very large casino with 100 games would pay a total of $32,800, or an average of $328 per game. These relationships are illustrated in figures 3-2 and 3-3.

The state law does not provide for a prorating of the fees for

Table 3-3. Nevada Annual State License Fees.

Number of Games	Annual Amount	Per Game
1	$100 total	100
2	200 total	100
3	400 total	133.33
4	750 total	187.50
5	1,750 total	350
6–7	3,000 total	428.57
8–10	6,000 total	600
11–16	1,000 each game	1,000
Over 16	16,000 plus $200 each game over 16	200

a partial-year operation, although there is the same limited transferability to new owners as in the case of the annual slot tax. The taxes on the annual basis are due and payable on or before December 31 for the coming calendar year. The penalty for late payment is mandatory and amounts to 25% of the total tax due. The annual license fee reporting form for Nevada is NGC-2.

Annual State License Fee for Nonrestricted Slot Machines The next state license fee is for nonrestricted slot operations.[10] The distinction is drawn between nonrestricted and restricted slot licenses. Restricted licenses operate less than fifteen machines at any one location. Nonrestricted licenses operate sixteen or more machines or any number of slot machines if they are operated in conjunction with other games such as 21, craps, keno, or bingo.

The amount of the tax is $80 per year for each slot machine. As previously discussed, the state of Nevada definition of a slot or coin-operated machine is based not on the internal reel mechanism count, but on the number of machines in the casino. The amount of the tax, although expressed as an annual rate, is payable in advance on or before the end of each quarter. There is no provision for the prorating of the fee during the quarter, and the availability of transfer to new owners is the same as previously discussed. The penalty for late payment is again a mandatory 25% of the fees due. The license fee reporting form is NGC-15.

Quarterly Flat License Fees The quarterly flat license fees are authorized under NRS 463.383. Their operation is very similar to the annual state license fee. This tax is based on the number of games being operated and is in addition to, and should not be confused

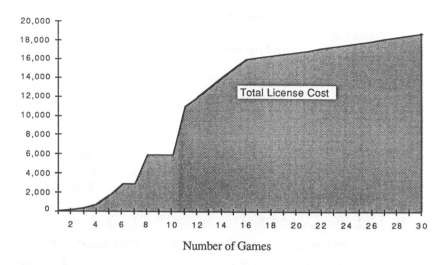

Fig. 3-2. State of Nevada annual game license fees.

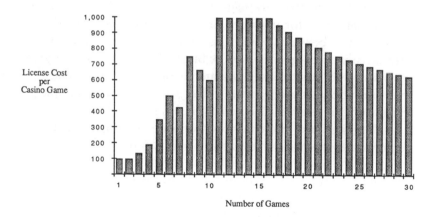

Fig. 3-3. Nevada state annual license fee per game.

with, the quarterly gross revenue percentage license fee previously discussed. The computation of the number of games in a location is the same as under the annual fee, and the scale of rates is presented in table 3-4. Note that these are annual rates, but again are payable on a quarterly basis. The payments are due and payable

Table 3–4. Nevada Quarterly Flat License Fees.

Number of Games	Annual Amount	Per Game
1	$50 total	50
2	100 total	50
3	200 total	66.66
4	375 total	93.75
5	875 total	175
6–7	1,500 total	214.29
8–10	3,000 total	300
11–16	500 total each game 1–16 inclusive	500
17–26	8,000 plus $4,800 each game 17–26	4,800
27–35	56,000 plus $2,800 each game 27–35	2,800
Over 35	81,200 plus $100 each game over 35	100

on the last day of the last month of each calendar quarter, for the ensuing quarter. The quarterly payment is in advance and should be based on the number of games expected to be in operation during that quarter.

The quarterly fees are initially much lower, but rise much more sharply until the maximum of $4,800 per game is reached for casinos with seventeen to twenty-six games and then fall to a rate of $100 per game for the very largest casinos. This pattern of increasing rates per game with a decrease for the largest number of games places the same heavy tax burden on those casinos with a medium-sized operation. There are no provisions for prorating of fees during a quarter, but the same general provisions apply to transfers of ownership. The standard penalty of 25% of the amount due is applied on a mandatory basis for late payments. The information for this fee is reported on form NGC-15.

Quarterly Restricted Slot License Fee   The last state tax is that applied only to restricted slot license operations.[11] These licenses apply to operations where there are fifteen or fewer slot machines at any location and where there are no other table games. These small operations are required to pay a fee of $35 per machine per quarter. The amounts are due and payable in advance for each quarter on the last day of the last month of the quarter for the ensuing quarter and are also based on the number of slot machines expected to be in operation. The same provisions of prorating, transferability of interest, and penalties apply for the nonrestricted slot machine tax as for other slot machine license fees. The reporting form is also NGC-15.

Casino Entertainment Tax   The next category of state tax is a unique Nevada tax levied not on the gaming revenues, but on the amounts paid for admission, merchandise, refreshments, or service while a casino is in "entertainment status"[12]—which is broadly defined to mean live music or other cabaret entertainment. This tax is based on the authority of NRS 463.401. The basic tax rate is 10% of the amounts collected under the above definition. In terms of total dollars collected, the casino entertainment tax is the second largest tax, following only the percentage gross revenue quarterly tax in revenue to the state of Nevada.

The casino entertainment tax has been subjected to numerous legal challenges for a variety of reasons. The principal problem is the difficulty of determining if a casino is in " entertainment status." Subtle differences—such as a lounge act playing in a glassed-in room, not an open space with access to the gaming area—have resulted in substantial additional tax assessments based on food and beverage receipts in the general casino area. These assessments have given rise to an equally substantial tax dispute. The general rule is that the tax applies clearly to expenditures made in showrooms and specific lounges, but does not apply to all beverage and food expenditures in restaurants—if there is no entertainment in the immediate area.

There were various changes to the law regarding the casino entertainment tax in the 1981 Legislature. The principal change is that the tax was formerly due on a quarterly basis, on the last of the month following the quarter for which the return applied. The law was amended to call for monthly filing of returns, by the last day of the month following, if the aggregate amount of tax due is $500 or more per month. All other returns would remain on a quarterly basis. The penalty for late payment of the casino entertainment tax is now 1% monthly of the amount due. All casino entertainment tax returns are filed on form NGC-11.

Miscellaneous State Taxes and Fees   There are a number of miscellaneous taxes and fees that are applied by the state. This discussion is limited to regular, repetitive fees and taxes and does not include fees such as investigatory fees, application fees for licensing, or other one-time fees levied by the state authorities.

The first miscellaneous taxes were levied on the dissemination of racing information by various news services. The amount of tax, as specified by NRS 463.450, is $10 per day for each race book serviced. The statute is silent on the various administrative aspects of the race book fees, but they are due on a quarterly basis, in arrears, on the last day of the month following the quarter. The same rates of penalty apply to late payment as for other state fees.

The second tax is the tax on pari-mutuel pools. These pools are taxed at the rate of 3% of the total handle. This rate is equivalent to the federal excise tax on wagers imposed on all race book wagering. The pari-mutuel tax of the state is applied only to wagering on any racing or sporting event other than horse or dog racing. The authority of the tax is NRS 464.040, and in Nevada it applies principally to the jai alai operations. The amounts are payable quarterly, in arrears, on the last day of the month following the end of the quarter.

The third tax is that levied on manufacturers, sellers, and distributors of devices or machines used in gambling.[13] This excludes pinball machines. The amount of the tax is $500 per year for a manufacturer's license, either initial or a renewal, and $200 for a seller or distributor's license, again either a new license or a renewal. The manufacturer's fees are payable annually, in advance, on or before June 30 of each year for the coming fiscal year. There are no standard reporting forms for these miscellaneous taxes.

Local Gaming Taxes in Nevada

The local taxes in the state of Nevada are divided into two categories. The first category is a single tax, called the county quarterly license fee. This tax was passed into law by the state on behalf of the counties. The payments are made to the county sheriff, and the monies are subsequently transferred to the county treasurer for use in the county general fund. The administration of the tax is entirely a local county matter, with only the enabling legislation being a product of the state. All gaming operations within the county must pay the county quarterly license fee, regardless of the additional county or city levies that must be paid.

The rates of tax under the county quarterly license fee are set under NRS 463.390 and are presented in table 3-5. The amounts of the taxes are specified on a monthly basis.

The amount of the county quarterly license fee is payable in advance, on a quarterly basis, and is due and payable on or before the last day of the end of the quarter for the ensuing quarter. There is provision for ownership transfer as outlined in NRS 463.386, and the taxes are generally transferable with the machines or games to

Table 3-5. Nevada County Quarterly License Fees.

Category	Monthly Amount
Card Games (nonbanking)	$25 per table per month
Table Games (21, Craps, etc.)	$50 per game per month
Slot Machines	$10 per machine per month

which they apply. The standard 25% penalty applies to late payment of this tax.

Local Ordinances   The second broad category of local taxes in Nevada are those imposed by local ordinances by the respective counties and cities. Appendix 3-1 to this chapter outlines the county and city levies in effect as of June 30, 1983. These local fees are very extensive and can vary widely from county to county and city to city. In spite of the variety, there are a number of common elements.

The local tax rates are generally imposed on all gaming establishments within their jurisdiction. Thus, a casino in an incorporated city would be liable to pay not only the taxes under the local county ordinances, but also the tax levied under city ordinances. If the casino is operated outside of the limits of the incorporated city, then it would only have to pay a single local tax—to the county. An exception to this rule is Clark County, where there is no county tax if the casino is within the incorporated areas, so that a casino in the city of Las Vegas would pay only the city of Las Vegas fees. A different program exists in Washoe County, where there is one rate for casinos in the incorporated cities of Reno and Sparks and a second, somewhat higher rate for casinos outside of the incorporated areas. In Washoe County, the casinos located in the city of Reno are responsible for the reduced Washoe County rate plus the city of Reno fees. Table 3-6 indicates the difference. These differentials are an attempt by local governments to recognize the duplicate burden of taxation and to provide some relief to the casinos.

Table 3-6. Washoe County Gaming Tax Rates.

| | RATE APPLICABLE TO: | |
| | Unincorporated | Cities of Reno |
Description	Washoe County	and Sparks
Poker and Other Nonbanking Games	$100 per year	$ 75 per year
Slot Machines	$ 40 per year	$ 30 per year
All Other Games	$200 per year	$150 per year

Local taxes in Nevada have a bewildering array of miscellaneous provisions. For example, in Washoe County, the taxes at the county level are not due until the first day of the quarter, but are still payable in advance. They do have a prorating schedule for payments of games and slot machines added during the quarter, but do not have any provisions for penalties for late payment, short of sealing the machines to prevent their use.

The State Legislature in 1981 passed a law, as part of a property tax and spending limitation program, to limit the amount of increases that local governments can implement in fees from year to year. Under NRS 463.395, local government gaming fees were limited to those in place as of April 27, 1981. This freeze on local government fees went beyond the general restriction imposed on other governmental fees, which limited the increases to cost-of-living increases plus the percentage of population increase in the jurisdiction of the local government. This move was to avoid having the local governments excessively increase local gaming fees and taxes.

Casino Taxation in New Jersey

The New Jersey laws with respect to casino taxation are presented below. In total, they have roughly the same structure as Nevada's, with license fees annually payable for the right to operate, coupled with a gross revenue tax at the state level. At present, there are no specific gaming license fees levied by the local government in Atlantic City.

Federal Taxation

The casino operations in Atlantic City are subject to the same federal taxes as Nevada operations. Since the present federal laws are applicable to sports and race book betting, neither of which is allowed within the casinos in Atlantic City, the federal levies do not have any effect in New Jersey. The old federal slot machine tax has been taken over by the state of New Jersey, in a fashion similar to that in Nevada.

New Jersey State Taxation

The taxation and fees for Atlantic City operations within the state of New Jersey are applied at the state level as follows:

1. State License Fee.
2. Annual Slot Tax.

3. Gross Revenue Tax.
4. Casino Reinvestment Tax.

State License Fees The state license fee is a single fixed amount, for the initial application and subsequent renewals. The initial fee was to be at least $200,000, with annual renewals not less than $100,000. The actual license fee is determined after the fact by considering all the costs of maintaining the control and regulatory activities of the respective state enforcement and control agencies. This cost is then allocated back to the casino in the form of a state license fee. The license fee is a flat dollar amount and is not to be determined on the cost of controlling individual casinos. These charges are determined by having the aggregate administrative costs of the control agencies shared by all casinos equally. The specific authority for the license fee is contained in *New Jersey Statutes—Annotated (NJSA 5:12-139)*. The license fee is not based on the number of games or slots in the casino, as is the case in Nevada. The annual license fee is nonrefundable and nontransferable. No mention is made in the statute of a prorating of part-year license fees or of a specific date for renewal of the license. Based on current practice, the licenses appear to run for one year from the date of granting and do not expire on a set date.

Annual Slot Fee This tax is New Jersey's version of the federal slot tax. The tax is authorized by *NJSA* 5:12-140 and amounts to $250 per machine per year. The fee is due and payable on July 1 of each year with regard to all slot machines in use on that date. Additional machines may be added on a pro-rata basis. The tax is nonrefundable but is transferable with the machine.

Gross Revenue Tax The gross revenue tax is authorized under *NJSA* 5:12-144. It calls for a tax of 8% on the gross revenue of the casino. Deductions are allowed for uncollected casino credit instruments (markers), but only to a maximum of 4% of the gross revenue, including markers. A sample calculation of the amount of tax due under the New Jersey Gross Revenue Statute is shown here.

The computation is very similar to that used in Nevada. The payment of the gross revenue tax is due weekly by authority of the Casino Control Commission, but the statutory period is monthly collection due by the tenth of the following month. There is a

March 15 deadline for filing the annual gross revenue report for the prior calendar year.

Gross Winnings: Cash and Credit	$6,854,358
Less: Credit Adjustment (the lesser of	
actual uncollected or 4% of gross winnings)	
Actual 212,000	
4% 289,574	
	(212,000)
Amount Subject to New Jersey Tax at 8%	$6,642,358

Casino Reinvestment Tax In addition to the 8% gross revenue tax, there is an additional 2.5% tax (authorized under New Jersey Public Law 1984, chapter 218).[14] This tax is to be paid if the gross investment made by the casino in the community or in authorized reinvestment projects does not meet or exceed 2.5% of gross revenue. This tax is either to assure the redevelopment of Atlantic City or to result in the payment of a like amount to the government, which will in turn be directed to such development efforts. A casino can offset this investment tax obligation by obtaining investment tax credits. These credits can be obtained by investing in Casino Reinvestment Development Authority bonds or by making direct investment in projects authorized by the CRDA. The amount of the casino's reinvestment tax credit is twice the amount of such investments. Thus, the 2.5% tax can be avoided by an investment equal to 1.25% of the casino gross revenue. The purpose of the tax credit provisions of the law is to encourage casinos to make the investments, rather than simply paying the tax. Table 3-7 presents a summary of the principal elements of each gaming tax.

Distribution of Tax Proceeds in Nevada and New Jersey

Of considerable interest is the distribution of the various license fees and taxes that are imposed on the casino operations. Table 3-8 and figure 3-4 indicate and illustrate the proceeds distribution for the various taxes in both New Jersey and Nevada. In general, the New Jersey distributions are quite straightforward, as are the distributions of the primary taxes in Nevada. However, the

Table 3-7.

Description	Applicable To	Amount	Due	Form #	Refundable	Pro-Rata	Transferable	Penalty
FEDERAL								
Wagering Tax	Pari-Mutuel wagers	.25% of wagers	Monthly	730	n/a	n/a	n/a	—
Occupational Stamp	Sports & race book employees	$50 per year	Annually in advance by June 30	11-C	N	Y	N	5 years' imprisonment + $10,000 fine
NEVADA								
Percentage Fees	Gross gaming revenue	Sliding scale 5.75%	Monthly by 24th after end	NGC-1	n/a	n/a	n/a	25% of tax due
Annual Slot Tax	All coin-operated machines	$250 per machine per year	Annually in advance by June 20		N	Y	Y	25% of tax due
Annual State License	Games but not "non-banking" & slots	Sliding scale $100 to $16,000 per year	Annually in advance by December 31	NGC-2	N	N	Y	25% of tax due
Annual Unrestricted Slot License Fee	Unrestricted slot licenses: slots 16 or 15 with other games	$80 per machine per year	Quarterly 1 month after end	NGC-15	N	N	Y	25% of tax due
Quarterly Restricted Slot License	Restricted slot	$35 per machine per quarter	Quarterly 1 month after end	NGC-15	N	N	Y	25% of tax due
Quarterly Flat Fees	Games—as in annual	Sliding scale $50–$2,800 per year	Quarterly 1 month after end	NGC-15	N	N	Y	25% of tax due

Table 3-7.

Description	Applicable To	Amount	Due	Form #	Refundable	Pro-Rata	Transferable	Penalty
Casino Entertainment Tax	All receipts when casino "in entertainment status"	10% of revenue	Monthly one month after end	NGC-15	N	N	N	25% of tax due
NEVADA—Misc. Wire Service	Dissemination of Racing Info.	$10 per day per location supplied	Quarterly—1 month end		N	N	N	25% of tax due
Pari-Mutuel Pool	Jai Alai—pari-mutuel other than horse or dog racing	3% of wagers	Quarterly—1 month after end		N	N	N	25% of tax due
Manufacturer & Distributor	Manufacturers & distributors of gaming devices or machines	Manuf. $500/yr. Distr. $200/yr.	Annual by June 30		N	Y	Y	n/a
NEVADA—Local County Quarterly License Fees	All games & slots	Nonbanking card games—$25 per mo. Table games—$50 per mo. Slots—$10 per mo.	Quarterly 1 month after end		N	N	Y	25% of tax due

Table 3-7. (cont'd.)

Description	Applicable To	Amount	Due	Form #	Refundable	Pro-Rata	Transferable	Penalty
NEW JERSEY								
State License Fee	All casinos	Initial Min.—$200,000 Renewal Min.—$100,000 no max.			N	N	N	
Annual Slot Tax	All coin-operated machines	$250 per machine per year	Annually in advance by July 1		N	Y	Y	
Gross Revenue Tax	Gross Gaming Revenue	8% of gross	Monthly		N	N	N	
Casino Reinvestment Tax	Gross Gaming Revenue less Qualified Investment or Tax Credits	2.50%	After 3 years Monthly		N	N	N	

Table 3-8. Distribution of Gaming Tax Collections.

FEDERAL TAXES

All proceeds to U.S. Treasury.

NEVADA STATE TAXES

Percentage Fees: State General Fund.

Annual Slot Taxes:
- First $5M to State Higher Capital Construction Fund.
- Balance to State Distributive Fund.
- $50 each machine to Multipurpose Pavillion Bond Fund.

Annual State Licenses: 10% of State Annual Fee and Annual Slot Unrestricted Slot License Fee is set aside for gaming administration costs with any unused portion being distributed equally among the 17 counties. The gaming administrative budget is subject to the State Budget Act, and historically has not exceeded 4% of collections.

Quarterly Flat Fees Quarterly Restricted Slot Licenses: State General Fund.

Casino Entertainment Tax, Wire Service Fees, Pari-Mutuel Pool, Manufacturer and Distributor Licenses: State General Fund.

NEVADA LOCAL TAXES

County Quarterly License Fees and Other Fees:
- County License Fees assessed under NRS 453.390 are distributed 25% to the State General Fund, 25% to County General Fund, and 50% to City General Funds. The latter 50% is retained by the county if the gaming casino is not located in a city or town.
- Other County fees assessed by county ordinances are retained in full by the county.

NEW JERSEY TAXES

State License Fee and Annual Slot Tax: Casino Control Fund—State Treasury.

Gross Revenue Tax and Reinvestment Tax: Casino Revenue Fund—State Treasury.

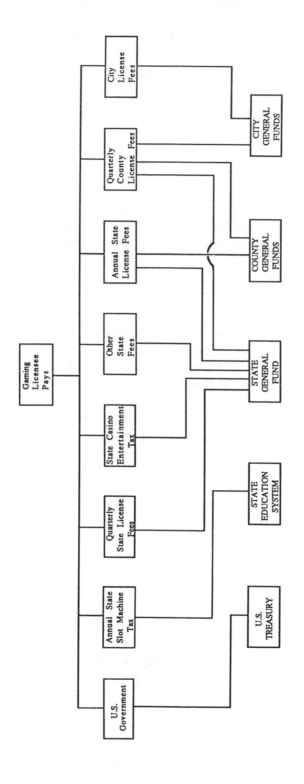

Fig. 3-4. Distribution of Nevada state direct levies on gaming.

Table 3-9. Example of Cash Flow Gaming Taxes Due.

Date	Tax	Amount per Unit	Total Due
June 20	Annual Slot Fee	$250	$600,000
June 30	Casino Entertainment	10% of $5,000,000 (estimated)	500,000
	Percentage Fees on	5.75% of $30,000,000	
July 24	Gross Revenue	(estimated)	1,725,000
July 31	Annual Slot Fee	$20	48,000
July 31	Quarterly Flat Fees	Sliding Scale	25,800
		Grand Total	$2,898,800

distribution of some of the minor taxes in Nevada, such as the county quarterly taxes and the slot taxes, can be very complex. This complexity has grown out of many years of sophisticated political negotiation.

Cash Flow Planning for Tax and License Payments

The amounts of money involved in the periodic payments of taxes and licenses can be significantly large for a casino operation. Also, the timing can be very critical. For illustrative purposes, imagine a Nevada casino, with 90 table games and 2,400 slot machines. The annual slot machine tax of $250 per machine would amount to $600,000. This amount would be due and payable on June 20 of each year in Nevada (or July 1 in New Jersey). This would be a significant cash outflow that would have to be properly anticipated in the casino operation. This June 20 outflow would then be followed by the May installment of the casino entertainment tax, which would be due by June 30. By July 24, the monthly installment of the percentage fees on gross gaming revenue would be due. On July 31, the annual nonrestricted slot license fee ($20 per quarter per machine times 2,400 machines equals $48,000) and the quarterly flat fees of $25,800 would be due and payable. Table 3-9 illustrates the computations of the taxes that would be due.

Hypothetically, then, in the 45-day period between June 20 and July 31, it would not be unreasonable to have a cash outflow for payment of taxes that would amount to almost $2,900,000. Although many of these tax payments would represent amounts already withheld from customers, such as the casino entertainment tax, all other taxes would have to be paid from the gross revenues generated. Under the heavy burdens of day-to-day operating expenses and capital needs for expansion and renovation, cash flow planning would be critical.

As a final note, the taxes indicated above do not include payments that would be due to a county or incorporated city for their respective licensing ordinances. Also, these amounts do not include payments of regular business, cabaret, or liquor licenses, which would be in addition to the gaming taxes.

Taxes on Shared Games and Slot Machines

In some circumstances, slot machines and occasionally table games located in a casino are actually operated by a separate person or business entity. These games and slot machines are often called *participation slots or games*. The standard business arrangement calls for the location (casino) to receive a portion of the profits and the machine or game owner to receive the rest. NRS 463.370 (4) specifies that the owner of the location (i.e., the casino) is responsible for the payment of the quarterly gross revenue percentage fees, but the amount of the taxes is shared by the owner of the game. The same general rule is applied to all other gaming taxes and licenses, except where specific local statutes or ordinances call for a different treatment.

In the implementation of these procedures, the location (casino) is considered to be the licensee and must assume the responsibility for payment of all taxes and fees. Then, quarterly (or for smaller locations annually), the total amount of fees paid is computed, the owner's share of these fees is determined, and the casino sends an invoice to the owner of the machine for his or her share of the fees. In this way, equitable sharing of the fees is achieved.

These arrangements can vary from owner to owner, and the specific terms of the participation agreement govern the sharing of the expenses associated with the operations. However, the statutes require that, under any circumstances, the location (casino) licensee is responsible for the eventual payment of the fees.

Accounting Issues of Gaming Taxation

There are several significant issues of an accounting nature that arise from state and local government taxation of gaming operations. These include accounting for the prepaid or accrued portion of taxes, licenses, and fees and the audit procedures to verify the prepaid or accrued portion of these taxes and licenses. The audit procedures are discussed in later chapters.

Prepaid Gaming Taxes and Licenses

Many of the license fees and taxes that have been described in previous sections of this chapter have to be paid in advance. This creates a very large prepaid taxes and licenses account on the books of most casinos. The most significant of these taxes in Nevada are the monthly gross revenue percentage fees. When a new casino opens, but before a license is issued, a bond must be posted or cash payment made by the casino in the amount equal to the first full month's license fees. This requirement is to assure payment of the tax amounts to the state. The prepayment is calculated under the statute by doubling the first-period payment, thus forming the prepayment. The timing and the amount of this double payment depend on the exact timing of the casino opening, the extent of the casino opening, and the statutory definitions.

For each month after the first month, the license fee is considered to be a fee paid in advance—but the amount is based on the gross gaming revenue of the preceding month. The duplicate first-period payment merely puts the new casino on the payment-in-advance basis from the start.

Financial Statement Presentation

Given the substantial amount of money involved in gaming taxes, several accounting treatments of the taxes are suggested.

Fees paid in advance such as state, county, and local flat license fees are typically treated as prepaid items. Since the prepayment is for a quarter, the amount is usually amortized on a monthly basis for interim reporting purposes.

There are a few taxes such as the federal wagering excise tax that are simply accrued as a liability payable at the end of the month, in a manner similar to other taxes payable.

The largest tax payments arise from the gross revenue percentage fees. Given the unique system of first-period prepayment, the accounting treatment can be quite complex. This complexity arises because the prepayment of the fee does not fit the strict definition of an asset. However, there are several alternative methods to account for this duplicate portion when paid and to assure the proper expense recording. One alternative is to record it entirely as an expense when paid. A second alternative is to record it entirely as a deferred charge. A third alternative is to divide the payment into expense and deferred portions in some manner.

If the duplicate payments were recorded entirely as an expense when paid, then there would be one extra quarter's tax expense recorded in the first year of operation. To avoid this distortion, some portion of the fee should be recorded as a deferred charge when paid.

This deferred charge is carried until the license is terminated. Since no additional fee is required if a licensee discontinues operations at or near the end of the calendar month, then, by inference, the duplicate portion of the payment has some future utility in a traditional asset sense and is suitable for categorization as a deferred asset.

An alternative treatment of the expense aspects of the prepayments is to regard one-half of the duplicate payment as a long-term deposit held by the taxing authorities against future liabilities, while regarding the other half of the payment as a prepaid expense item. The proper accounting treatment under this prepaid method is to compute on a monthly basis the gross revenue percentage fees actually due and payable. Once the monthly amount is known, the previously established prepaid tax deposit is then amortized by the computed amount and the appropriate expense recognized. This provides the most accurate matching of revenue and expenses in the period in which the revenue was earned and the liability incurred.

Another alternative accounting treatment with respect to expenses is to classify the entire doubled payment amount initially as a prepayment of expense. These items are held at that amount and not amortized to expense. However, a monthly accrual of expense is made in order to match revenues and expenses. When the next tax payment is made, the accrued liability is eliminated, while the prepaid expense remains in place.

The Accounting Principles Committee of the Nevada CPA Society has recommended that the recurring license fee be accrued for the period in which the revenue is earned and the license fee is calculated.[15] This revenue measurement focus is considered the primary objective of the financial statement. If material, the duplicate portion for the first full quarter of operation should be recorded as a deferred charge. The deferred charge should not be expensed unless and until the license is terminated. There is no recommendation with regard to the classification of the expense portion of the payment as prepaid expense or as a deposit, as long as the proper periodic expense accrual adjustment is made.

Appendix 3-1. Casino Taxes Including Local Government Gaming Taxes.

	COUNTY LEVIES	QTRLY FEE
Carson City		
Stud or Draw Poker, Panguingui		97.50
Roulette, "21," Chuck-a-Luck, Craps, Big Six, Hazard		180.00
Keno, Bingo, Race Horse Pool, Baccarat, Wheel of Fortune		172.50
Slot Machines (each separate mechanism)		40.00
Clark		
Bingo, Keno, "21," Craps, Big Six, Baccarat, Faro Bank, Race Book, Roulette		150.00
Sports Book		150.50
Draw or Stud Poker		75.00
Regular Slots		30.00
Double Slots		60.00
Triple Slots		90.00
Las Vegas Convention Authority Gaming Fees		
Slots, 12 or less		1.00 each
more than 12		2.50 each
1 game		10.00
2–5 games		25.00 each
6 or more games		40.00 each
Douglas		
Baccarat, Roulette, "21," Wheel of Fortune, Craps, Keno, Bingo, Race Book, Pai-Gow, Sic-Bo		350.00
Poker		275.00
Slots, 250 machines or less		38.00
Slots, over 250 machines		50.00
Elko		
Poker, Panguingui		
Wells, Carlin, Elko		75.00
All other areas		111.00
Slots		
Wells, Carlin, Elko		30.00
All other areas		42.00
Table Games		
Wells, Carlin, Elko		150.00
All other areas		186.00
Esmeralda		
Slot Machines		30.00 each

Humboldt
  Slot Machines   39.00 each
  All other games   210.00

Mineral
  Slots,
    Mina, Montgomery Pass   33.00 each
    All other areas   35.00 each
  Craps, Roulette, Bingo, Keno, Panguingui 155.00
  Poker   80.00

Pershing
  Slot Machines and games   12.00

Storey
  Slots   30.00 each
  Table Games   150.00

Washoe
  Poker, Bridge, Whist, Solo, Panguingui
    Unincorporated Areas   104.44
    Incorporated Areas   75.00
  Slot Machines
    Unincorporated Areas   41.77
    Incorporated Areas   30.00
  All Other Games
    Unincorporated Areas   208.88
    Incorporated Areas   150.00

CITY LEVIES

Caliente
  Poker, Big Six, Faro, Race Horse Keno   15.00
  Bingo, Tango, Keno, Race Horse Pool, Sports Pool 6.00
  Slot Machines   9.00

Carlin
  Slot Machines   20.00 each

Elko
  Craps, "21," Bingo, Roulette, Faro, Keno, Fan Tan 50.00
  Race Horse Keno   100.00
  Poker   30.00
  Slot Machines   15.00 each

Ely
  Slot Machines   30.00 each
  Craps, "21," Roulette, Panguingui, Keno, Poker, Bingo   40.00

Fallon
  All Card Games   7.50
  Mechanical Percentage Games   15.00
  Slot Machines   3.00

Henderson
  Big Six, Bingo   75.00
  Bridge, Whist, Solo   15.00
  Chemin de Fer, Race Horse Book   280.00
  Craps, 1 Table   57.00
  Craps, 2 or more Tables   140.00
  Keno   70.00
  Keno, per chair in addition   1.50
  Roulette, "21," Hazard, Faro Bank   70.00
  Panguingui   30.00
  Slots   28.00
  Slots, Penny   50.00
  Stud Poker   35.00

Las Vegas
  Slot Machines
    1–5 Machines   25.00
    More than 5 Machines   30.00
    Penny Slots   50.00
  Stud or Draw Poker   50.00
  Panguingui   30.00
  Bridge, Whist, Solo   15.00
  Chemin de Fer, Baccarat   250.00
  Roulette, "21," Hazard, Faro Bank, Wheel of Fortune,
    Big Six   150.00
  Craps, 1 Table   150.00
  Craps, 2 or More   250.00 each
  Race Book   400.00
  Race Horse Information   250.00
  Bingo   75.00
  Bingo, per chair additional   1.50
  Keno   300.00
  Sports Book   100.00
  Games not specified above   50.00

North Las Vegas
GAMING FEES:

Bingo	62.50
Bingo, per chair additional	1.50
Keno, Race Horse Keno	250.00
Keno, per chair additional	1.50
Roulette, "21," Hazard, Faro Bank, Wheel of Fortune, Big Six	125.00
Craps	150.00
Chemin de Fer, Baccarat	200.00
Bridge, Whist, Solo, Panguingui	32.50
Stud or Draw Poker	50.00
Race Horse Book	300.00
Sports Book	100.00
Slots, less than $1	25.00
$1 Slots	50.00

GAMING TAXES:

Slots, 12 or less machines	1.00 each
Slots, More than 12 machines	2.50 each
1 game	10.00
2–5 games	25.00 each
6 or more games	40.00 each

Reno

Slot Machines, Electronic Gaming Devices, each	26.25
Roulette, Craps, "21," Baccarat, Dai Situ	
1–3 games	187.50 each
4–9 games	212.50 each
10–19 games	237.50 each
20 or more games	262.50 each
Poker, Panguingui	37.50
Race Horse Keno	300.00 each
Bingo, Tango, Keno	375.00 each
Race Horse Pool	312.50
Chemin de Fer, Race Horse Services	250.00
Chuck-a-Luck, Hazard, Big Six, Faro	62.50 each
Sports Pool	75.00
Punch Boards, per room	5.00
Jai Alai	1,000.00
Jai Alai, per chair additional	2.25

Sparks

Faro, Chuck-a-Luck, "21," Hazard, Big Six, Roulette, Baccarat, Craps	105.00

Tango, Chinese Lottery, Bingo, Race Horse Pool	150.00
Stud or Draw Poker	75.00
Panguingui	36.00
Keno, Race Horse Keno	225.00
Race Horse & Sports Book	300.00
Slot Machines, Electronic Gaming Devices	30.00
Punchboards	6.00
Pool (where percentages are taken)	90.00

Wells
Slot Machines, Electronic Gaming Devices	7.50
Poker	30.00
All other table games	15.00

Winnemucca
Slot Machines	30.00
Poker	75.00
All other table games	150.00

Yerington
Slot Machines	30.00
Draw or Stud Poker, Panguingui	75.00
Keno, "21," Roulette, Bingo, Craps	150.00

♠ ♡ ♣ ◇ II

Accounting for Casino Operations

CHAPTER 4

Casino Revenue Flows

Introduction

This chapter discusses the basic concepts of casino revenue accounting, which represents the truly unique aspects of casino accounting control, systems, and procedures. The importance of understanding casino revenue flows cannot be overemphasized. The diverse revenue flows, the complexity, and the mixture of revenue transactions with exchange or cashiering transactions create an atmosphere where even sophisticated laymen may have difficulty understanding how casino revenues flow. A second important need is to recognize that casino revenues can indeed be controlled, the controls tested, and eventually the entire casino operation subjected to auditing scrutiny.

Casino Accounting Organization

The first step in understanding the casino revenue flows is to understand the accounting personnel, their working relationships, and the overall accounting organization that has the responsibility for the casino revenue accounting operations.

The casino accounting organization is set up in five distinct levels. The first consists of the operating personnel who are present in the public casino areas, including pit clerks, change booth personnel, and to some degree even the dealers on individual games. These operating personnel have a primary responsibility for the revenue reporting process or, in the case of dealers, have some limited reporting duties in addition to their regular game responsibilities.

The second level consists of accounting personnel who occupy semipublic positions and who conduct intermediate-level

95

revenue collection activity. Examples of this level are cashiers in cages, personnel connected with the fill and credit procedures, and those persons connected with the issuance of casino credit or markers, including credit approval and record-keeping.

The third level consists of those who have relatively little public exposure. These persons have the highest degree of responsibility for the revenue collection procedures. Those in this area include count room personnel, vault personnel, and persons involved in the maintenance of marker and check cashing activity. Many supervisors (such as cashier supervisors) are also in this category.

The fourth level consists of those persons who have top revenue reporting responsibility, including overall income statement reporting. This group includes the senior financial management, such as internal auditors, controllers, and financial vice-presidents.

Finally, the casino has other traditional accounting personnel dedicated to functions such as food and beverage accounting, hotel room revenue accounting, accounts payable, and payroll and general ledger accounting.

Casino Control Objectives

It should be stressed that since the fundamental product of a casino is service to the customer, and the principal inventory item is money, the accounting controls exercised by the accounting department cannot and should not be overly centralized. There must be many clerks and controllers and many control points. In this way, each and every operating department can assure the proper recording of transactions and the proper conduct of the appropriate controls in each area.

Figure 4-1 indicates the financial operating structure of a typical hotel-casino. The main principle of organization is to achieve maximum control, principally through separation of duties of various individuals. This fundamental principle is based on the belief that if many persons are involved in processing and reporting a transaction, then theft can only occur through collusive fraud. The risks of this occurring are lessened by a substantial division of duties in the accounting and record-keeping area. The separation of the responsibilities for various revenue reporting activities among several departments may even result in financial reporting person-

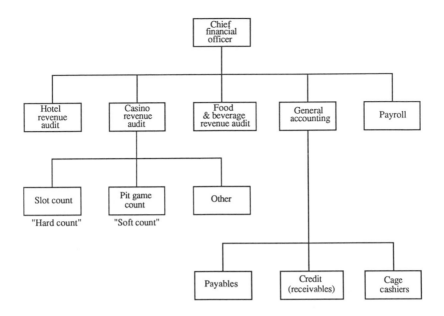

Fig. 4-1. Casino financial organization structure.

nel having several different supervisors. This maximum separation of duties helps to maintain a program of effective internal control.[1]

There may be as many as three distinct groups of accounting and financial reporting personnel involved in the casino revenue flows and the casino operations:

1. Casino Operations.
     Dealers.
     Pit clerks to record game transactions.
     Drop teams.
2. Cage Operations.
     Cage cashiers.
     Credit cashiers.
3. Count Rooms.
     Hard coin and soft currency count personnel.

All of these personnel are involved in various degrees with the revenue reporting process. In any casino, there is both extensive involvement of virtually all operational personnel in the internal control over revenue procedures and a heavy involvement in the record-keeping for all aspects of the casino operations.

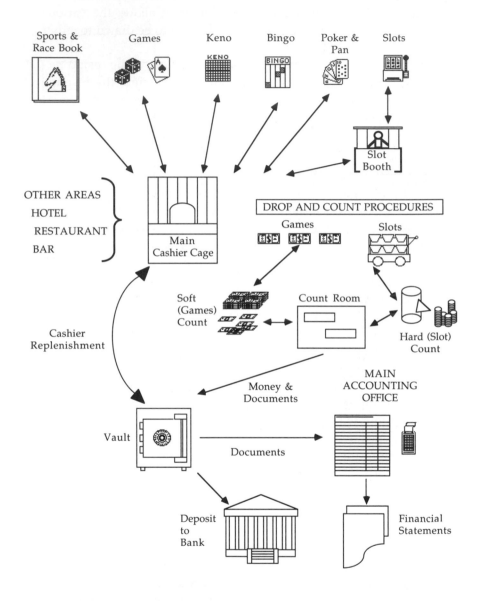

Fig. 4-2. *Principle revenue flows in the casino.*

Description of Principal Revenue Flows in the Casino

The principal revenue flows in the casino are illustrated in figure 4-2. This diagrammatic representation allows the various parts of the accounting process in the casino to be drawn together into one cohesive illustration.

The principal components of revenue flow in the casino recognize a primary separation between the flows into the revenue stream from slot and game operations. Each of these revenue areas has separate and distinct operating characteristics, staff, and procedures.

Cashiering Transactions

In addition to the principal revenue flows that exist in the casino, there are also large numbers of cashiering transactions. These transactions are indicated by the two-headed arrows in figure 4-2, which show not only revenue flowing into the casino, but also the exchange or cashiering transactions that occur in the casino. These activities are of somewhat less significance, since the balances in various areas are maintained on an imprest basis. Also, these cashiering flows do not have any impact on casino revenue, but are only transactions of changing money from one form to another. However, to the uninformed observer, they can be misunderstood for revenue transactions and may distort some of the control procedures.

It is important to realize that these cashiering functions must not interfere with the process of revenue generation, nor should they be included in the revenue flow so as to distort the actual operating results or the statistical reporting derived from the revenue reports. In order to clarify these cashiering transactions, they are discussed in each major area where they occur.

Slot Machine Cashiering

The principal cashiering activity in the slot machine area revolves around the exchange of currency for coins and tokens that can be played physically in the slot machines. These exchanges, or cashiering activities, take place between the gaming customer and the cage personnel, or between the customer and the change personnel located on the floor of the casino, or between the customer and the slot booth personnel. The cashiering activity is one of the most critical functions for the slot department for two reasons.

First, the change person is the first line of public relations for the casino. If this individual is not personable and pleasant, then the customer will be somewhat less inclined to play the slot machine. Second, the slot person must be physically present and conveniently located in order to assure that the customer has a ready supply of coins that can be played in the slot machine. Casino customers have indicated that as long as they have coins, they are likely to play the great majority of them in the slot machines and will not carry them home or exchange minor amounts of coin into currency when they stop playing. Casino customers tend to play the slot machines until all their coins are gone—at which point the decision is made either to stop play or to change more currency into coin and continue playing.

From time to time, the change persons on the floor are not justified from the standpoint of the volume of business, and the slot booth becomes the sole area of exchange. In addition to the customary exchange of currency for coin, the slot booth may also perform various other minor duties, such as recording and paying out promotional items, and/or serving as a security point for control over the slot machines. Also, the slot booth serves as a secondary bank or storage area for coins, at which floor slot change persons can exchange their excess currency for additional coins, which are in turn sold to customers of the casino.

An interesting sidelight has evolved from the role of the carousel barkers or runway personnel. These are change personnel who are in charge of a set of large-denomination machines, usually a bank of twenty or thirty $1.00 slot machines. Their function is not only to provide change in tokens for the players; they also have microphones and serve as carnival barkers, encouraging customers to continue to play. The microphones also allow them to announce the frequent winning jackpots.

Table Games Cashiering

The cashiering function of the table game is much more straightforward. The cashiering usually takes place between the customer and the dealer on a 21 game or a boxman on a crap game. In this exchange process, the customer offers currency, markers, or other denominations of chips, which are exchanged for gaming chips. On the table games, the currency is deposited in the table drop box, where it is counted along with the other items in the drop and count procedures. Chips exchanged are merely added to the table game inventory.

Keno, Bingo, and Race and Sports Book Cashiering

In these game activities, the interaction between the customer and the casino usually does not involve a lot of cashiering. The only thing approaching it would be the situation where the customer pays for a sports bet, keno ticket, or bingo game with a bill of larger denomination and change is returned to the customer. This operation is more of a sales transaction than a true cashiering activity.

Poker Cashiering

In poker or other card room transactions, the cashiering activity is very significant. Chips may be bought and sold from the customer at a separate cashier's cage located in the immediate vicinity, or cashiering activity may take place in the poker game itself.

These separate card room cashiers exist for several reasons. Since card rooms are often located in portions of the casino away from the central cashier, play is facilitated by the convenience of a nearby cashier. Also, since card rooms often use smaller-denomination chips than other games, they can be controlled more effectively through their own cashier. Finally, since card rooms typically operate on a commission basis called the rake-off, it is easier to control dealer's banks if most of the cashiering activity is directed to the cashier and not to the dealer.

Main Cashiering

Many of the exchanges of a cashiering nature take place at the point of sale—on the table game or at the slot machine. However, it is common practice, particularly in smaller casinos, to have most if not all of the cashiering transactions occur at the main casino cashier. The cashier's cage is a central point for most of the recording of the activities in the casino.

For example, if the slot booth is depleted of coins, the coins from the reserve vault storage area are first transferred to the cashier's cage and then exchanged with the slot booth. All fills and credits, either to reduce or to increase table game inventory, also originate in the cashier's cage.

The casino cashier may be a part of these exchange transactions of special types. For example, the issuance of casino credit is for accounting purposes only an exchange transaction—a cashiering activity. In this case, the document (a counter check or a marker) is exchanged for coins or chips or, in rare instances, for currency. This exchange is most frequently handled by a cashier. Cashiers also have a role in the cashiering transactions with the central vault. In these transactions, various coins or chips are exchanged from the vault and are put back into the cashiering stream of the casino after they have been counted and deposited with the vault.

Accounting for Casino Revenue

This discussion of casino revenue flows is broken into two distinct parts. The first is devoted to explaining the various operating definitions and procedures used to compute casino revenue. The second is an explanation of the detailed accounting procedures of the revenue flow for each of the types of games. The flow of the accounting details is discussed in a logical procedure from the game to the drop and count procedures and finally to the vault.

In casino revenue accounting, the key definition is that of *win*, defined as the total amount of casino income.[2] It is legally defined in the laws of Nevada as gross gaming revenue. It should be stressed that win is the net amount of win—after all winning wagers have been paid. The concept of win is similar to that of net sales revenue for a commercial business.

Win can also be defined as the difference between the total amount wagered or played and the amounts repaid to winners. Technically, then:

$$\text{WIN} = \text{DROP minus PAYOUTS}$$

A second definition of use in understanding casino revenue flows is that of *drop*. Drop is a measure of the total wagering activity in a casino. The term is reserved for table games. When used in connection with a slot machine, drop is the number of coins in the collection bucket located under the slot machine and is called the *slot drop*. A closely related concept in slot machines is the *handle*, which measures the total amount of money deposited into a machine. The handle can be measured by the use of meters in the slot machine.

However, in the case of table games, the winning and losing bets are determined by the dealer; either the winners are paid or the losing bets are collected. The losing bets are returned to the table tray, if the bets were placed in chips, or are deposited in the drop box for bets made with something other than chips. There is no effective way to measure the total wagering activity, and only the net effect of the wagering—that is, the win—can be measured. In this situation, the drop cannot be accurately determined.

Drop (for table games) can be a misleading measure, since in some casinos it has come to mean the total amount of money, foreign chips, and other documents placed in the table drop box. In other casinos, drop is interpreted to mean the total amount of *money only* in the drop box. Drop is a widely used measure of total gaming activity and should be used with extreme care. Various interpretations of drop and some of the limitations on the use of this concept are discussed in the next section of this chapter.

Hold and the related concept of *hold percentage* are defined in a somewhat less exact sense. Hold is the total amount retained by the casino and represents the same concept as win. The hold percentage is a calculation that allows the casino to compare the actual percentage profit margin on games or slot operations with the theoretical percentages that should be retained or held, given the statistical and odds structure of the game.

Hold percentage is the percentage of gaming revenue retained by the casino, divided by the total amount of casino gaming activity. Thus, the hold percentage is used to determine overall gaming efficiency, but it is also used to compute the performance of various games, both by shift and by table, and for each of the slot machines. Hold percentage could be presented as:

$$\text{HOLD PERCENTAGE} = \text{WIN} / \text{DROP}$$

Limitations in the Use of Casino Revenue Definitions for Slot Machines

In the slot machine area, the computation of the various items of revenue is fairly easy. This is primarily due to the fact that the mechanical nature of the slot machine, together with various measuring devices, called meters, allows an accurate recording of the different components in the computation of slot machine revenue.

The first measure, that of the total amount of money put in, is the *slot handle* or *coins in*. This amount of money can be metered, and most frequently is the single most important control reading utilized by the casinos in their slot machine performance reporting. With the advent of multiple coin machines, as many as five coins can be inserted for each physical pull of the handle. In these cases, as well as for multiple reel machines, the number of handle pulls does not equal the number of coins put in. Therefore, the definition could be stated as:

COINS IN = HANDLE

The second measure of slot machine activity is the money that is paid out. These paidouts must be defined in two main parts. First, there are the coins paid out directly by the machine. In this situation, the amounts of money paid out can be monitored by the use of meters. The second part is the money paid out by hand by various slot personnel, including change persons, jackpot payoff persons, or the slot booth personnel or cashiers. These paidout items typically are for larger amounts or may include amounts used to refill empty hoppers.

In recent times, in an effort to control the labor costs in the slot operation, the size of the machine paidouts has risen, and the capacity of the slot hoppers has been increased. Typically, the slot hopper pays any amount up to 200 coins automatically. After this level has been reached, a manual payoff is required.

The third measure of slot machine activity is the amount of money that is retained by the slot machine. Typically, this money is deposited in the drop buckets. This amount is known as the *slot drop*. The amount of money in the drop buckets is the amount of money inserted into the machine—the slot drop minus the amounts that are automatically diverted by the slot machine to refill the payout hopper. This diversion is accomplished automatically when the machine senses that the number of coins in the payout hopper is too low. At that time, coins inserted and retained by the machine go to the hopper, rather than going to the drop bucket directly.

The fourth and final measure of slot machine revenue is the

key concept: *slot win*. The slot win can be defined as the total money retained by the machine minus any paidouts. Since the slot drop has already taken the coins paid out automatically by the machine into account (through the indirect refilling of the slot hopper from which the machine jackpots are paid), the computation of slot win is as follows:

$$\text{SLOT WIN} = \text{SLOT DROP minus JACKPOT PAIDOUTS}$$
$$\text{minus HOPPER FILLS}$$

Casino Revenue Definitions for Table Games

The simplicity of the revenue definitions and related calculations for the slot machine operations is unfortunately not present in the computation of casino revenue for various table games.

The first concept of revenue measurement that must be abandoned is that of measuring the total handle or drop in the table game environment. The concept of total handle in the casino, where handle represents the total betting activity, is desirable from a management control standpoint, but is virtually impossible to measure. This would require some form of extensive reporting of the amount of each and every wager placed on a table game. This reporting, although attempted in a limited sense in the past, was found to slow the process of the game so badly that it reduced the overall profitability of the game, and upon final analysis it was not sufficiently accurate to warrant the high cost of gathering the information and recording the transactions.

Because the total amount of wagering activity is unrecorded, various casinos have developed what could be called a surrogate measure of total casino betting activity. This measure is still called *drop*—but is defined as the total amount of money found in the table drop box when counted. The table drop box is a money receptacle attached to each table, which contains currency, accounting documents, and other items saved for record-keeping for the table game. Each shift and each table has a separate drop box.

The concept of drop as a measure of total casino activity would be valid if the results of all betting activity were reflected in the contents of the drop box. In other words, if the drop box held the working cash fund for the table, then the results at the end of the shift would represent the total sales of the table, in the same way that a restaurant or bar cashier's bank represents the total sales.

This is unfortunately not the case. Only if the operating procedures of the casino are stable over time, and if the same items are placed in the table drop boxes, can the computation of table drop figures be of any use as an indicator of total volume of betting activity of the casino. It should be stressed that drop is only one component of the calculation of true casino win and is not a primary indicator of casino income.

Complications of Revenue Calculations

In the case of table games, several additional factors complicate the calculation of table game revenue. They are:

1. Fluctuations in table game chip inventories.
2. Fill and credit activity between the table and the cashier.
3. Other items in the drop box.

These factors and the impact that they have on the process of revenue measurement are discussed in detail below. Let us initially assume a situation that is very simple to understand with respect to table revenue.

EXAMPLE 1   Table game entirely in cash, with no use of chips and no table game inventory

Cash Count	Drop	Game Win
$500	$500	$500

Table Inventory Fluctuations   Most table games contain a working bank of a specified amount. This table bank consists almost entirely of chips of the casino, together with a minor amount of silver currency or $1.00 slot machine tokens. For a 21 game, the amount of the bank could vary from $1,500 to $6,000. For a crap game, the bank amount could vary from $10,000 to about $25,000. These chips are sometimes known as *checks* and are used in the cashiering functions that the dealer performs. The customer's money is converted into casino chips, which the customer then uses to play on the tables. The use of currency for play on the tables is discouraged. As a result of this cashiering activity, the table inventory may fluctuate, even though no playing activity has taken place.

In order to portray accurately the win activity of the table game, the inventory fluctuations from the beginning of the shift to the end of the shift must be recorded and taken into account in the computation of the win or loss for the table and for the particular shift. Recording the table inventory is accomplished by the use of a document called the *table inventory card*. This form is also sometimes known as an *opener* or *closer* because of the functions that it performs—recording the inventory on the table bank at the close of one shift and at the beginning of the next shift. The amounts of chips of each denomination are recorded, and the first copy of the document is placed in the table drop box—before it is removed from the table. The second copy of the two-part form—the opener, which was recorded at the same time—is then deposited in the new shift table drop box as the first transaction of the coming shift. When the drop box is opened for purposes of counting, the opening and closing inventory documents are then present, allowing the determination of opening and closing inventory for the shift. In this way, the process of merely cashiering chips for cash on the table can be taken into account and does not distort the results of the game.

For example, without the inventory records, the appearance of a $50 bill in the drop box would apparently indicate that the game has won $50 for that shift. However, if the customer merely stopped at the table to exchange the money for chips, played one hand, and then moved on to another table, the real operating result would only have been one hand won or lost, not $50 won.

Thus, the change in the inventory of the table tray would have to be taken into account. When the inventory changes were computed, the true amount of the win or loss could be determined. This example also stresses the validity of the concept of win as the key accounting determinant. Notice that the drop is indeed $50, but it was merely the result of cashiering activity and not the result of table play activity. If a table is subjected to a lot of cashiering, with little play activity, the relation of drop to win, as expressed in the hold percentage, is very low. This indicator could lead to concern regarding the operation of the game that might be totally unfounded.

The impact of these inventory fluctuations can be indicated in the following example:

EXAMPLE 2   Table game uses a table tray inventory and is conducted in both cash and chips

| Game Bank | | Cash | | Game |
Begin	End	Count	Drop	Win
$1,000	$900	$600	$600	$500

The game bank fluctuations (increases or decreases) must be added to the cash count in order to determine the proper game win figure. In general, the computational flow of the game win can be summarized from the foregoing elements.

GAME WIN = DROP plus ADJUSTMENTS

where ADJUSTMENTS = INVENTORY CHANGES IN GAME BANK

Note that the total amount of cash in the drop box ($600) is the composite of two factors, the cashiering activity of $100 plus the game win of $500. Thus, in this case the game has exactly the same profit as was indicated in example #1.

Fill and Credit Activity   From time to time, the working inventory of the table either becomes depleted or builds up to unnecessarily large amounts. There may also be too many chips of a particular denomination on the table. In order either to replenish the tray (inventory) or to redistribute the denominations, a *fill* (addition to) the table or a *credit* (subtraction from) the table is made. The detailed handling of these types of transactions is discussed at considerable length in later chapters; for the present discussion, the impact of adding chips to the table or removing them from the table must be taken into account so that the measurement of the table inventory is not distorted. For example, without the consideration of the fill and credit activity, a table game could be losing a considerable amount of money, but the drop box might still contain some money (from cashiering activity) and the table inventory count could be about the same at the end of the shift as it was at the beginning of the shift.

In this situation, another dimension must be added to the computation of game win. The effects of the fills and credits on the table game inventory must be measured. Example #3 shows the expanded computation.

PART II. ACCOUNTING FOR CASINO OPERATIONS

EXAMPLE 3 Fill and credit activity is reflected in game results

Game Bank		Cashier		Cash		Game
Begin	End	Fills	Credits	Count	Drop	Win
$1,000	$900	$1,000	$0	$1,600	$1,600	$500

GAME WIN = DROP plus ADJUSTMENTS
where ADJUSTMENTS = INVENTORY CHANGE plus/minus
FILLS OR CREDITS

or expressed in fuller terms, indicating each component,

GAME WIN = DROP plus CLOSING INVENTORY plus CREDITS
minus OPENING INVENTORY minus FILLS

If a substantial amount of money was added to the table, then the cashiering amount must have been very large, if the table still won. Thus, the cash amount rose to $1,600, resulting in the game win remaining at $500.

The computation of fills and credits can be further illustrated in the case where the game was a large winner and, as a result, the chip inventory built up on the table. In this circumstance, one of two things could take place. First, the table inventory could be left to build up, and the increase would be reflected in the table inventory card. Second, the excess chips could be removed from the table by a credit. In practice, the table inventory is usually kept close to a standard or par amount, and the excess chips are customarily removed with a credit to the table.

EXAMPLES 4 and 5 Table inventory buildup is reduced through use of a credit

Game Bank		Cashier		Cash		Game
Begin	End	Fills	Credits	Count	Drop	Win
$1,000	$1,300	$0	$ 0	$200	$200	$500
$1,000	$1,000	$0	$300	$200	$200	$500

In these cases, the game bank fluctuations (increases) must

be added to the cash count in order to determine the proper game win figure, as well as considering the impact of adding money to the table (fill) or removing it from the table (credit).

In general, the computational flow of the game win can be summarized from the foregoing elements in the following manner:

GAME WIN = DROP plus ADJUSTMENTS
where ADJUSTMENTS = INVENTORY CHANGES plus/minus
FILLS OR CREDIT

or expressed in fuller terms, indicating each component,

GAME WIN = DROP plus CLOSING INVENTORY plus
CREDITS minus OPENING INVENTORY minus FILLS

Complications of Drop Box Counts

In all of the previous examples, drop has been regarded as the total cash count of all currency contained in the table drop box. There are other components of the drop that can cause some complications if not clearly understood. From time to time, the drop box may be used as the repository for other items of accounting significance. Some of these can cause distortion of the drop count and the resulting game win computations.

The first example of an addition to the drop box is that of foreign chips, meaning chips from other casinos, usually restricted to well-known casinos in the immediate area. For example, a Reno chip could probably not be played on the table in a Las Vegas casino, unless it was from a sister casino. It is customary to allow a limited amount of gaming on the table using chips that may belong to another casino. In the situation where these chips are played and lost, the dealer deposits them directly into the drop box. They are separated during the count process and redeemed from the issuing casino at some later date. When the contents of the drop box are counted, the foreign chips are considered to be the same as cash, with the face value (denomination) of the chip included in the count of the currency in the drop box.

Another example of an item that may distort the drop box is the issuance of credit instruments and check cashing, both of which may take place at the table. In both of these situations, chips from the table are usually given to the gaming customer in return for a marker. Thus, the table inventory is depleted by the cashiering transaction without any form of document or reimbursement to indicate that the change was due solely to a cashiering activity.

The solution to this dilemma is twofold. First, some casinos utilize a special type of cashier credit, similar to a regular credit slip for chips, to indicate the transaction. The marker or check is transferred directly back to the central cashier in exchange for the table credit. Other casinos utilize a separate reporting system, where the chips are only temporarily advanced to the customer at the table, and the table is subsequently reimbursed from the cashier in exchange for the marker instrument. In some situations, the marker is held in the pit until the end of the shift and then forwarded to a central cashier. In this case, the pit cashier issues the credit slip to the table.

In the first instance above, the marker is treated as money and is included in the drop count figure. In the second case, the item is treated as a special form of credit slip and is included as a separate item along with more customary fill and credit activity. Since the handling of these marker instruments is largely under the control of management, this serves to illustrate the fact that the amount of the drop can be changed merely by the type of revenue accounting system in use in the casino or by management's decision to count or not to count certain items.

These treatments of credit instruments in the drop box are indicated in examples #6 and #7.

EXAMPLE 6   Marker activity reflected in drop results

Game Bank		Cashier		Marker and	Cash		Game
Begin	End	Fills	Credits	Check Cashing	Count	Drop	Win
$1,000	$900	$600	$0	$1,000	$200	$200	$500

If the situation in example #6 assumed that the check cashing credits were to be included in the drop, then the revised drop figures would be as shown in example #7:

DROP = CHECK CASHING plus CASH COUNT

EXAMPLE 7   Marker activity with cashier credit included in cash count

Game Bank		Cashier		Marker and	Cash		Game
Begin	End	Fills	Credits	Check Cashing	Count	Drop	Win
$1,000	$900	$600	$0	$1,000	$200	$1,200	$500

The Fallacy of Drop and Drop Percentages

Notice in all the examples that the amount of game win, the gross revenue produced from this particular game during this shift, is a constant $500. Because of various factors, mainly different types of cashiering activity, as well as managerial definition of what should be counted in the drop, the drop figure could fluctuate from a high of $1,200 to a low of $200. These examples serve to indicate how improper reliance on the drop figures can yield improper indications of game performance.

For the various situations, the drop and hold percentage could have fluctuated as indicated below:

Example	DROP	WIN	HOLD P.C.	Explanation
1	500	500	100%	All Cash Transactions
2	600	500	83.3%	Table Inventories Used
3	1,600	500	31.25%	Cashiering Activity
4	200	500	250%	Inventories Not Adjusted
5	200	500	250%	Inventories Adjusted
6	200	500	250%	Marker Activity
7	1,200	500	41.6%	Redefine Drop to Include Marker Credits

It should be stressed that, under certain conditions, the use of drop figures and hold percentages can be an aid to the management of the casino. Where the casino has stable operating procedures and experience and no substantial changes in the definition of what is included in drop, the measure of drop can be a useful indicator of the total activity in the casino. In this situation, severe fluctuations in the drop or the hold percentages can signal that something has changed. The discovery of the reasons for the change is left up to management. Also, drop can be used as a way to measure the aggregate volume of activity in the casino. Under most circumstances, the hold percentage remains fairly constant; with increased volume of activity, assuming the constant drop definition and consequently a constant hold percentage, then the gross gaming revenue of the casino is increased.

Theory and Practice of Hold Percentages

Hold percentages are utilized by a variety of persons to indicate the odds structure on a particular game.[3] For example, it has been widely calculated that the hold percentage on a keno game is approximately 28%–30%, while the hold percentage on a crap game (assuming pass or don't pass bets) is as little as 1.6%. A 21 game is assumed to hold about 5% (not taking into consideration card counting or differential betting strategies). These theoretical computations of the hold percentages for various games in the casino are based on statistical analysis of the odds structure and make three significant assumptions:

1. That the gaming activity is limited to a single transaction. That is, only one person is playing the game. In reality, there may be any number of persons playing a single game. Typically, there may be four to five players on a 21 game, with approximately seven to nine persons at a crap table during the average game playing period. This level of activity can vary from day to day, from shift to shift, and from season to season.

2. That the odds are calculated based on a single bet, with the odds determining the payoff and the hold percentage. The best example here is the pass (don't pass) bet on the craps table where the odds are 1.6% for the house. In reality, however, there may be a wide variety of bets placed on any single roll of the dice, and the actual house result over time is not determined by a single bet but the weighted average of the different types of bets placed on the table. For example, the "hard way" bets in the center of the layout have different odds structures than the number bets and also have different payoffs, as well as different hold percentages.

3. The third assumption is that the amount of betting activity is known and can be measured. In reality, for most table games, the total amount wagered cannot be determined accurately and cannot be tracked for any extended period. Thus, the aggregate hold percentage for the crap table can be a bewildering array of several factors, including the total amount of money bet on the

table. While percentage figures are supposed to be immune to dollar fluctuations, the larger volume of activity does have significant impact on the hold percentage, which tends to increase as the volume of dollars placed as bets increases.

In practice, then, the amount of money held by a crap game can be portrayed not merely as 1.6% of the amount bet, but rather as the complex weighted average of the following factors:

TOTAL WIN = the odds on different types of bets
WEIGHTED BY the amount of betting activity for each type of bet
TIMES the impact of multiple players

In reality, it is assumed that a 21 table holds about 18%, while the craps and other games are assumed to hold about 15%–20% over the long period.[4]

An interesting counterexample exists for a keno game. In the operation of a keno game, the total amount wagered is recorded and is known. Based on the known amount of wagers and the recording of the amount of money bet in each of the various categories allowed, a theoretical yield for the game could be computed. Experience has shown that the actual hold percentage is approximately 28%–30%, very close to the theoretical maximum based on the odds structure of the game.

Validity of the Hold Percentage Comparisons

The validity of hold percentage comparisons that are performed by various casino managers, as well as by regulatory agencies, could be called into question. First, as noted in the discussion of drop, the main component of the hold percentage is subject to wide fluctuations depending upon the internal management definitions of what is drop and the internal accounting for various types of table transactions. Second, the hold percentage can vary on an individual game according to the number of persons playing and the mix of the bets placed on that game and the length of player stay.

At best, an analysis of drop percentages is meaningful to discover any changes in game performance over time, with the assumption of long-term statistical stability underlying all of the analyses. Thus, if a game has held 20% consistently for all shifts, for all seasons, then a decrease to 15% could be viewed as a serious problem that should be investigated. However, there are many factors that could have caused the drop, and each should be carefully examined to assure the correct identification of the problem.

If a significant increase in the size of the bets made occurred on a table game, for example, due to the presence of a single high roller, then the hold percentage would probably go down. If the player was at the table for a substantial period of time, the hold percentage on that table would decrease significantly. In the past, the decrease in hold percentage would simply have been called a losing shift and occasionally the dealer or boxman would have been dismissed, often for unspecified reasons. But the tacit understanding was that the reason for the poor hold percentage on the losing shift was probably employee theft. Today, however, it is known that the real reason for the reduced hold percentage in spite of the high dollar betting activity was the impact of the changing pattern of betting on what was otherwise a stable process. The employees most likely were not stealing, but were merely the victims of a changed statistical measure—the lower hold percentage.

Revenue

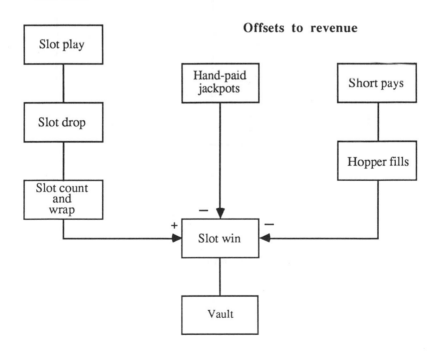

Fig. 4-3. Slot machine revenue flow.

Individual Casino Revenue Flows

Once the flows of revenues for slots and games are understood, all of the revenue flows in the casino can be summarized in flowchart form. Figures 4-3 to 4-8 present the individual revenue flows for slot machines, table games, keno, poker and card rooms, bingo, and sports and race book, respectively.

After removing the effect of the cashiering activity, the remaining revenue flows are quite simple.

All revenue transactions begin with the play and conclude after appropriate count and recording in the casino vault. The various components that constitute additions to revenue or deductions from revenue are presented on the flowcharts.

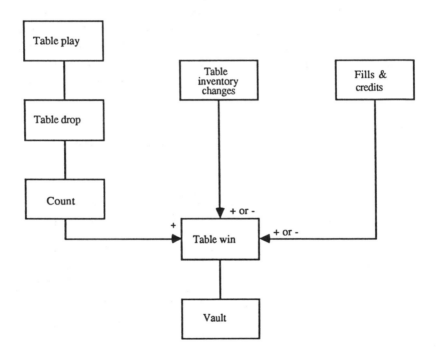

Fig. 4-4. Table games revenue flow.

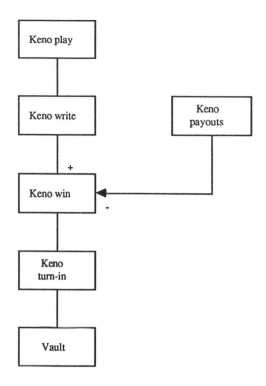

Fig. 4-5. Keno revenue flow.

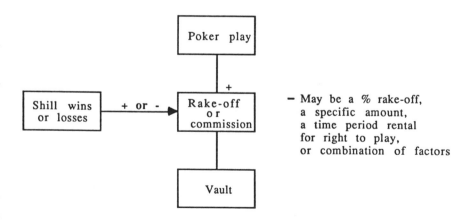

Fig. 4-6. Poker revenue flow.

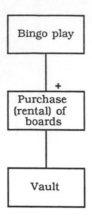

Fig. 4-7. Bingo revenue flow.

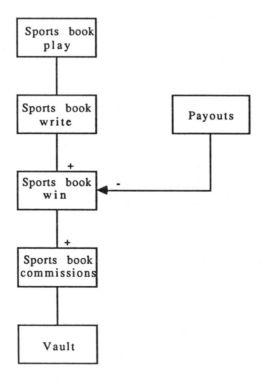

Fig. 4-8. Sports and race book revenue flow.

CHAPTER 5

Slot Machine Accounting

Introduction

This chapter describes the various components of slot machines, their operation in a casino environment, and the procedures relating to slot machine accounting. It also examines in detail the process of revenue determination for slot machine operations.

Slot Machine Components

Slot machines are customarily 20 to 24 inches wide, 16 to 18 inches deep, and 36 to 48 inches high. They are usually built as tabletop units and weigh about 100 pounds. Although they are relatively portable, slot machines are usually attached to a cabinet that is used to store the drop buckets that collect the coins played in the machine.

The principal components of the slot machine are described below and illustrated in figure 5-1.

1. The first is the coin receptacle. This is a slot into which the coins or tokens used by the slot machine are inserted. The mechanism is the same as used in a multitude of coin-operated devices throughout the nation. The coin receptacle can handle multiple coins, which can be inserted sequentially.

It is a fairly expensive proposition physically to change the coin denomination of a slot machine. Estimates by Bally Manufacturing in 1985 indicated that the cost for parts and labor would be approximately $200 per machine.[1] This high cost was the primary reason for the widespread adoption of $1.00 slot tokens in the casinos of Nevada following introduction of the downsized Susan B. Anthony dollar, which replaced the larger Eisenhower dollar. To avoid the great expense of changing the coin receptacle on their

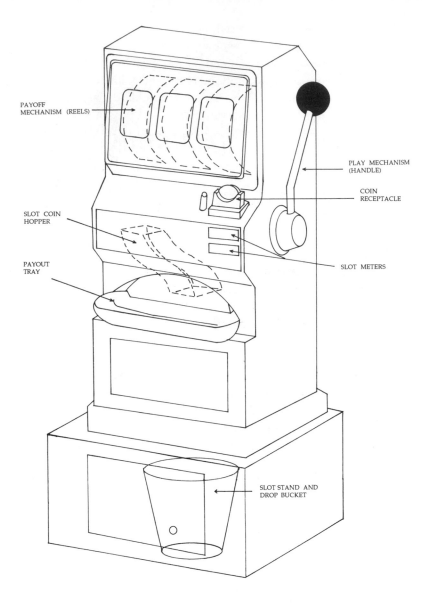

PAYOFF
MECHANISM (REELS)

PLAY MECHANISM
(HANDLE)

COIN
RECEPTACLE

SLOT COIN
HOPPER

PAYOUT
TRAY

SLOT METERS

SLOT STAND AND
DROP BUCKET

Fig. 5-1. Typical slot machine.

$1.00 machines, various casinos applied for and received permission from the U.S. Treasury Department and the Nevada Gaming Control Board to mint tokens and use them in their $1.00 slot machines.[2]

   2. The second component of a slot machine is the play mech-

anism. This is the method by which the play of the machine is initiated—in most slot machines, by pulling a handle. The slot machine handle initially was designed as the way in which the mechanical reels were put into motion. However, with the advent of the new electro-mechanical and all-electronic slot machines, the handle is more important in its function of tripping a switch that initiates the physical movement of the reels—impelled by a motor, rather than by the mechanical action of the handle. Thus, in many new slot machines, the handle may or may not be connected physically to the inside of the machine. It is interesting to note that in order to preserve the "psychological integrity" of the new slot machines, the handles are often manufactured in such a way as to duplicate exactly the feel of a true mechanical handle. Other play mechanisms for various coin-operated devices include a button that must be pushed to initiate the play electronically; in a few cases, the play mechanism is automatically initiated by the mere insertion of a coin.

3. The third element of the slot machine is the payoff mechanism. In a traditional slot machine, this is made up of the reels and the specification of the sets of symbols or combinations on the reels. It is this play mechanism that determines the payout to be made by the machine. These reels typically are set three or four on a common axle and are put into motion either electronically or mechanically. When the reels stop, they are locked into place by a series of ratchets, one per reel. Once the reels are locked in place, there is a sensing device, such as a metal rod or a light beam, that tells if a predetermined payoff has been achieved. At this point, the payoff mechanism is set into action to deliver the payoff.

4. The next component is a slot hopper. The slot hopper is a storage area, which is usually deep within the machine, and should not be confused with the display hopper that is shown on the front of many machines. The display hopper does not have anything to do with the operation of the machine, but is used as a device to attract customers.

The slot hopper is customarily filled at the beginning of the casino operation or whenever a new slot machine is put on the floor. The average slot hopper load, in terms of the amount of money, depends on the denomination of the machine, the proposed payoff schedule, and other factors. Once the initial slot load has been placed in the hopper, the slot machine begins operations.

Most typically, the machines are filled with the minimum

amount necessary to commence operations. For a $0.05 slot machine, the standard slot load is $30–$50; for a $1.00 slot machine, the standard slot load is $200–$300. Table 5-1 illustrates the standard slot loads for various denominations of slot machines together with the actual amounts taken from the physical count of machines that have been on the casino floor for a number of years.

When a payout is indicated by the results of the reel positions, the hopper automatically pays out the number of coins necessary. If the payouts from the hopper are too numerous, the slot hopper may become depleted. A low level is usually determined by a mechanical or electronic sensing arm inside the machine. When the sensing arm is too low, it automatically causes a diverter to come into place. When subsequent coins are put into the slot machine, instead of falling directly into the drop bucket (which is usually located in the cabinet below the slot machine), they are diverted into the slot hopper to replenish it. Once the hopper level has been restored, the diverter arm moves back, and the coins are once again directed into the drop bucket.

5. The next component is the slot payout tray. This is a metal tray that receives the payout of coins from the slot machine. The trays are usually specifically designed to provide maximum resonance when the coins are dropped into the tray. This noise is to create the impression of a large payout, regardless of the number of coins actually dumped into the tray.

6. The next component of the slot machine is a measuring device called a slot meter. The slot meters described in this section are the meters that are internal to the machine and not the meters visible to the public that indicate the amounts of jackpot payoffs that could be won on a particular machine. The purpose of these meters within the machine is to enable the casino and the gaming regulatory authorities to measure the amount of slot machine ac-

Table 5-1. Typical Slot Machine Hopper Loads.

Denomination	Standard Load	Sampled Load
$1.00	$300–400	$334
.50	200–300	331
.25	100–200	208
.10	80–200	162
.05	40–50	35

Standard loads are based on prevailing industry practice.
Sampled loads are based on audit sampling procedures for a major Nevada casino.
The differences show the impact of long-term changes in slot loads.

tivity. Nevada law requires any machine manufactured after 1965 to be equipped with these meters.

A slot machine customarily contains two meters, the coin-in meter and the coin-out meter. Of the two, the coin-in meter is more important, since it measures the total amount of coins actually played on the slot machine. In the process of accounting for slot activity, the meter readings are taken on a regular basis in conjunction with the slot drop. The actual count results are compared to the meter readings, and the meter readings are adjusted when necessary. Early slot meters were mechanical in nature and tended to be very inaccurate. The reliability of the meters has been improved recently with the advent of all-electronic machines.[3]

When the slot meters are reliable, they can be a very powerful method of controlling and reporting on gaming activity. The coin-in meter allows recording of the total number of coins played on the machine. The coin-out meter allows a careful record of the jackpots that have actually been paid by the machine. In this way, using the coin counts, the actual performance of the machine can be measured and compared to its expected theoretical performance.

7. The final component of the slot machine is the stand it customarily sits on. This slot stand serves many purposes. The first is to elevate the machine to the most convenient playing height. Second, the cabinet stand itself is used to store the drop buckets. The operation of the slot machine usually provides that the money played either goes directly to the slot hopper to replenish it, as previously described, or into a collection area. In most modern machines, the collection area is located below the machine in the locked slot stand. The coins drop either into a canvas bag attached to the bottom of the machine or into a plastic bucket. The bucket or bag holds the money won by the machine until it can be emptied by the regular slot drop and count procedures.

Electronic Slot Machines

The advent of electronic slot machines and other electronic coin-operated gaming devices has created a new environment for slot operations, with a number of challenges as well as opportunities.

Electronic slot machines are the most recent development in a trend toward more electronic components within slot machines. The first slot machines, popularized in the 1920s and 1930s, were totally mechanical. There are relatively few of these machines, manufactured by the Pace and Mills Manufacturing companies, still in existence.

The first step in the development of slot machines was the introduction of some electronic components. The payoff mechanisms were probably the first component to be electrified. As electronic slot technology developed, there were machines that had only three mechanical parts—the handle, the case of the machine, and the reels. The rest of the parts were electronic. Finally, machines have been produced that could be considered totally electronic, with the reels being replaced by a television-type screen showing the results of the play, a button in place of the handle, and a totally electronic payoff mechanism controlled by a microcomputer chip!

The electronic machines have great potential but have not yet been proven in play, and some slot professionals feel that there are problems with their introduction into the casinos.

On the positive side, the electronic circuitry tends to be much more reliable in operation than prior mechanical machines. This lack of mechanical wear and tear results in fewer problems in the operation of the electronic slots. In addition, the use of various electronic components allows the operator to keep better records of what is going on in the machine. The meters are more reliable, and the microprocessor controls allow more detailed self-diagnosis of internal operating problems.

On the negative side, the same electronic circuitry is very difficult to test and validate since the electronics themselves must be tested. This testing must be done to assure that the components perform in the manner in which they are intended and that there are sufficient safeguards against either random unintentional or deliberate disruption of the electronic circuitry. For example, some electronic slot machines, when first introduced, tended to pay off the entire jackpot hopper whenever a certain type of walkie-talkie was used by a security guard standing near the machine. Adjustment of internal components eliminated that problem, but the threat of this type of problem still exists—electronic jamming of slot machines by thieves is a possibility.

Another unknown factor is the stability of these electronic components over time, the expected life of the component, and what happens if a critical component fails. Because of the relatively short time that electronic slots have been in use, the answers to these questions and their impact on the slot machines and the casino are not yet known.

The final uncertainty with regard to these new machines is the feeling that the repair and maintenance technology is rapidly changing. Instead of needing a skilled mechanic to repair slot machines, the new era of slot repair will require degrees and training in electronics.

The limited experience with these machines in Nevada has indicated that consumer acceptance of the all-electronic games has not been as high as had been anticipated. Many persons still prefer the feel of the old mechanical machines. Nevertheless, the electronic machines have proven to be very reliable and more trouble free than their mechanical counterparts. The jury is still out on the long-term acceptance of these machines, but they are definitely here to stay until another innovative technology is developed.

Slot Machine Denominations

Information published by the Nevada Gaming Control Board indicates that the various denominations of slot machines have radically different financial and operational characteristics. This section discusses some of these differences.

The denominations of slot machines are typically $0.05, $0.10, $0.25, $0.50, and $1.00. Very occasionally there are machines that take special tokens (other than the standard $1.00 tokens), whose value can range up to $5.00. There are very few $0.01 slot machines left in Nevada, and most of these have been relegated to antique stores or museum shelves.

The number of slot machines in use in Nevada is indicated in table 5-2, according to geographic area and casino size. The Gaming Control Board statistics are taken from the 1985 issue of the *Gaming Abstract*.[4] There were a total of 77,045 slot machines in Nevada in 1984 for all casinos with revenues in excess of $1 million per year. Of these machines, 34.4% were $0.05 machines, 20.4% were $1.00 machines, and 37.9% were $0.25 machines. The table shows that the distribution of machines varies widely from area to area, with the largest number of slot machines being located on the Las Vegas Strip, with 21,866 machines; followed by the Reno-Sparks area with 19,179 machines; Downtown Las Vegas with 12,731 machines; and Douglas County (South Lake Tahoe) with 6,840 machines.

In each of these areas, the percentage of slot machines of each

Table 5-2. Statewide Slot Machines (1984).

Casino Location	# of Loc.	NUMBER OF MACHINES DENOMINATION						
		.05	.10	.25	.50	$1.00	Other	Total
L.V. Strip	38	6,637	364	8,965	211	5,012	677	21,866
Downtown L.V.	24	4,684	246	4,957	111	2,336	397	12,731
Laughlin	5	1,058	57	1,197	15	454	29	2,810
Reno-Sparks	30	6,620	1,347	6,444	335	4,367	66	19,179
Douglas Cty	7	2,127	521	2,471	134	1,400	187	6,840
Elko	11	1,192	105	974	40	456	45	2,812
Balance of State	33	4,226	341	4,177	216	1,096	151	10,807
Total	148	26,544	2,981	29,185	1,062	15,721	1,552	77,045
% of Total		34.4	3.9	37.9	1.4	20.4	2.0	100.0

Casino Location	PERCENTAGE DISTRIBUTION OF MACHINES DENOMINATION				
	.05	.25	$1.00	Other	Total
L.V. Strip	30.4	41.0	22.9	5.7	100.0
Downtown L.V.	36.8	38.9	18.3	6.0	100.0
Laughlin	37.7	42.6	16.2	3.5	100.0
Reno-Sparks	34.5	33.6	22.8	9.1	100.0
Douglas Cty	31.1	36.1	20.5	12.3	100.0
Elko	42.4	34.6	16.2	6.8	100.0
Balance of State	39.1	38.7	15.7	6.5	100.0
Statewide	34.4	37.9	20.4	7.3	100.0

denomination is also indicated in table 5-2. These differences in number of machines and mix of denominations of machines can be explained very easily by the varied marketing emphasis in each of these areas. The casinos are merely providing the mix of slot machine denominations desired by their unique customer group. Since the customers are very different between Las Vegas and Reno, it is reasonable to expect considerable variations in the slot machine denomination mixes of the two locations.

The mix differences can be most clearly indicated in the $0.05 and $1.00 slot machines. The highest percentage of $0.05 machines is in the Elko area with 42.4%, followed by 37.7% in Laughlin, 36.8% in Downtown Las Vegas, and 34.5% in the Reno-Sparks areas. The difference is most noticeable between the Downtown and Strip areas of Las Vegas (36.8% and 30.4%, respectively). However, there are some striking similarities between areas such as Douglas County (South Lake Tahoe) and the Las Vegas Strip (31.1%

and 30.4%) and between Downtown Las Vegas and Reno-Sparks (36.8% and 34.5%).

With regard to $1.00 machines, the differences between the style of operation in the respective market areas seem to be significant. The percentage of $1.00 slot machines varies from a high of 22.9% on the Strip to a low of 16.2% at Elko.

If a preliminary analysis of the slot mix is plotted against some of the traditional indicators of quality of gaming customer, you would expect fewer $1.00 slot machines in higher-quality

Table 5-3. Slot Machine Distribution by Casino Size (1984).

| | | NUMBER OF MACHINES | | | | | | |
| Location and Size | # of Loc. | DENOMINATION | | | | | | |
		.05	.10	.25	.50	$1.00	Other	Total
Downtown L.V.								
$1–10 M	10	867	45	793	3	543	23	2,274
10–20 M	5	1,189	45	901	23	467	182	2,807
over 20 M	9	2,628	156	3,263	85	1,326	192	7,650
L.V. Strip								
$1–10 M	12	681	29	754	16	259	83	1,822
10–20 M	8	1,947	70	2,044	42	799	176	5,078
20–60 M	12	2,269	87	3,789	83	1,998	202	8,428
over 60 M	6	1,740	178	2,378	70	1,956	216	6,538
Reno-Sparks								
$1–10 M	17	2,591	537	1,570	143	1,024	14	5,879
10–20 M	5	890	86	833	43	840	—	2,692
over 20 M	8	3,139	724	4,041	149	2,503	52	10,608

| | | PERCENTAGE DISTRIBUTION | | | | |
| Location and Size | # of Loc. | DENOMINATION | | | | |
		.05	.25	$1.00	Other	Total
Downtown L.V.						
$1–10 M	1	38.1	34.9	23.9	3.1	100.0
10–20 M	5	42.4	32.1	16.6	8.8	100.0
over 20 M	9	34.4	42.7	17.3	5.8	100.0
L.V. Strip						
$1–10 M	12	37.4	41.3	14.3	7.0	100.0
10–20 M	8	38.4	40.3	15.7	5.6	100.0
20–60 M	12	26.9	44.9	23.8	4.5	100.0
over 60 M	6	26.6	36.4	29.9	7.1	100.0
Reno-Sparks						
$1–10 M	17	44.0	26.8	17.5	11.9	100.0
10–20 M	5	33.1	30.9	31.2	4.8	100.0
over 20 M	8	28.6	38.1	23.6	8.7	100.0

areas. This is exactly the case in the higher-quality Douglas County (South Lake Tahoe) market, which has fewer $1.00 slot machines than Reno-Sparks (20.5% and 22.8%, respectively). The Las Vegas Strip market appears to be redirecting its efforts away from a premium player since it has a significantly larger number of $1.00 slot machines (22.9%), which appeal to lower-quality players.

Table 5-3 shows a more detailed analysis of the number of slot machines in three selected markets: the Las Vegas Strip, Downtown Las Vegas, and the Reno-Sparks area. For each of these areas, the size of the casino is a second determinant. On the Las Vegas Strip, the only significant difference in denominations of machines appears to be that casinos with greater annual revenue tend to have fewer $0.05 machines and more $1.00 machines. This clear pattern of fewer $0.05 machines and greater numbers of $1.00 slot machines in larger casinos is exhibited both in Downtown Las Vegas and in the Reno-Sparks area.

An interesting question arises here. Is the greater number of $1.00 slot machines in the larger casinos a cause or effect? That is, does the greater earning power of the $1.00 slot machine create the situation where the casino revenue is significantly greater, or is the greater number of $1.00 slot machines the natural result of having players in these casinos who have more money to spend?

Profitability of Various Denominations

One of the most interesting statistics regarding slot machine operations is the amount of gross revenue that can be earned by a slot machine. Table 5-4 indicates the median win per unit for various denominations of slot machines located in the different geo-

Table 5-4. Median Slot Machine Annual Win per Unit (1984).

Location	DENOMINATION				
	.05	.10	.25	.50	$1.00
Downtown L.V.	$7,751	$9,217	$15,848	$16,380	$28,530
L.V. Strip	9,483	12,134	18,127	24,492	36,233
Laughlin	12,249	15,797	23,966	19,465	50,130
Reno-Sparks	8,235	8,654	15,317	15,114	27,085
Douglas Cty	8,589	12,366	19,422	17,938	29,614
Elko	6,487	7,641	12,038	13,941	25,297
Balance of State	7,266	8,120	15,372	13,474	24,063
Statewide	7,876	8,878	15,891	15,610	29,614

graphic areas of Nevada. It is interesting to note that even within the various denominations there tends to be a wide variation in the earnings of these machines. For example, a $0.05 slot machine earns from $6,487 in Douglas County (South Lake Tahoe) to a maximum of $12,249 in the Laughlin area. This difference seems to be very small when compared to the fluctuation that occurs in the earnings of a $1.00 slot machine. The low for these machines is $25,297 in Elko, with a maximum of $50,130 in the Laughlin area.

This difference in earnings, both from the various geographic areas and for the slot machine denominations, is due to a number of factors. With respect to the denominations, the superiority is based solely on the volume of money that can be played on a $1.00 slot machine. (It takes twenty handle pulls for a $0.05 machine to equal just one handle pull for a $ 1.00 slot machine.) This increased volume of money has been offset by having the $1.00 slot machine set at a payoff rate much greater than the $0.05 slot machines. The combination of better return coupled with the attractive locations of the $1.00 slot machines in high-volume or high-traffic areas tends to result in very high rates of play, which in turn means good earnings for the casino.

Also, it should be stressed that the figures in table 5-4 are the *median* win per unit figures. There are some casinos that operate various slot machines in each geographic area that have performance results both better and worse than those indicated. The Gaming Control Board *Abstract* indicates these higher and lower levels of earnings as upper and lower quartile win per unit, respectively.

Table 5-5 indicates the differences that exist in the win per unit for the various denominations of slot machines when categorized by the gross revenue of the casino for the Las Vegas Strip, Downtown Las Vegas, and the Reno-Sparks area. The results are quite dramatic for the Las Vegas locations, with the $0.05 slot machine win being about 80% higher and the $1.00 slot machine win being about 190% higher for the larger casinos. In Downtown Las Vegas, a very similar situation exists. The differences in the Reno-Sparks area are somewhat less pronounced, but still very important. For $0.05 as well as $1.00 slot machines, the difference is still 60% and 130% more win per unit, respectively, for the larger clubs.

It is interesting to note that there is also a strong geographic difference in the win per unit for the slot machine denominations. For example, in the $1–$10 million category, the earnings of the $0.05 slot machines are very similar between the Las Vegas Strip

Table 5-5. Median Slot Annual. Win per Unit (1984).

Location		DENOMINATION			
and Size	.05	.10	.25	.50	$1.00
Downtown L.V.					
$1–10 M	6,812	5,590	7,401	4,702	19,728
10–20 M	8,009	9,771	17,822	13,333	30,288
over 20 M	10,621	11,965	21,111	27,364	48,989
L.V. Strip					
$1–10 M	5,951	7,951	11,417	6,921	17,398
10–20 M	8,906	11,957	17,634	24,890	30,704
20–60 M	11,056	14,588	19,092	22,801	37,841
over 60 M	12,192	13,919	29,467	37,070	57,808
Reno-Sparks					
$1–10 M	5,823	5,963	12,728	10,296	21,891
10–20 M	9,262	10,031	17,826	16,626	32,561
over 20 M	9,347	9,767	19,173	21,322	50,232

and Downtown Las Vegas, but there is a 50% difference between the Reno-Sparks area and the Las Vegas area average. With respect to $1.00 slot machines, the Reno-Sparks area machines seem to be more profitable than the Las Vegas machines for the small casinos.

However, once the focus changes to the larger casinos, as in the case of those that produce over $20 million in gaming revenue, the differences in the $0.05 slot machine between Las Vegas and Reno are very significant. A machine on the Las Vegas Strip earns up to 30% more than the same machine in a Reno-Sparks casino of the same revenue size, but the revenue in the $1.00 slot machines is only 15% greater in Las Vegas. Only in certain cases does the win per unit in the Las Vegas area exceed the win per unit in the Reno-Sparks area: the $1.00 slot machines in the casinos in Reno are slightly ahead of the same units on the Las Vegas Strip in all size categories except the very largest casinos.

Slot Machine Mix

Slot mix is a term that describes the physical layout and the denominations of machines, as well as the exact types of machines, in the casino. The primary objective of the slot mix is to have a successful slot operation. This section is concerned with examining the factors that underlie this success.

The basic variables that are crucial to slot success are floor location of the slots; coin denomination of the slots; and payoff schedule of machines and hold percentage.[5]

Floor Location

The floor location of the slots is perhaps the most important factor in determining the success of a slot operation. The first element of the floor location is to plan the casino so that service facilities such as restaurants and show rooms are in the center of the casino. In this way, customers coming into the casino for many purposes will pass the gaming areas.

The next layer outside the service core is the pit area, with the outside layer being the slot operations. This circle theory of location also uses the idea of interception, with very few direct routes being available from the center of the casino (and the primary service areas) to the exits and entrances. With these deliberately circuitous paths, the flow of customers can be directed around the slot machine area, without easing their exit from the casino. The longer the patrons stay in the casino, the greater the likelihood that they will spend some additional money.

Other features of floor location include having a choice or mixture of slot denominations available. There is no single rule in this area. Some casinos mix the denominations of slot machines so there is no uniform pattern. Harrah's pioneered the "block style" of locating the slot machines in orderly rows or blocks of slot machines of the same denomination.

A relatively new phenomenon is the use of the concept of a slot carousel or a group of $1.00 slot machines located in a certain area of the casino. These slot carousels are staffed by a separate change person who may also act as a barker to attract people to play these high-value machines.[6]

The final aspect of floor location in the slot mix is the concept of service and security control over slot areas. It is desirable to utilize every square foot of space in a casino to produce revenue. This can be accomplished by putting slot machines in every conceivable nook and cranny. However, when the casino is busy, the ability of the slot service personnel, slot change personnel, and security guards to oversee these nooks and crannies is significantly reduced.

Coin Denomination

The coin denomination of the slots in the casino is a second factor in the success of a slot operation. There is a conventional attitude that to be successful in a certain area, you simply install the slot machines in the ratio that has already been demonstrated to be effective in your market area. This is nothing more complicated than looking at the latest *Gaming Abstract* and choosing the ratio or proportion of slot machine denominations indicated. This procedure does not always work, however. The popularity of the $1.00 slot machines has called this conventional wisdom into question. Recently, more sophisticated marketing analysis has used coin counts and revenue generated to analyze the demand for slot machine play of a certain denomination and in a certain area. The available supply of machines is then compared to the ideal demand; if necessary, new machines are introduced or machines are removed in order to adjust the slot mix to meet the player demand.[7]

Payoff Schedule and Hold Percentage

The third factor influencing the slot mix is an interrelation of payoff schedules with the casino hold percentage. In the structure of payoffs of the various machines there are two extremes. The first is what could be called a jackpot-only machine, which pays only if a single jackpot sequence is achieved. This single jackpot is sufficiently large to outweigh the lack of small payoffs. The second type of machine is called a multiple-payoff machine, which may have much more frequent but smaller payoffs. The proper mix of these machines is essential since they seem to appeal to vastly different groups of players. Although psychological literature suggests that the concept of selective reinforcement in small, frequent payoffs is preferable to most persons, the casino must have all types of machines in order to accommodate all types of player preferences.[8]

The payoff schedules also relate to the use of casino hold percentages, a widely accepted procedure to be able to determine what a slot machine should theoretically hold, based on a given number of plays and the known reel patterns and payoff schedule. This theoretical hold percentage can be calculated using a form similar to the one indicated in figure 5-2. The computation of the hold percentage on a multiple-jackpot machine is shown in figure 5-3. Note that on this machine the payoff percentage is approximately 95%, with a hold percentage of 5%. The casino must make the initial determination of the hold percentage for the slot machine at the time the machine is ordered from the manufacturer. Once the machine is ordered with the reel strips (symbol strips) in

IDENTIFICATION _____

POSITION	REEL 1	REEL 2	REEL 3	REEL 4
1				
2				
3				
4				
5				
6				
7				
8				
9				
10				
11				
12				
13				
14				
15				
16				
17				
18				
19				
20				
21				
22				
23				
24				
25				
TOTAL				

PLAYS PER CYCLE

Combination	A	B	C	D	E	F	G	H	I
WIN	1ST REEL	2ND REEL	3RD REEL	4TH REEL	Total # of HITS A*B*C*D	PAID PER COIN E×F	PAID PER CYCLE	AMOUNT PAID ON FLOOR	PAID BY MACHINE G-H
NON WIN	1ST REEL	2ND REEL	3RD REEL	4TH REEL	TOTAL HITS	TOTALS			

PLAYS PER CYCLE

[ ] Plays per Cycle X _____ = TOTAL WIN (enter below)

$ _____ Total Win

Minus _____ PAID minus

Equals _____ WIN Equals

====== Percent of ======

WIN   TOTAL WIN   Machine Win

Prepared By: _____

Date: _____

Type of Machine: _____

Model: _____

Inventory No: _____

Location: _____

Fig. 5-2. *Slot payoff analysis.*

IDENTIFICATION 5¢ (#94)

POSITION	REEL 1	REEL 2	REEL 3	REEL 4
1	7	7	7	
2	BE	PL	PL	
3	PL	BA	BE	
4	OR	CH	OR	
5	PL	BA	BE	
6	CH	OR	PL	
7	PL	BA	BE	
8	BA	BE	OR	
9	PL	BA	BE	
10	OR	CH	PL	
11	PL	BA	BE	
12	CH	OR	BA	
13	PL	BA	BE	
14	BA	BE	OR	
15	PL	BA	BE	
16	OR	CH	PL	
17	PL	BA	BE	
18	CH	OR	OR	
19	PL	BA	BE	
20	BA	BE	PL	
21	BL	BA	BE	
22	OR	CH	OR	
23				
24				
25				
TOTAL	22	22	22	

PLAYS PER CYCLE 10648

Combination WIN	A 1ST REEL	B 2ND REEL	C 3RD REEL	D 4TH REEL	E Total # of Hits Apl'cd	F PAID PER COIN EFF	G PAID PER CYCLE	H AMOUNT PAID ON FLOOR	I PAID BY MACHINE G-H
CH xx	3	18	22		1188	2	2376		
CH CH x	3	4	22		264	5	1210		
BA BA BA	3	10	1		30	100	3000		
BE BE BE	1	3	10		30	18	540		
PL PL PL	10	1	5		50	14	700		
OR OR OR	4	3	5		60	10	600		
777	1	1	1		1	100	100		
TOTALS							8526		

Combination NON WIN	1ST REEL	2ND REEL	3RD REEL	4TH REEL	TOTAL HITS
BA BA x	3	12	22		792
BE BE x	1	19	22		418
PL PL x	10	21	22		4620
OR OR x	4	19	22		1672
7 7 x	1	21	22		462
BA BA BA	3	10	21		630
BE BE BE	1	3	12		36
PL PL PL	10	1	17		170
OR OR OR	4	3	17		204
777	1	1	21		21

PLAYS PER CYCLE 10648

[10648] X 5¢ = TOTAL WIN (enter below)
Plays per Cycle

$ 10648 Total Win $ 532.40

Minus 8526 PAID minus 426.30

Equals 2122 WIN Equals 106.10

19.93% Percent of =

WIN   TOTAL WIN   Machine Win

Prepared By: _____
Date: _____
Type of Machine: _____
Model: _____
Inventory No: _____
Location: _____

Fig. 5-3. Slot payoff analysis.

place, and the corresponding mechanical or electronic determination of the payoffs set, it is a very significant effort to change the reel strips and circuitry in order to alter the payouts. The casino must therefore decide ahead of time, based on its judgment of the competitive environment, just how much of the customer's dollar it is going to retain for itself.

New Jersey and Nevada have adopted vastly different attitudes to this problem. In New Jersey, the casinos are required to have no machines that hold in excess of 15% of the customer's dollar. In Nevada, there is no specific limit of that nature, and the state depends on competition and marketing pressures to assure that the hold percentages are at a reasonable level. The only formal requirement in Nevada is that the payoff schedule must be prominently displayed on the front of the machine.[9] The current mix of slot machines in northern Nevada indicates that the 15% New Jersey guideline is about the standard for the mix of all machines in the casino. This, however, varies widely by denomination, with the majority of the $1.00 slot machines holding between 5% and 10% (considerably less in percentage terms than other denominations, but considerably more than other machines in terms of total dollars held).

Casino design and the slot operation often go hand in hand. An understanding of the traffic flow in and around slot machines in the casino can be critical to the success of the machines. If the casino is catering to slot machine customers, and particularly if it is handling large numbers of organized bus tour customers, then particular attention must be paid to the flow from the buses into the casino with a minimum of difficulty.

There is a final slot machine fallacy that must be put to rest: the changing of the payoff structures on slot machines. Various stories circulate that there are summer and winter sets of reels for slot machines and that they are changed during the off-season to increase the payout to the customer during these slow business periods. The reality is that the process of payoff changing is long, difficult, and expensive and is only done as part of a major shift in attitude or management style in the casino. Much more frequent is the process of moving the various slot machines from location to location in the casino. It is quite common to have a machine that does not perform well in a certain location moved to another location; due to the different environment, it may become a productive machine.

Slot Machine Accounting Definitions

The definitions that are used in conjunction with slot machine operations are generally pure, since the mechanical or electronic aspects of a slot machine allow for the precise measurement of the various betting transactions. This exact measurement is not possible on other casino pit or table games. For this reason, the accounting definitions for the slot operation are not only important for understanding the operation and revenue of the slot operation, but form the basis for understanding revenue concepts for the casino in general.

Slot Handle

Slot handle is the total amount of money played in the slot machine. It is customarily measured by the coin-in meters and is also known in some areas as the *handle pulls*. If the number is expressed in handle pulls, then it must be converted to a dollar amount according to the machine's denomination. (Some confusion may arise in the case of multiple-coin machines, where up to five coins can be played on a single physical pull of the handle. In this case, the handle figure would be the five-coin total amounts.)

Slot Drop

Slot drop is the total amount of money in the drop bucket. As previously described, when the money goes through the machine, it is usually deposited in the drop bucket located in the cabinet underneath the slot machine. The slot drop is the amount of money put into the machine less two items: the amount of money diverted to refill the slot hopper and any jackpots paid automatically by the machine. The slot drop is a close measure to the slot handle or total gaming play on the slot machine.

Slot Win

Slot win is the net amount won by the machine. In various operating situations, there are many different interpretations of the win amount. For example, if all the payouts are paid automatically by the machine, then the win equals the amount in the drop bucket or the slot drop. This computation assumes that there are no inventory changes in the amount of money in the slot hopper. If there are dramatic or material changes in the level of the slot hopper, then the win is calculated as:

$$\text{WIN} = \text{DROP plus or minus INVENTORY CHANGE IN}$$
$$\text{THE SLOT HOPPER}$$

If payouts or jackpots are paid by the machine and by the slot personnel (so-called hand pays or hand jackpots), then the amount of these hand-paid jackpots must be deducted from the total drop to arrive at the win. The computation then becomes:

$$\text{WIN} = \text{DROP plus or minus INVENTORY CHANGE IN}$$
$$\text{THE SLOT HOPPER}$$
$$\text{minus HAND-PAID JACKPOTS}$$

or, more simply stated, if slot hopper inventory changes are not material:

$$\text{WIN} = \text{DROP minus HAND-PAID JACKPOTS}$$

Finally, there is one other alteration to the process of computing the win. In some circumstances, a jackpot of a machine that is supposed to be paid automatically may be short a certain amount. This causes a circumstance known as a *short pay*. In this situation, two complementary actions take place. The first is that the patron who won the jackpot must be paid the total amount due. This creates a hand-paid jackpot. In addition, the reason for the short pay is either because of machine malfunction or else because the slot coin hopper is empty and must be refilled before it can be put back into service. In this case, an additional element in the computation of win is introduced. This element is called a *slot machine fill*.

$$\text{WIN} = \text{DROP plus or minus INVENTORY CHANGE IN HOPPER}$$
$$\text{minus HAND-PAID JACKPOTS}$$
$$\text{minus FILLS MADE TO THE SLOT MACHINE}$$

Again, if the inventory change in the hopper is not material, then a simple expression of the relationship is:

$$\text{WIN} = \text{DROP minus JACKPOTS minus FILLS}$$

For all practical purposes, the hopper levels are not measured to determine the amount of win on slot machines during the year. However, it is a customary year-end audit procedure to test sample some of the slot hoppers in order to assure that the hopper fills are close to the standard slot loads. Depending upon the results of this year-end sampling procedure, the reported slot machine win for the year can then be adjusted either up or down to match the actual amount held in the slot machine hopper.

Hold Percentages

Hold percentage is a vital management concept in the casino and is very important in the slot machine area. The hold percentage is theoretically expressed as the percentage of the money that is held by the slot machine when measured against the total money put into the machine.

The hold percentage is the win dollars divided by the total play dollars. If the machine calculations are based on the number of coins, the hold percentage can be expressed as the number of coins won divided by the total coins played. This second computation is eased by the use of the coin-in meter figure to determine the denominator of the equation.

$$\text{HOLD PERCENTAGE} = \text{WIN \$} / \text{TOTAL PLAY \$}$$
$$\text{or} = \text{Number of Coins Won} / \text{Number of Coins In}$$

The hold percentage is a particularly powerful measuring device in the case of a slot machine. Because of the ability to measure the total coins played, there can be a meaningful analysis of the comparison of the theoretical hold percentage and the actual hold percentage.

Comparison of Hold Percentages

The comparison of theoretical hold percentage and actual hold percentage can form the basis for diagnostic and managerial analysis of slot operating results. From slot meter readings, together with the machine specifications, a theoretical hold percentage can be calculated. With this measure, the comparison of actual hold results to the theoretical hold results identifies the machines that could be classified as losers and winners.

The deviation of the actual hold percentage from the theoretical hold percentage is a signal of mechanical, electrical, or other performance problems. If the number of coins in is sufficiently large, a valid comparison of these two measures can result. The necessity of having large numbers of coins in to compare cannot be overemphasized since the inevitable nature of statistical fluctuations may make the short-run variations extremely erratic and possibly misleading.

Figure 5-4 indicates a sample slot winner and loser report, where the theoretical hold (called the *par*) is compared to the actual hold percentage (% of coins in), with the positive and negative differences identified.

In certain casinos, the faith that is placed in the coin-in meters is somewhat less, either due to the older age of the machines or as a result of previous poor results of coin meter performance. In this case, the comparison of theoretical to actual hold is very difficult, so other surrogate measures of hold percentages are used. One such measure is expressed as:

$$\text{HOLD \%} = \text{\$ AMOUNT WON} / \text{\$ DROP AMOUNT}$$

Although this number cannot be absolutely determined, if it is assumed that the hopper levels are largely unchanged, then the drop amount should be closely related to the coins in. The effect of this changed formula is to use a more reliable counting basis (the actual physical count of the coins in the drop bucket), rather than the somewhat unreliable meter measurement to determine the actual hold percentage. Although the hold percentages may vary from the theoretical setting of the machine, the long-term stability of this new surrogate measure of hold percentage can be used as an excellent indicator of the mechanical reliability of the slot machine.

Slot Machine Personnel

Slot personnel, essential to the effective operation of the slot department, are divided into three categories: slot management, repair and maintenance, and change persons. Each of these groups has a unique contribution to the operation of the slot department and plays a role in the internal control over the slot machine accounting system.

Date	Coins in	Drop	% of Coins in	Regular Jackpots	Fills/ Shorts	% of Coins in	Win	% of Drop	% of Coins in	Par	Diff.	Confidence Level
$1 MACHINE NO. 112 TYPE 3 PAY O PLENTY												
CURR	6388.00	2104.00	32.9	--	100.00	1.6	2004.00	95.2	31.4	22.3	9.1	W 95
W 060880	5035.00	2345.00	46.6	--	--	0.0	2345.00	100.0	46.6	22.3	24.3	W 99
W 061580	3933.00	1150.00	29.2	--	200.00	5.1	950.00	82.6	24.2	22.3	1.9	--
W 062280	2272.00	502.00	22.1	--	200.00	8.8	302.00	60.2	13.3	22.3	-0.9	--
$1 MACHINE NO. 820 TYPE 9 THREE LINE $ SIGN												
CURR	16720.00	2249.00	13.5	26.00	200.00	1.2	2023.00	90.0	12.1	4.6	7.5	W 85
W 060880	40496.00	2056.00	5.1	--	--	0.0	2056.00	100.0	5.1	4.6	0.5	--
W 061580	30617.00	2087.00	6.8	--	--	0.0	2087.00	100.0	6.8	4.6	2.2	W 70
W 062280	20800.00	1443.00	6.9	--	--	0.0	1443.00	100.0	6.9	4.6	2.3	W 70
$1 MACHINE NO. 827 TYPE 8 THREE LINE PAY												
CURR	66849.00	1946.00	2.9	--	--	0.0	1946.00	100.0	2.9	6.1	-3.2	L 75
W 060880	31074.00	2790.00	9.0	--	--	0.0	2790.00	100.0	9.0	6.1	2.9	W 70
W 061580	13421.00	2098.00	15.6	--	--	0.0	2098.00	100.0	15.6	6.1	9.5	W 90
W 062280	22871.00	1235.00	5.4	--	--	0.0	1235.00	100.0	5.4	6.1	-0.7	--

Fig. 5-4. Slot winner and loser report.

Slot Management

Slot management is usually limited to one manager per casino, who has exclusive responsibility for the slot operation and reports to the casino manager or general manager. Unfortunately, most slot managers are repair and maintenance personnel who have been promoted. They usually do not have a keen sense of slot marketing or of what appeals to customers. This often results in a technically strong slot department with the latest machines in excellent repair, but the marketing of the machines and the related activities such as organization and layout of machines are left to chance.

Slot Repair and Maintenance

Slot maintenance is usually staffed with a minimum of one person per shift for approximately every 100 machines in the casino. The slot repair personnel are responsible for the maintenance and repair of the slots on the floor, for handling inspections if there is a short pay or improper jackpot payoff, and for assisting management in verifying the jackpots. They are also responsible for various maintenance and repair functions in the slot repair shop.

There are two very significant problems with respect to the slot maintenance function. The first is that the maintenance personnel must, of necessity, have the keys to all the slot machines in the casino, giving them instant access. Coupled with this condition is the fact that the average slot mechanic is not highly trained or highly compensated. This creates a very difficult situation where the incentive to steal (arising from low wages) and the opportunity (having key access) are frequently present on the slot floor.

The second problem arises from the present shortage of skilled slot machine repair personnel. As a result, casinos are less and less selective about their hiring, causing the quality of personnel to suffer. In addition, the new demand for electronics training has created a situation where the shortage of skilled, reliable staff has been further accentuated.

Slot Change Personnel

These individuals are the closest to the slot machine accounting functions. Slot personnel typically consist of change persons on the floor of the casinos and persons located in slot booths. The slot change floor personnel perform two separate and distinct jobs, which are often combined for ease of execution but are radically different from an accounting standpoint. These dual roles are those of slot change and jackpot payoffs. From the viewpoint of accounting complexity, as well as exposure to loss in the casino, the major emphasis must be on the function of jackpot payoffs. In this area, the personnel must be trained not only to record the transactions correctly, but to be aware of potential irregularities in the payoff procedures. They must also be carefully trained in the approvals that must be secured for jackpots of any major size.

Slot booth personnel can act independently of the floor personnel or can be their supervisors. Depending on the size of the casino slot area, the volume of operation, and the number of floor personnel, the number of slot booths can vary widely. A minor activity of slot booth personnel can be to act as a coupon redemption center and a place where give-away coins can be obtained. Finally, the slot booth can provide some security and surveillance from its elevated position on the slot floor.

The change function of the slot personnel can be controlled very well by the use of the concept of imprest balances, both for individual change persons and for the various change booths located throughout the casino.

Slot Accounting Procedures

There are two main flows of accounting information in the slot area: the cashiering functions, as typified by the various change functions, and the casino revenue flow procedures, encompassing the drop, the jackpot payout procedures, and other activities.

Cashiering Functions

Figure 5-5 indicates the general nature of money flow in the casino slot machine operation. Most of the money flow is between the customer and the machines, from the customer to the various change personnel, from the change personnel to the slot booth, and, finally, from the slot booth to the vault. In the cashiering function, the exchanges of money are always made on an even-money exchange basis. For this purpose, all of the accounting and control elements in the slot area can be operated toward a specific imprest balance. The only changes in the amount of money are for shortages or other irregular transactions. For virtually all of the other transactions, the amount of money on hand at any point is con-

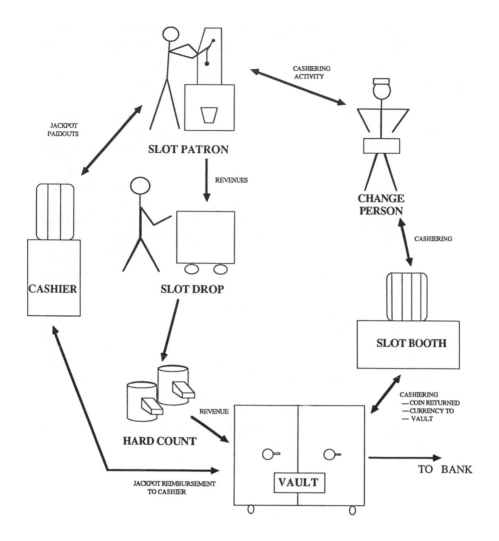

Fig. 5-5. Slot machine accounting flow.

stant, with only the physical composition of coin or currency changing. When the amount of currency builds up, either with the change person or in the slot booth, the currency is exchanged for coins from the other sources.

It is important to note that the coins that are derived from the revenue cycle of the slot operation, even under the operating policy of depositing the revenue of the day in the bank, never leave the casino. It would be an enormous physical task to transfer that much coin. Instead, the coin is exchanged for currency in the vault, the currency is deposited in the bank, and the coin is held in the vault or recycled to the slot booth and back to the patrons.

Revenue Functions

The second major flow in the slot area is the flow relating to the revenue function of the slot operation. This flow is indicated as revenue in figure 5-5. The principal component of the revenue flow in the slot area is the action of the patron dropping a coin in the slot machine, and that coin then finding its way to the drop bucket in the cabinet beneath the machine.

At the proper time designated for the slot drop (discussed in detail later), the coins are removed from the drop bucket and are physically transported through the casino to the coin counting room. All of this, of course, is accomplished under tight security. Once the coins are in the coin count room, the process known as the *hard count* commences. This process is usually accomplished by mechanical, high-speed counting machines. Once the amount of coin is determined, it is wrapped in standard denominations and is transported to the vault. When it arrives in the vault, the revenue reporting is completed by the inclusion of the jackpot paidouts, and the final slot revenue or slot win is determined. The coin is either held in the vault or transferred to the coin storage area of the slot booth in exchange for currency. The amount of the slot win is then deposited in currency in the bank.

Slot Accounting for a New Casino

One of the most significant accounting issues arises when a new slot machine is put into operation or when the casino is first opened with all new machines.

The key accounting transaction at this operational stage is the necessity to account for the amounts of money that are put into the slot hopper initially (the initial hopper load) as capital transactions and not to record them improperly as mere offsets to the slot revenue.

The initial slot hopper loads should be observed by the independent accountant, in order to verify their amounts. This eases the subsequent auditing process since the amount of fluctuation in the amount of slot hopper load can be accurately determined. The amount of money that is placed in the slot hoppers is accounted for as a deduction from the accountability (the cash balance) of either the vault or the cashier's cage, depending upon the preference of the casino management. From an accounting viewpoint, the journal entry to record initial slot hopper loads at standard fill amounts would be:

DR Cash on Hand—Slot Hoppers	999,999	
CR Cash on Hand—Cashier's Cage		999,999

Slot Hopper Load Problems

There are three main problems associated with the process of slot hopper loads. The first is the concept of slot load creep. In this situation, the amount of the slot hopper loads may increase over time. This increase may be the result of several factors: poor record-keeping, so that the amount of the original load is unknown; deliberate underfilling of the hoppers when the casino is opened (this is quite likely, since most of the casinos are cash poor when opening); and as an unintentional result of machines getting out of adjustment and overfilling the slot hoppers.

The problem of slot hopper load creep arises from the fact that, if the original load is lower than the amount shown in the hopper at the end of the fiscal period, the sum of the revenue that was truly earned during the time period does not wind up in the drop buckets and most likely is not reported as income. The amount of slot creep can be significant, and slot loads do tend to increase over time.

Accuracy of the revenue reporting process can be achieved by having the amounts of the slot loads checked periodically by physical inspection and counting of the amount of money in the slot hopper. If the amounts of money in the hoppers have increased significantly above the standard amounts or the original slot loads that were recorded, an appropriate adjustment should be made to the revenue ledger. Another alternative would be physically to reduce the amount of the hopper load back down to the original amount and to indicate the difference as additional revenue.

The second issue is determining the correct amount of the hopper load. If the slot load is substantial in terms of dollars, then the casino has a higher level of exposure to slot cheats; if the machine is dumped improperly, the amount of the loss could be significant. The opposite side of the issue is that most machines can pay the majority of the day-to-day jackpots automatically. Thus, in

an effort to keep the hand-paid jackpots at a minimum and to minimize the labor costs, the machines may be loaded up with coins
in order to pay virtually all jackpots automatically.

Finally, the customary slot loads for each denomination of
machine are indicated in table 5-1. The amounts indicated are the
standard hopper loads, compared with the amounts actually in use
in a casino and the amounts uncovered as a result of sampling the
loads in slot machines at year end, which indicates a moderate
amount of hopper creep.

Detailed Slot Revenue Procedures

The slot revenue procedures are concerned with four distinct
phases. These are:

1. Slot Drop—the physical removal of the coins from the machines.

2. Slot Wrap and Count—the count of coins in exact amounts
and the preparation of the coins for reuse in the casino by wrap-
ping in standard denominations.

3. Revenue Accounting—the recognition of win and the entering of amounts into the revenue ledgers of the casino.

4. Recirculating the Coin—the transfer to the vault and cashier's cage for subsequent reuse.

Slot Drop

The first element of the slot drop is the scheduling of the
times and personnel involved in the drop procedure. First, the
days of the week on which the drop will be performed must be
determined. There are several considerations. Depending upon
the size of the operation and the volume of activity, the drop may
have to be done on a daily basis. However, most casinos use a
schedule of two or three times a week. The twice-a-week schedule
is keyed on what times are most suitable to have the machines
empty and the coin counted and wrapped so that it will be ready
for operation again during the busiest time of the week. For this
reason, casinos usually schedule the drop on Monday or Tuesday,
coupled with another drop immediately before the weekend, usually early on Friday morning.

A second fact is the time of day of the slot drop. For most
casinos, the slot departments are quiet during the early morning
hours, and the slot drop is scheduled at this time for several reasons. First, the security problems are lessened if fewer people are

around, and the inconvenience to the customers is minimized if the drop is done during the early morning from 2 A.M. until 6 A.M. There is a firm requirement that the time selected for the drop of the slot machines be reported to the Gaming Control Board. Also, once the time of the slot drop is set, it cannot be changed without notifying the Control Board. The slot drop must thereafter be performed during the time specified by the casino to the Control Board. (In some instances, casinos have run short of coin during the weekend and have had to schedule a special slot drop to clean out their machines with the permission of the Gaming Control Board.)[10]

Slot Drop Team   The slot drop team, as previously mentioned, usually consists of three members, two of whom remove the drop buckets and empty them into another bucket or into numbered bags. (In some casinos, a duplicate set of buckets is available in order to speed the removal by merely inserting the new empty bucket into the drop stand.) The third person acts as a security guard and may or may not perform some of the meter reading functions.

The membership of the count team is very restricted by regulation. The general rule is that no owners of the casino can participate in the drop procedures, and the members of the count team must be independent of the slot management. In most instances, the work of emptying a large number of slot machines (anywhere from 150 to 1,500) can be a strenuous, back-breaking job that very few owners would be interested in participating in anyway. Persons with exceptional physical stamina are usually recruited for this job and are supervised by the cashier or vault personnel.

Slot Drop Procedures   The slot drop must be accomplished according to the operational and control guidelines provided by the regulatory authorities. Since the drop is one of the key areas of control, and since there are usually carefully written guidelines for the conduct of the drop, drop procedures tend to be highly standardized from casino to casino.

The slot drop occurs in the following sequence.

1. The supervisor of the count team gets the key to the coin room from the responsible person. The key is usually kept in the

main cashier's cage. This person signs a key control ledger indicating the time the key goes out.

2. The count team gets all necessary materials, including a set of drop buckets or a set of numbered bags. These bags help to keep the drop from each machine separate to meet the regulatory reporting requirements.

3. The keys to the slot machines and the slot stands are signed out.

4. Each machine is individually opened. The contents of the drop bucket are kept separate. This rule is important because it is the only way that management can subsequently determine how much each machine has made or lost.

These segregation procedures vary widely. One system is to empty the buckets into a series of coin sacks, each with an identifying number, or else into unmarked bags, with some form of identification such as a disk or tag indicating the machine number added to each bag. Other count systems utilize duplicate sets of buckets, with each bucket numbered for the machine. The full bucket is removed and the corresponding empty bucket replaced in the slot drop stand.

Another procedure is to take the money out of the drop bucket and count it immediately, usually by use of a sensitive scale or portable counter located on a cart that is pushed through the slot area. Once this count has been done for the machine, the drop is recorded, and all the coins of a certain denomination are then merely dumped into a large bucket on the coin cart. The key accounting and control requirement at this stage is that the drop associated with each machine must be separately identified.

5. Before moving to the next machine, another member of the slot team opens the slot machine itself and records the meter readings on a special reading sheet. This sheet must be completed in ink. The meter readings for both coins in and coins out are recorded if available. Meter readings from progressive slot machines are done on a daily basis.

6. When the cart is full, or all the machines have been emptied, or dropped, the count team moves the slot cart to the slot count area where the next phase of the process, the slot wrap and count, takes place.

The essential control elements in this process can be briefly summarized as follows. First, the keys to open the stands where the drop buckets are located are subject to a high degree of control.

Second, the drop bucket contents of each machine are carefully segregated by machine number and denomination for subsequent managerial and revenue reporting. Third, the use of the count team, with no members of a slot managerial position, creates a control through the segregation of duties. Fourth, the recording of the slot meter readings provides a backup measure against which the actual coin drop results can be evaluated.

Slot Wrap and Count Procedures

The problems of the slot count procedures could be characterized as having to count the kernels of corn in a grain elevator. There is an avalanche of coins to be counted because of the periodic drop procedure. In an attempt to simplify the measurement process, the initial count of coins is usually established by weight. This initial count is used by management as a preliminary indication of the operating results and is followed by a more accurate wrap and count figure.

The use of only a weigh mechanism to account for the slot drop is a simplification of the count procedure, but, as a result of the 1979 weigh fraud in Las Vegas, there has been greater concern over the accuracy and controllability of the weigh machines.[11]

Some of the Nevada casinos have what could be categorized as very unusual layouts for their hard count rooms. A typical slot count room layout is indicated in figure 5-6, showing the very large amount of coin to be determined by weight. The coins are then transferred by automatic conveyor to a bank of wrap and count machines. The coins are counted and then physically transferred to the slot coin vault area. It is interesting to note that the slot vault area is under the administrative control of the controller's office.

Detailed Count Procedures After the slot drop has been accomplished, the first step in the count is the recording of the individual slot drop by machine and by each machine's denomination. The results of the individual machine counts are then consolidated into a count of all coins of a single denomination. Thus, for example, all $0.05 coins are counted together. The results of the individual machine counts and the summary within denominations are then recorded. The results of the count are usually recorded on the slot drop record sheet. A sample of the form is shown in figure 5-7. The same machines that count the coins by denomination also wrap the coins automatically. The wrapped coin is then put into

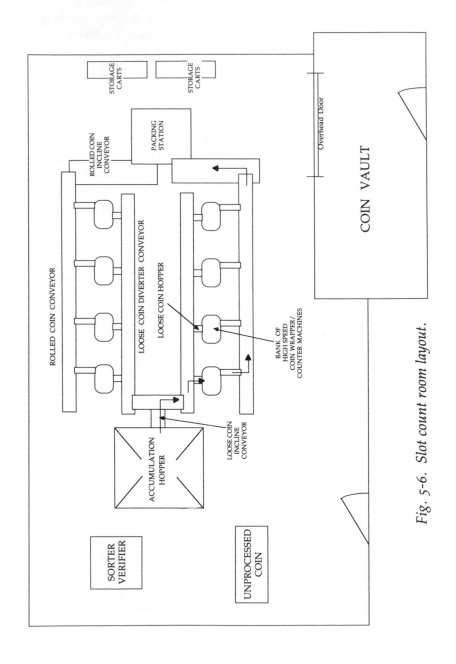

Fig. 5-6. *Slot count room layout.*

SLOT DROP COUNT

Date _____

Count Team _____

MACHINE NO.	IN	OUT	DROP	COUNT	EXTENDED

Fig. 5-7. Slot drop count.

metal boxes (referred to as cans) in standard denominations. (For example, a can of nickels holds fifty rolls of nickels, each worth $2, for a total value of $100.) These cans are then stacked in the counting area; when the count for all the coins has been completed, the coins are physically transferred to the vault with the accompanying paperwork.

There are important reconciliations made between the initial weigh count, if used, the summary of the count by machines, the denomination count, and the total count. These amounts must agree throughout the process to assure good accounting control over the slot drop. At the completion of the count and the reconciliation process, and after any differences have been identified, the members of the count team all sign the documents attesting to the amount of money, and the physical transfer to the vault takes place. At this time the vault cashier signs a transfer sheet, witnessing the transfer of the drop to the vault.

Computation of Slot Win

The counting of the slot drop is physically the most difficult part of the process of determining the slot win, but it is only one part of the total process. All the other elements of the slot win must now be brought together.

The other elements of the slot win are the jackpot paidout documents and the slot fills and slot short pay documents. Again, various casinos have different procedures, but the essential elements are common to all. This process of combining slot win components can be accomplished in several ways.

1. The first alternative is for the slot manager to take coin from the slot drop and actually "buy back" the fills and paidout jackpots from the cashier's cage.

2. The second method is a more indirect exchange in which the paidouts and the fills are transferred from the cashier's cage to the vault, and the cashier's cage is replenished with coin. The vault cashier then assumes the responsibility for combining the paidout documents with the drop calculations in order to determine the overall win.

3. The process of actually calculating the win is usually done with a computer report, with the vault cashier only completing the input forms for the data processing department.

4. Finally, the documents could be sent to the accounting de-

partment, where all the computations for the slot win are performed.

Accounting Department Role

Usually all of the components of the slot win—including all reports and paperwork from the vault—are sent to the accounting department. In order to complete the necessary statistical reporting required by the regulatory authorities, the accounting department combines the following information into the computerized slot accounting system:

1. Slot machine meter readings for each machine.
2. Slot drop figures for each machine.
3. Slot paidout, including fills, short pays, and jackpots for each machine.

This information either is entered directly into the computer via a terminal or is entered on summary sheets, from which the information is later transcribed into machine-readable formats.

At this time, the slot drop figures are also verified from the count recap sheets, and the jackpots are verified from the jackpot paidout summary sheet kept in the cashier's cage to check the paidouts that occurred during the shift.

The format and the use of the various forms of the slot reporting system are discussed in detail later in the chapter. After the computer run has been processed, it is distributed to the members of the slot department and general manager, and copies are retained in the accounting department.

The slot win figures, after the slot reporting system computer run has been completed, are then transferred to the revenue system via the summary general ledger postings.

Slot Operational Transactions

The operational transactions in the slot department that require documentation for accounting purposes, as well as understanding from a flow standpoint, revolve around transactions in the change booth and by the various change persons.

The basic control element in the slot area is the maintenance of an imprest balance for virtually all change funds. Thus, the change booth, although it may contain as much as $25,000 to $50,000, is exactly like a large petty cash fund. At any time, the total of all cash, coin, and paid outs should equal the imprest balance. At the end of the shift, or whenever the amount of money available is insufficient to meet the operating needs of the casino, the paidouts are cleared and the coin levels restored.

The process of clearing the paidouts takes place between the slot booth and the cashier's cage of the vault, depending upon the flow utilized in that particular casino. The process is uniquely simple: buying back all the paidouts in the slot booth. There may be some formal recap or summary sheet prepared to attach to the various paidout forms. The exchange process is usually verified by having both the slot cashier and the vault cashier sign for the accuracy of the coin exchange. These exchange documents are then audited by the internal audit staff or by the accounting department at some later date.

Finally, each of the slot booths has end-of-shift checkout procedures and a summary coin count form that must be completed. The purpose of this form is to record the ending balance and composition of the cash and coin in the slot booth and to serve as a transfer document to the oncoming slot booth attendant.

The operational transactions between the change persons and the slot booth are the exact parallel of the operational transactions between the slot booth and the cashier. In the case of the slot personnel, when the coin levels get too low, the change person can buy coin from the slot booth to replenish the stock. This purchase can be accomplished by some combination of paidout vouchers such as jackpots and cash.

There are different organizational philosophies as to the responsibilities of the change persons for jackpots. In some casinos, the slot change persons have authority to pay only certain jackpots, and all those over a certain amount must be paid from the slot booth or the cashier's cage. In other casinos, all jackpots must be paid from the cashier's cage.

End-of-shift procedures of the slot change persons usually are not documented in writing, but are merely the process of mutually counting the money in the storage drawer and the change apron and handing it over to the oncoming person.

Audit Problems of Slot Transactions

The basic audit and control problems of the slot operational transactions revolve around the validating of various paidout items, including the slot fills, the jackpots, the short pay documents, and the various kinds of coupons that are typically redeemed at the slot area.

Paidout Procedures—Generally The slot paidout procedures are of three types: promotional items such as free nickels; jackpots paid to players; and fills of machines that require the hopper to be replenished, or short pays where the contents of the hopper were insufficient to pay the required jackpot.

Items 2 and 3 are treated as offsets to the slot win, while item 1 is a promotion item and is not usually accounted for as an offset to slot win, but is considered a promotional expense. This separate treatment means that the later accounting for these types of promotion items must be separated from the other paidout items.

Jackpot Paidouts Whenever a player wins a jackpot that is not automatically paid directly by the machine, the following procedures come into play. The first consideration should be for the security and propriety of the jackpot—is it legitimate?

The legitimacy of the jackpot can be assured by answering the following questions. First, is the machine in order? Has the machine been cheated or altered in any way to produce the jackpot, or has the machine been manipulated in some improper manner?

The second consideration is whether the amount of the jackpot is correct for the reel setting that appears. This question must be answered because there are many opportunities for errors in paying jackpots caused not just by cheating, but by inattention of the jackpot personnel to the correct amount to be paid.

Third, what approvals are necessary in order to pay this jackpot? Depending upon the size of the jackpot, various casinos have different levels of necessary approval. Table 5-6 indicates the typical approval schedule for jackpot payouts in a Nevada casino.

Finally, a jackpot must have some documentation. This documentation must take at least three separate forms. The first is the

Table 5-6. Slot Jackpot Approval Schedule.

Jackpot Amount	*Responsibility*
All Hand Pay	Slot Manager
	Change Employee
	Security
Over $500	Games Shift Manager

accounting forms that serve as input to the revenue determination process, the second is the verification of the propriety of the jackpot, and the third is external documentation such as IRS reporting.

Correctness of the Jackpot   The issue of the correctness of the jackpot can be solved very easily by consulting the displayed slot payout schedule. Nevada law provides that the machines must prominently display the payouts appropriate to the various winning reel symbol combinations. The jackpot payoff person has to be very careful to pay only the correct amount. Overpaying jackpots can be a major source of revenue loss for a casino and can occur either through carelessness or through a deliberate attempt to cheat the casino. Overpaying could also be an attempt by the change person to curry favor with the customer, in the hopes of gaining a gratuity.

Documentation of the Payout   The documentation of the payout is accomplished by filling out a jackpot payout ticket, a multipart form, which includes a variety of identification information. Typically, the information includes:

1. Machine number and location.
2. Denomination of the machine.
3. The winning combination of reel symbols that constituted the jackpot.
4. The time and date of the jackpot.
5. The amount of the jackpot.
6. The signature of the jackpot payoff person and at least one supervisor. If the amount of the jackpot is large, additional information and the signatures of supervisory personnel may be required.

In addition to preparing a jackpot payout form for each jackpot, the cashier or the slot booth personnel usually prepare a summary form listing all jackpots paid during a shift. This serves as an ongoing control to prevent successive cheating of one machine or group of machines since a pattern of large jackpot payoffs would be indicated.

Another control feature that could be used to document the payout of a jackpot is taking a Polaroid or other instant picture of the face of the machine. This would verify that the payout was made for the actual winning combination, not merely the jackpot payoff person paying a confederate.

Finally, documentation of large payouts requires customer

identification, both for casino control purposes and for required IRS reporting. In addition, if the jackpot is very substantial, some casinos impound the machine and have either a slot mechanic or the Gaming Control Board personnel inspect the machine for any evidence of faulty operation or tampering. The maintenance report of the slot mechanic might also be filed with the jackpot payout ticket.

Withholding Rules and IRS Reporting

There are specific rules regarding the withholding and reporting of slot machine jackpot winnings to the IRS.

First, the IRS requires the withholding of monies from the jackpots that are paid to nonresident aliens. In Nevada, the most common occurrence is the winning of large jackpots by Canadian or Mexican nationals. The rate for Mexicans is 30% of the jackpot, and for Canadians 15%. This amount must be withheld from the jackpot payout and remitted to the IRS by the casino accounting department.

Second, large jackpots must be reported to the IRS for winners who are U.S. citizens or resident aliens. This is informational reporting only and does not require any withholding. In this case, the federal form W-2G is completed, with one copy given to the winner, one copy retained by the casino, and one copy filed with the IRS.

In both cases, the withholding and the reporting come into play if the slot jackpot exceeds $1,200. When this occurs, two forms of positive identification must be supplied by the winner. Also, for U.S. citizens and resident aliens, the individual's social security number must be provided since this is the basis for reporting the income.

Special Accounting for Large Jackpots

From time to time, a very large jackpot may be won. Under these circumstances, the payoff must be made in the proper manner to assure that the jackpot is properly recorded as an offset to the slot machine revenue. However, the slot payoff may exceed the amount of money available in the cage. The mechanism for this large payoff is temporarily to increase the amount of money on deposit with the slot cage or vault. This is usually accomplished by a check being issued from the accounting office and temporarily used to increase the vault accountability and, in turn, the cashier's cage. Once the slot payoff is made, the jackpot payout is then cleared back through the cashier to the vault, and the respective balances are reduced to their former levels.

Other Paidouts

There are two other types of paidouts that occur in the course of slot machine operation: short pays and hopper fills. These paidouts are exceptional items and must both be carefully controlled to prevent abuses and cheating and to assure proper accounting for the payout.

Short pays occur when the hopper of the machine is empty and the total amount of the jackpot indicated is not automatically paid by the machine. A short pay may be for the entire amount of the jackpot or for some portion of the total jackpot. Slot machines usually have a pay meter to help in controlling the short pays by indicating if the correct number of coins was really paid by the machine.

Hopper fills are circumstances where the hopper of the slot machine is empty and requires additional coins to be put into it. In most circumstances, barring some technical malfunction, whenever there is a short pay with an insufficient jackpot, the hopper is empty and should require refilling. Therefore, it is a general but not absolute rule that whenever there is a short pay, there should be an accompanying hopper fill.

Because of the severe control problems, and the strong possibility of outside cheating, the short pay procedures should be subject to special control. For example, if a jackpot is properly paid by a machine, but the customer scoops some money from the tray and puts it in his pocket and then claims that the machine has malfunctioned, it is very difficult for the casino to refuse to make the additional payment unless the act was observed by casino personnel. Typical short pay procedures should include verification that the slot hopper is indeed empty, by having a slot mechanic or floor person examine the slot machine. One additional control technique would be for the short pay document to contain some information about the customer involved. In case of repetitions of that situation with the same customer, the likelihood of cheating could be explored.

The documentation for a short pay or a hopper fill should be generated from the casino cage; while the money required for a short pay could come from the change booth, it is best that hopper fills originate from the cage only, and that the amounts be transmitted to the empty machine by a security guard and a slot floor supervisor. Once the fill has been completed, the documentation becomes part of the cage accountability until the end of the shift or the day and is then cleared back to the vault for inclusion in the hard count results.

From time to time, miscellaneous paidouts for customer slot machine refunds may be made directly to customers. If these refunds are small in amount, they can be executed without approval directly by the slot booth or change person. However, some form of documentation should be generated; if the amounts become too large, then some form of control over the change persons could be implemented. Some casinos have a no refund policy, but in other casinos, the refunds are occasional and form part of the over and short calculations for change persons.

Slot Participation

Slot participation is a situation where the slot machines in a particular location are not operated solely by the owner of the location but are owned and operated by another individual or group. This is equivalent to having a leased department operating within a department store.

The slot participation most commonly occurs in a small, desirable location, which may not actually be a casino, but where the landlord has neither the marketing expertise nor the management ability to manage slot machine operation. Typically, a small bar owner might have three to six slot machines that are operated by a slot route operator, much like any other coin-operated vending route.

In casinos, leased or participation slots are not unusual. In some circumstances, certain types of machines may be of significant cost or unusual nature so that the casino owner may not wish to tie up capital in the machine or may wish to have a way to try the machine before committing to a purchase. In these circumstances, the casino may have several types of participation slots.

From a legal standpoint, a participation agreement is different from the mere leasing of machines from an equipment leasing company. Lease payments or installment purchases of machines may also use revenue divisions (similar to a participation agreement) to guarantee the repayment of the capital costs of the slot machines. In participation, both parties share in all aspects of the slot operation. Thus, the accounting procedures must reflect this joint operation.

Participation Agreements

The underlying agreement between the landlord and the slot operator is the controlling document, which in turn helps to clarify the accounting responsibilities for the operation of the participation slots. Typically, the participation agreement spells out the essential terms of the joint operation. The key ingredient is the split that should be made of the total profits generated by the slot operation. The usual split in most Nevada casinos is 50/50, with the casino receiving half the income and the slot operator receiving the other half. However, splits of 45/55 are not unusual, and some situations have resulted in the location receiving as much as 65%, while the operator receives the balance of 35%.

In addition to determining the split of profits, the agreement should spell out the responsibilities for payment of various costs incurred in the operation. These costs include the labor to supervise the slot machines, the responsibility for maintenance and repair, and, most importantly, the responsibility for payment of gaming taxes and licenses. Finally, the agreement usually calls for the adoption of a set of uniform operating procedures that are required to account for the win and the losses of the slot machines.

Participation Accounting

The basic procedures surrounding the accounting for participation slots are centered around two things. The first is the procedure used when a shared machine is dropped and the drop subsequently counted, and the second is how the various payouts are documented and collected.

The drop of the participation machines is usually performed jointly by a representative of the operator and a representative of the casino. This drop is usually done at some time other than the time when the drop of the casino's own machines is accomplished. Again, this time must be set, adhered to, and properly reported to the Gaming Control Board.

Once the drop has been accomplished for each machine using identification procedures similar to those used for house machines, the drop is wrapped, accounted, and summarized. Next the various hopper fills, short pays, and jackpot payouts are collected, and the net win is determined. Then, based on this win figure, the various shares are allocated. The usual procedure is that the entire amount of the coin is sold from the participation drop to the vault, in exchange for cash, and the split is paid to the operator in cash at that time. Most participation agreements call for the cash determination to be regarded as preliminary and subject to final accounting correction.

The various payout documents used in the participation slots require the use of forms separate from the house documents. This creates the situation where there may be two entirely separate sets of slot accounting documents present in the casino, which calls for a great deal of care. First, the documents must all be carefully controlled and safeguarded against loss or improper use. Second, care must be taken to assure that the correct documents are used for each machine. In the case of a jackpot, the machine must be identified as being a participation machine or a house machine using the correct jackpot payout document. Third, and finally, there must be a careful computation of the win amount; any errors are liable to result in the real loss of funds since there is an independent third party taking money out of the casino.

Progressive Slot Machines

Progressive slot machines are slot machines that have several distinctive features. These machines typically have a set of one or two meters located in a prominent display above the slot machine itself. The meters are set so that, for every third or fifth coin inserted, the figure indicated on the meter increases by some fixed amount, usually the denomination of the coin used in the machine. Progressive slot machines thus have meters that show increasingly higher amounts until one major jackpot is won.

The progressive slot machine accounting procedures are particularly important since these machines usually have money amounts that are many times the maximum jackpot available in other slot machines of the same denomination.

Progressive Slot Accounting Controls

To assure the accuracy of the meter readings, gaming control regulations and casino procedures call for daily readings of the meters on all progressive machines. These daily readings serve to verify that the amounts are constantly increasing, unless won, and have not been improperly adjusted downward by the casino. In fact, Nevada Gaming Control Board Regulation 5.110 prohibits reduction of the amount of money indicated on meters in a progressive slot machine.

The win of the progressive slot machine is determined in exactly the same manner as the win of other slot machines. The drop procedures are identical to other machines, and the wrap and count and reporting of the win are all the same. The increase in the liability for payout of the substantial progressive jackpot at some future date, although not representing a strict liability of the present period, is usually accrued by the casino with the amount of liability recorded as an offset to the win reported on these slot machines. The issues involved in the propriety and recording of this liability, and the offsetting reduction of income, are indicated in chapter 11, which deals with income taxation issues of progressive slot machine operation.

Remote and Linked Slot Machines

In 1986, a special high-payoff type of slot machine was introduced in Nevada. The slot program was called "Megabucks" and was intended to compete against the multimillion-dollar jackpots of state lotteries. This program was unique in that it combined the characteristics of a participation slot machine and a progressive slot machine, as well as linking as many as 125 machines at separate locations into one central progressive meter and central point. Another unusual feature of this program is that the slot machine supplier assumed the entire responsibility for payment of the jackpots. Jackpots are usually split between the location and supplier in the same ratio as net revenue in most participation agreements.

Due to the multilocation nature of the slot machines and their electronic linkage, this slot system has intensified security as well as adding some unique telecommunication and electronic security features.[12]

Slot Maintenance

The key concept of slot maintenance is the decision to balance the cost of maintenance of the slot machines against the potential or actual loss of income that may occur from improper operation of the slot machine resulting from lack of maintenance. This section discusses some of the issues relating to slot maintenance and the cost of these maintenance procedures.

Maintenance Access

The first issue of slot maintenance is who has access to the inside of the slot machine and consequently to the contents of the hopper and payoff mechanism, which may be set up for improper payoffs. Access to slot machines is not severely limited in most casinos. For each shift, there are a number of slot floor mechanics who have keys that allow them access to all machines in the casino. A few casinos have established separate access procedures where a security guard or senior supervisor must be present when opening sensitive machines because of their location, the amount of money contained in them, or their jackpot size.

In cases where a machine is removed from the floor for repairs, there are procedures for the removal of the contents of the slot hopper before the machine is sent to the repair shop. The contents are usually bagged, identified, and deposited with the cage cashier for safekeeping until the machine is returned to the floor, at which time the hopper contents are taken from the cashier and redeposited in the slot machine.

Access Controls

The second aspect of concern to a slot operator is preventing improper access that could lead to alteration of the machine or theft of the contents of the hopper. The procedures used by most casinos include exclusive custody of keys by only a few persons for each shift, thus limiting the number of persons who have access to the machines. This limiting must be balanced against the need for service of the machines for legitimate malfunctions and the need for many keys in the casino during busy periods. A related issue—the possession and control over slot keys—is crucial, since it is a major physical task to change the locks on a slot machine. If a key is improperly duplicated or lost, many casinos may actually not change the locks, but elect to take their chances with the stray key by maintaining a close watch on the slot machines because of the excessive cost of rekeying all of the machines.

Another control over access is a procedure whereby every time that a machine is opened, for whatever reason, the time, date, reason for opening, and signature of the person opening the machine must be written on a card located inside the machine. This control works well, because if a machine is being opened excessively, or is suspected of being raided, observation coupled with verification of the signature may tell who the culprit is. If a machine is opened without the notation being executed, the person responsible could be warned not to do it again; if found subsequently committing the same offense (which is likely to occur if a theft is being perpetrated), the person could be fired. New advances in electronic card key control systems could also help to alleviate these problems by allowing access codes to be changed easily if the existing keys were compromised through unauthorized duplication or loss.

More sophisticated automatic slot control systems that use microprocessors in each machine connected to a central control computer allow the opening of a machine to be automatically recorded and would trigger a signal to the security staff, who could verify that the machine was being opened for legitimate purposes.

Maintenance Records

The heart of any good slot maintenance system is the necessity of having proper signaling systems to identify which machines are likely to be in the greatest need of repair and to spot those machines that are in trouble. A second component of this is a good record-keeping system to keep track of maintenance that has been done on the machines, together with the ability to generate a schedule of preventive maintenance.

One element of a slot win reporting system is a component that allows the reporting of heavy losers and heavy winners in machines. If the machine performance is badly out of line with the expected norm, then an exception or maintenance report could be generated. This applies both to those machines that are too loose, and lose too much, and to those machines that are too tight, and win too much, resulting in improper play for the customer. Maintenance records are necessary in order to tell if a machine is truly in need of repair or may just have appeared on the loser's report as a result of a statistical anomaly.

A final comment is in order with regard to the slot repair area where off-the-floor maintenance is performed. Access to this area should also be restricted, so that no one can tamper with a machine prior to its being placed on the floor. Also, internal maintenance procedures should be in place to assure that all machines are tested prior to being returned to the floor to ensure that they are performing correctly.

Slot Management Systems

There are many systems currently available that process information in a variety of ways to assist the process of managing a slot operation. These systems are broken into two types and offer a basic set of management reports with various detailed systems providing a variety of optional reports.[13]

The key distinction between the types of systems lies in the degree of interaction between the slot machines themselves and the automated reporting procedures. The simplest type of system is one that relies solely on data inputted from the machines themselves in a manual mode. In this type of system, the reading of the meters is combined with the drop count and other manual accounting data, comparisons are made, and various types of reports are generated. The second type of reporting system uses the direct input from the small microprocessors located inside the slot machines as inputs to the control computer from which the data reports are then generated. Usually this automatic information is compared with manual data input by the accounting processes of drop and count, and comparison reports are prepared.

The manual systems have as their principal benefit cost-effectiveness since they can be implemented without internal modifications of the individual slot machines themselves and, when coupled with the existing program of meter reading that occurs during the drop procedures, can be highly efficient. The electronic systems, on the other hand, are dependent upon having complex electronics resident in each slot machine, which must be linked to the central computer. This can be both a complex and an expensive task.

Slot Management Reports

Some of the typical reports that are generated by a slot management system include:

Accounting Reports:
1. Summary of slot drop/jackpot/fill and win activity by machine, by denomination, and with overall totals.
2. Summary of all slot jackpots and fills by numeric sequence.
3. Summary of all slot meter readings, including both regular and progressive machines.
4. List of year to date and month to date reports of win by denomination and with overall totals.

Performance Reports:

1. Comparisons of actual to theoretical performance.

2. Listing of most significant deviations, both winners and losers.

3. Identification of large transactions, jackpots, fills, or short pays.

4. Lists of unusual transactions, such as where win exceeds drop.

The most desirable component of a slot management system is the ability to generate exception reports, which help to identify problems before they become significant. Where problems already exist, the use of instantaneous electronic reporting is clearly preferable but is considerably more expensive. Once again, the cost of the control must be weighed against the benefit to be derived from the control.

Other Slot Issues

Slot Cheating

Slot cheating is more properly the subject of an entirely separate book. For purposes of the current discussion of accounting systems and controls, control of slot cheating can be accomplished by three distinct actions. The first is the recognition of the need for care, supervision, and control of the slot operation at all levels. The second is the insistence upon adherence to systems of reporting, documentation, and "paperwork" properly reflecting all transactions in the slot area. Third, there should be a recognition of the role that accounting information can play in providing early warning of irregularities in slot machine performance.

From an accounting standpoint, there are several things to keep in mind if slot cheating has taken place in a casino. The first is that the reduction of revenue resulting from the cheating has already been reflected in the records for the period. Thus, no further write-down of revenue or recognition of expense or loss is necessary. The process of cheating is self-correcting insofar as accounting record-keeping is concerned. Second, accounting can be of some assistance in documenting the amount of likely loss by presenting statistical comparisons of performance from regular periods of operation to the loss periods. Thus, timely reporting of slot machine performance can be an effective control against large slot losses.

Token Machines and Free Play

Several casinos have special token slot machines that offer free play for specific prizes but usually not for direct cash payoffs. The accounting for these special promotion or token machines is handled in the following manner. First, the tokens are usually given away, and the number in open circulation should be controlled. Customers should be encouraged to play the tokens and not to carry them around. Second, the prizes offered as a result of winning on the token machines should not be recorded as offsets to gaming wins from other machines, but should be recorded as promotional expenses and not as jackpots. The recording as a jackpot would improperly reduce the overall gross win on the slot machines and would result in the underreporting of taxable income for state gross revenue purposes.

Minimum Payoffs

The New Jersey Gaming Control Act specifies that there must be a minimum level of payoff of 85% for all the machines in the casino. Recent administrative actions have sustained this rule as applying to all machines individually in the casino and not merely to the overall slot payoff. Thus, care must be taken to assure that, in both design and maintenance and operation, the payout does not drop below these minimum points.

CHAPTER 6

Games Accounting

Introduction

This chapter deals with accounting for the principal table games utilized in a casino, which generally include 21, craps, roulette, baccarat, and big 6. All of these are considered to be banking games—that is, the house or casino participates for profit. In addition, there are several other casino side games that are introduced from time to time. In recent years, games such as sic-bo, pai-gow, and fan tan have appeared as novelties with distinctive appeal to certain segments of the gaming customers. The long-term prospects for continuation or widespread adoption of these games are very slim.

It is interesting to note that some games, such as faro, that were very popular in earlier days of Nevada gaming have all but disappeared from casinos. This gives rise to the feeling that the number of games customarily utilized in a casino is very limited. In Nevada, it is apparently popularity with customers and competitive pressures that determine whether a specific game is retained or eliminated. In New Jersey, the state regulations have specified the types of games allowed, and new game approvals can only come through administrative and regulatory action.

There are hundreds of new games being invented each year;[1] however, of that large number, very few are even considered and even fewer win the approval of the gaming regulatory authorities. Recent statements by members of the Nevada regulatory agencies have indicated that they are unhappy about having to consider and evaluate a large number of so-called carnival games each year. These authorities have said that they are not going to look very favorably on applications for new games unless they have demonstrated some substantial merit. While this attitude may be a simple way of conserving the scarce resources of the regulatory agencies in evaluating these new games, the restraint on the inventiveness of various game designers and manufacturers, as well as the apparent restraint on the dynamics of the free market, may contribute to a lack of innovation or resistance to change on the part of the industry.

Importance of Various Games

The financial importance of the various casino games can be measured in a number of ways. The first is the contribution of the different games to the total gaming revenue of the various areas. The profile presented in table 6-1 was derived from the *Nevada Gaming Abstract*. From that table, it is apparent that the predominant games in Nevada are 21 and craps. Together, these two games account for approximately 80% of the total table revenue for each of the major areas of the state. Roulette is fairly stable at 2.3% to 6.0% of the revenue, but the other games can vary widely, as in the case of baccarat on the Las Vegas Strip. Another observation is that 21 is much more popular in the northern Nevada area, while craps seems to be more popular in the southern part of the state.

A second measure of the importance of the different games can be determined by an analysis of the win per unit that each type of table game produces. Table 6-2 indicates the average win per unit for the year. From an analysis of this table, certain important facts appear. First, the amount won by a single crap table is dramatically larger in southern Nevada than in other areas of the state. The win is almost double the win per unit in South Lake Tahoe, and almost three times the win in Reno. The win per unit on 21, although somewhat larger in the southern part of the state, does not show as much variation between the north and the south.

Market Differentiation by Game Mix

Each of the various markets within Nevada has distinctly different characteristics, not only with respect to the win per unit of the games, but also in the number of games of each type, as well as the ratio of table games to slot machines. These differences can serve to identify the different markets in Nevada.

Table 6-3 indicates several crucial ratios. The first is the mix of 21 games to crap games. The second is the mix of slot machines to 21 games, the so-called slot to game ratio. Based on the number of games and the number of slot machines, the results indicate that there are considerable differences among the four primary markets

Table 6-1. Percentage Contribution to Gaming Revenue of Table Games (1984).

Location	21	Craps	Roulette	Other	Total
L.V. Strip	46.7	26.6	6.0	20.7	100.0
Downtown L.V.	44.9	33.2	2.3	19.6	100.0
Laughlin	54.6	23.7	4.2	17.5	100.0
Reno-Sparks	56.6	18.0	4.1	21.3	100.0
Douglas Cty	55.3	16.9	3.9	23.9	100.0
Elko	66.0	17.7	2.9	13.4	100.0

Slots and Table Games (1984).

Location	Total Slots	Total Games	Total
L.V. Strip	45.2	54.8	100.0
Downtown L.V.	61.5	38.5	100.0
Laughlin	76.4	23.6	100.0
Reno-Sparks	64.4	35.6	100.0
Douglas Cty	51.8	48.2	100.0
Elko	65.0	35.0	100.0

Source: *Gaming Abstract*, 1984.
For casinos $1 M and over in revenue.

Table 6-2. Average Win per Unit (1984).

Location	Craps	21	$1.00 Slot	$0.05 Slot
L.V. Strip	1,348,050	334,546	48,004	9,828
Downtown L.V.	816,001	182,062	38,541	8,839
Laughlin	597,169	140,627	58,062	12,867
Reno-Sparks	527,404	173,894	39,614	7,475
Douglas Cty	780,777	214,534	40,170	8,795
Elko	275,632	106,451	32,621	7,186

Source: *Gaming Abstract*, 1984.
For casinos $1 M and over in revenue.
Averages are reported, since in some areas median win per unit figures are not available.

Table 6-3. Game Mix and Slot to Game Mix (1984).

Location	GAME MIX RATIO			SLOT TO GAME MIX RATIO		
	21	Crap	Ratios	Slots	21	Ratios
L.V. Strip	974	138	7.1	21,866	974	22.4
Downtown L.V.	399	66	6.0	12,731	399	31.9
Reno-Sparks	650	65	10.0	19,179	650	29.5
Douglas Cty	355	31	11.5	6,840	355	19.3

in Nevada. This game mix is consistent with the marketing image that an area wishes to present and that the casinos' customers are comfortable with. The customers in Las Vegas demand more crap tables and fewer 21 tables, while in northern Nevada the opposite situation exists, with more 21 tables and fewer crap tables.

This concept is also exemplified, in some measure, by the comparison of the ratio of slot machines to 21 games. The ratio is very high in the markets where lower-stakes gamblers are playing, such as Downtown Las Vegas and the Reno-Sparks area. The high roller markets on the Las Vegas Strip, and to a lesser degree in South Lake Tahoe, seem to prefer more table games to slot machines.

This concept is also carried through in the appeal to the customers of the various table games. In southern Nevada, the high rollers tend to prefer more crap tables and fewer 21 tables, while the more modest players of northern Nevada seem to prefer more 21 tables than crap tables.

An argument could be made that the proposed game mixes utilized in the various casinos of New Jersey are of two distinct types: the new clubs to the area and the clubs that had Nevada experience. The Nevada clubs obviously brought the Las Vegas Strip game mix and slot to game mix to their operations. However, when faced with a different customer market, they have been forced to adjust their gaming mix to meet the preferences of their eastern customers. The most significant result has been a reduction in the number of table games and a relative increase in the number of slot machines, coupled with a slow but subtle change in the number of 21 tables and crap tables.

A final observation regarding the various markets has been the trend over time of the ratios indicated in table 6-4. The trend for each of the various markets indicates several things. The Las Vegas Strip seems to be becoming a more pedestrian market, with slot machines being added at a rate exceeding the additions of 21 tables. The South Lake Tahoe market is adding 21 tables at a faster rate and is becoming more like the Las Vegas Strip. Finally, the differences between the South Lake Tahoe area and the Las Vegas Strip and Reno are still significant, with the ratio of slot machines to games being notably higher in northern Nevada and with slot machines being added in the Reno-Sparks area at a faster rate than 21 tables. The former distinctiveness of the Las Vegas Strip as the premium market (with a very low slot to table game ratio) has ap-

Table 6-4. Slot to Game Mix Statewide (1976–1984).

| Year | L.V. STRIP | | | DOUGLAS COUNTY | | | RENO-SPARKS | | |
	Slots	21	Ratios	Slots	21	Ratios	Slots	21	Ratios
1976	11,419	623	18.3	5,031	232	21.7	9,433	413	22.8
1977	13,167	673	19.6	5,402	256	21.1	11,174	456	24.5
1978	14,764	720	20.5	5,939	288	20.6	12,639	515	24.5
1979	16,860	795	21.2	7,374	362	20.4	17,722	708	25.0
1980	19,290	937	20.6	7,666	447	17.1	18,824	691	27.2
1981	18,988	854	22.2	6,983	381	18.3	19,397	700	27.7
1982	20,112	927	21.7	7,033	374	18.8	19,122	710	26.9
1983	23,154	1,046	22.1	6,817	453	15.0	18,627	644	28.9
1984	21,866	974	22.4	6,840	355	19.3	19,179	650	29.5

parently been surpassed by the South Lake Tahoe market. However, the clear distinction of the Reno-Sparks area as the basic low-stakes gaming market has been preserved.

Regulation of Games and Game Approval

In addition to the traditional licensing procedures associated with a new casino or new owners, there is also a significant process involved with the approval and licensing of any new casino game. There are several steps in the process.[2] First, a prototype of the new game must be produced and made available to the Gaming Control Board for evaluation. The second step is an exhaustive evaluation by the Gaming Control Board, including an analysis of the odds structure, the ability of the game to be controlled properly, and, finally, the apparent or indicated profitability or popularity. If the game meets all of these criteria, then it is approved and can be licensed in accordance with the procedures outlined in chapter 2.

Description of the Games

The description of the most popular casino games and the structure and the odds on the various games can be found in many books dealing with the subject. One of the most comprehensive is *Scarne's Complete Guide to Gambling*.[3] This excellent volume serves as a complete reference to the operations of various casino games, and it includes virtually all casino carnival and private games that have achieved any degree of widespread popularity.

There are several physical aspects of the casino games that are of accounting significance: the play areas, the cash handling areas, and the drop boxes.

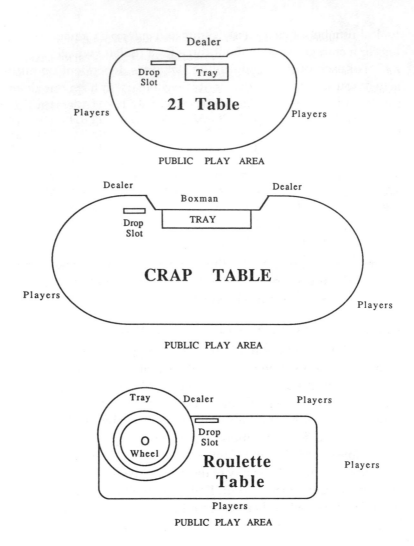

Fig. 6-1. Physical layout of casino games.

Figure 6-1 indicates the layouts and respective play areas and cash handling areas for the 21, craps, and roulette games. Note that a 21 game is set up to accommodate approximately seven players, while craps can handle fifteen players, and the roulette wheel is set up for about seven players. The number of playing positions is important to the games since the total amount of casino revenue is a function of the game odds, the betting limits, the pace of the game, and the number of people betting on the game. The

PART II. ACCOUNTING FOR CASINO OPERATIONS

typical number of customers is four to five for a 21 game, eight to ten for a crap game, and about three for a roulette wheel.

For each of these games, the staffing is dependent upon the activity on the table. However, it is customary to have one dealer for a 21 game, two or three dealers (actually two dealers and one boxman) for a crap game, and one dealer for the roulette wheel.

Cash Handling Areas

The cash handling area for the 21 table and the crap table is known as the *table tray*. The table tray is a series of coin racks that hold chips of various denominations. These racks generally allow more chips to be held than the average table tray inventory. The trays, when at standard, are usually physically about one-half full. The additional space is to accommodate the play transactions. The tray is organized with the high-denomination chips in the center, with the successive outward rows on both sides containing chips or coins of lesser denomination. It is also customary for the dealer to mark every fifth or tenth chip with a marker (usually a $1.00 token). This marking allows the dealer and the pit boss to count the table tray quickly and accurately without counting the individual chips on the rack. Figure 6-2 illustrates a 21 table tray.

The table tray for a crap game is somewhat different in appearance; the tray is not a horizontal storage area, but rather stacks of chips held on the back edge of the table, in a slightly reclining position, as shown in figure 6-3. The chip inventory storage area is considerably larger for a crap game than for a 21 game, but the same procedures with regard to chip denomination and stacking of chips with markers apply.

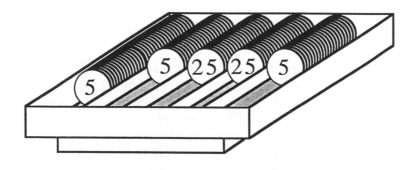

Fig. 6-2. Table tray.

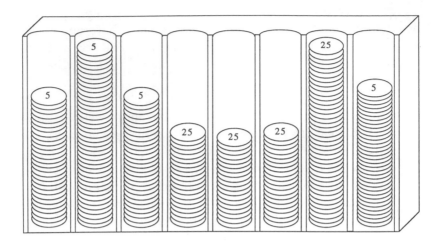

Fig. 6-3. Crap table inventory.

The table inventory for a roulette wheel is located in a separate area. In general, there is not a rack to accommodate the chips, but rather an area on the back edge of the table, usually behind a partition, where all the chips are stacked in denominations. Markers inserted in the stacks are not generally used. One significant factor is that in roulette, because of the widespread practice of allowing bets of smaller amounts, there are often fractional-denomination chips stored on the table. For example there may be $0.10, $0.25, or $0.50 chips on the roulette table to accommodate the play, but on the other table games the only chips are of larger denominations, usually starting at $5.00. Figure 6-4 shows the roulette bank.

Each of the various chip trays or table inventories is equipped with some form of locking cover, so that when the table is not active the chips can be secured on the table without having to remove the tray to the vault for safekeeping. As a practical matter, the locking cover on the table inventory is used only if the game is expected to be closed down for a fairly short time. If the period is expected to be extensive (usually more than one to two days), then the recommended procedure is to remove the table tray completely from the table and return it to the vault for safekeeping.

The dollar amounts contained in the table tray inventory vary

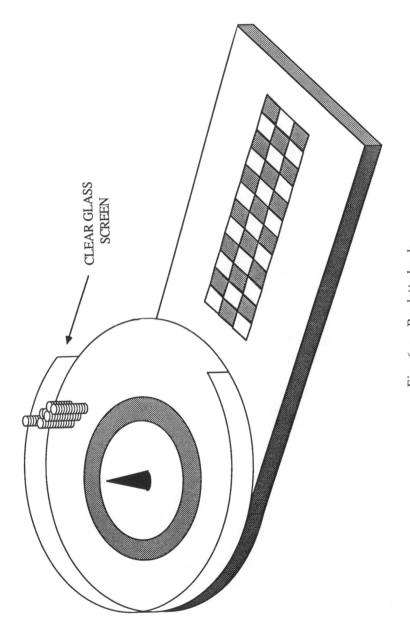

CLEAR GLASS
SCREEN

Fig. 6-4. Roulette bank.

from club to club. However, typical amounts held on the table tray are:

Game	Value of Table Inventory
21	$2,500–$3,000
Craps	$6,000–$9,000
Roulette	$2,500–$3,000

Other casino games such as baccarat have a much larger table tray inventory amount due to the larger average bets placed in the baccarat area. Big 6 and other games usually have a table inventory of an amount similar to a 21 table.

Accounting Procedures for Table Inventories

There are a number of steps that must be taken whenever a table inventory is established in the casino, when a new game is added, or when a game is closed on a permanent basis.

The first step in preparing the table inventories upon the opening of the new casino is to determine the amounts of inventory that should be held on each game. Within the total dollar amount, a determination also must be made of the various denominations of each chip or token to be placed on the table.

The second step is to record in some manner the amount of "table accountability" that should go to each table. This process typically arises from the process of establishing a dollar amount of accountability for the vault or the cashier. At either of these places, the total amount of cash and chips on hand must always be added together in order to arrive at the total amount for which the vault or cashier should be responsible. Once this overall amount has been set, the coin and chips are separated into the various table inventories. These inventories are placed on the table, and the cashier accountability is reduced or offset by the amount of inventories placed on the tables. It is important to recognize that the process of establishing an original table inventory must be regarded as a capital transaction and not a revenue transaction, which would improperly affect the revenue flow of the casino.

When year-end counts of table inventories are performed, the amounts indicated on the table inventories are then added into the cashier or vault amount in order to arrive at the total cash on hand in the casino. A second important reason for the year-end count of the chips and coin on each table is the necessity to identify them by denomination. In this way, when they are compared to the figure that is kept for the total number of chips purchased, the reconciliation of the chips outstanding and the resulting chip liability can be determined.

The accounting entries for the original establishment of the casino working funds, as well as the table inventories, are outlined below.

1. The casino is established with an investment of cash.

DR Cash in Bank	100,000	
CR Owners Equity		100,000

2. The chip stock is purchased; $100,000 worth of chips costs $2,000.

DR Chip Expense	2,000	
CR Cash in Bank		2,000

3. The chip stock is placed into an inventory control, usually in the vault.

DR Chips on Hand—Control Account	100,000	
CR Chip Liability		100,000

4. The vault bank is established with $50,000 cash.

DR Vault Bank—Control Account	50,000	
CR Cash in Bank		50,000

At this point the vault accountability equals $150,000: $50,000 in cash and $100,000 in chips.

5. A casino cage bank is established with $25,000 cash and $50,000 in chips.

DR Casino Cage Bank—Control Account	75,000	
CR Chips on Hand—Control Account		50,000
CR Vault Bank—Control Account		25,000

NOTE: At this point chips are accounted for as if they were cash. Vault accountability is now $75,000 and the new cage accountability is $75,000.

6. The table inventories are now established (assume in round numbers): $24,000 in chips and $1,000 in coin.

DR Table Inventories	25,000	
CR Cage Accountability		25,000

Chip Liability

At any time, a casino may have a liability to redeem gaming tokens held by customers that may have been purchased or won in the casino and not yet been presented for redemption. The total liability of the casino for the unredeemed gaming tokens is the difference between the total amount of chips on hand in the control account and the amount of chips originally purchased.

Depending upon the original method used to record the purchase of the gaming chips, there are various methods of determining the chip liability. Two such methods are shown in this section. If the chip purchase account and the chip liability account were originally used, then these two accounts are usually netted against one another, and the difference is carried on the balance sheet as the chip liability. This method of determining the chip liability is outlined below.

1. Chip liability upon casino opening (see entry #3 above).

DR Chips on Hand	100,000	
CR Chip Liability		100,000

The chip liability would be $0 at this time.

2. After a year of operation, all the chips in the casino are counted. If, for example, the chips on hand totaled only $95,000, the account would be adjusted in the following manner:

DR Miscellaneous revenue	5,000	
CR Chips on hand		5,000

The reduction of chips on hand by a credit to that asset-control account is offset by a reduction of the revenue. (A recognition of an expense could also be used. An adjustment to increase to cash on hand could also be used to balance the credit entry to chips on hand.)

If one of the last two methods is used, then there must be some periodic adjustment of the revenue of the casino. This revenue adjustment takes place whenever the chip liability reaches a certain dollar amount and is achieved by reducing both the income and the chip liability by corresponding amounts. The method above is preferred because it results in the immediate reduction of revenue, since chips outstanding have not really been sold and are not revenue because they may be redeemed.

At this point, a closing entry is prepared to net these two accounts. The chip liability would be $5,000, representing the difference between the debit balance of $95,000 in chips on hand, and the credit balance of $100,000 in chip liability.

DR Chip Liability 95,000
    CR Chips on Hand 95,000

3. Any additional purchases of chips during the year would affect the account listed in #1 above by the amount of additional chip purchases.

Chip Liability—An Alternative Method

Another accounting and recording method to arrive at the chip liability at the end of the year is through the use of the chip purchase account. The entries and the closing entry to create the chip liability are indicated below.

1. When the chips are purchased, the following entry is recorded:

DR Chips on hand 100,000
    CR Chips purchased 100,000

2. When the chips are counted at the end of the year there is only $95,000 on hand, necessitating an adjustment of $5,000. Since the chips have been exchanged for cash and have been reported as income, the revenue account is first adjusted in the following manner:

DR Miscellaneous revenue 5,000
    CR Chips on hand 5,000

This reduces the balance in the chips on hand account to $95,000.

3. At this point, a closing entry is created to close the chips on hand account and the chips purchased account. The residual to balance the closing entry is to establish the chip liability account.

DR Chips purchased 100,000
    CR Chips on hand 95,000
    CR Chip liability 5,000

Under either method of accounting, the amount of the unredeemed chips (or chips not physically present in the casino) would be determined to be $5,000.

The same procedure would be followed to account for the liability associated with the unredeemed $1.00 tokens used in the slot machines. These tokens are accounted for in virtually the same manner as more traditional gaming tokens.

Drop Boxes

The second key accounting control element in the table game area is the drop box. The drop box is attached to each gaming table, and a separate drop box is used for each shift during which the game is operated.

The physical nature of the drop box is shown in figure 6-5. In general, the drop box is a sturdy metal box that is hinged on one side so that it may be completely opened. It also has a slot in the top through which items can be deposited, but which does not allow items to be removed from the box.

The drop box also has two key locks. The first lock secures the drop box to the table. In order to remove the drop box, the key must be used. When the key is inserted into the box to remove it from the table, the slot on top is automatically closed by a panel that slides across the entry slot. The second key is necessary to open the hinged side of the box so that the contents of the drop box may be examined and counted. When the drop box is emptied, the second key is inserted in order to reset the slide that had previously closed the top of the drop box.

Finally, Nevada gaming regulations require that each drop box be clearly identified, that the shift and the table number be painted or attached to the box in a prominent manner, and that the identification be readable from a distance of some ten to fifteen feet.[4]

The drop box normally contains several items. The most prominent contents are cash and currency. In addition, all foreign chips (chips from other casinos) are also deposited in it. During the count procedure, they are considered to be the same as cash. The drop box also contains copies of the fill and credit slips that were processed from the various transactions to increase or reduce the table tray inventory. Where the casino operating procedures use a table inventory document, the drop box contains the appropriate shift inventory opener and closer. Finally, various kinds of casino coupons are routinely collected in drop boxes, although they are not customarily included in the count of the contents.

In general, the drop box should not contain house chips or

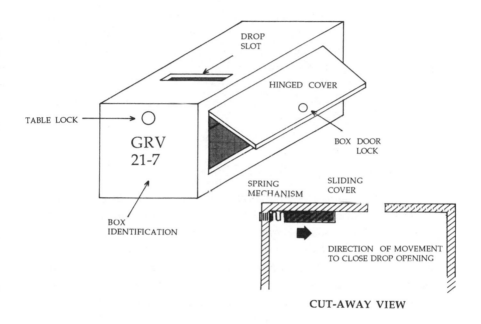

DROP
SLOT

HINGED COVER

TABLE LOCK

GRV
21-7

BOX DOOR
LOCK

SPRING
MECHANISM

SLIDING
COVER

BOX
IDENTIFICATION

DIRECTION OF MOVEMENT
TO CLOSE DROP OPENING

CUT-AWAY VIEW

Fig. 6-5. Table drop box.

tokens and may, again depending on the accounting procedures, contain various types of documents evidencing marker or credit transactions at the table.

The process of opening, inspecting, and counting the contents of the drop box, together with the physical controls over the handling of empty and full boxes, is discussed in the sections on drop and count procedures.

Table Accounting Procedures

The second major section of this chapter is a discussion of the detailed table accounting procedures. Each of the components used in the computation of the profit of the various games is examined in detail. These primary components are the inventories on the table, the fill and credit activity, and the drop and count procedures at the end of the shift. For each of these three principal areas, there is a discussion of how the various operational procedures are executed and how the transactions are accounted for.

Accounting by Shift and Game

The first element in determining the accounting for table games is the recognition that the basic accounting unit for revenue purposes is the individual game. Within the day-to-day flow of the game, the shift is also the smallest time unit for which accounting separation is maintained. For this reason, there are mandatory procedures for the recognition of game revenues on a shift-by-shift basis, with appropriate cutoff and count procedures being performed at the end of each shift.

The shifts of the casino may vary according to the tradition and the management needs of the individual casino. In a Nevada casino, the operation is organized around a 24-hour working day, with graveyard, day, and swing shifts. The 8-hour graveyard shift begins late at night, usually from midnight to 3 A.M. The day shift usually corresponds to a customer day shift of 8 A.M. to 4 or 5 P.M. The swing shift covers the evening hours from 4 P.M. to midnight. These three shift times may be adjusted from casino to casino, but the general pattern is maintained.

A second important consideration for shift-by-shift table accounting practices is the necessity of recognizing shift change procedures that may have an impact on accounting control, as well as operational efficiency. First of all, the end of the shift for the casino dealers may not exactly correspond to the shift end for accounting procedures, which may commence about half an hour before the end of the shift and may continue to other shifts before being considered complete. Second, in a large casino, to avoid mass confusion, the shift change time may be staggered from area to area in the casino over one–two hours. Finally, the shift change times for the supervisory personnel customarily involved in the end-of-shift count procedures may also vary from the shift times for the table dealers and other operating personnel. One suggested sequence of change in the shift procedures is outlined below.

Procedure	Personnel	Time Frame
1. Final fills & credits are made	Off-going supervisory personnel	20–30 minutes before shift change
2. Briefing	Oncoming & off- going supervisory personnel	15–20 minutes before shift change
3. Table inventories taken	On-coming & off-going supervisory personnel	5–10 minutes before shift change
4. Drop boxes taken from vault to pit	Security personnel	5–10 minutes before shift change
5. Drop boxes—old removed & new put on game	Security and all supervisory personnel	As close to shift change as possible
6. Dealer shift change	Dealers	After old drop box is removed
7. Supervisory personnel change	Off-going supervisory personnel	After all other procedures are complete

It is important to recognize that there is a lot of activity during the shift change. Smooth transitions, proper execution, and necessary recording are important to good accounting records.

Table Inventories

The first component of the computation of the amount of win on a table is the calculation of the changes that have taken place in the table tray inventory between the beginning and the end of the shift. This table inventory fluctuation can have a significant effect on the computation of the win of that table for a particular shift.

The table inventory process depends largely upon the system used by the individual casino to account for its table inventories. The first system is to try to bring the table inventory up to (or down to) a certain par amount at the end of each shift. Although this cannot be done exactly without disrupting the play at the table, experienced pit supervisory personnel can usually determine what amount is required to bring the table to the standard or par amount. The increase or decrease required under this par method is accomplished by an end of shift fill or credit from the cashier to the table, which is then included in the shift computation of win or loss.

In general, the par method of inventory can be performed without the use of table inventory documents or counts since the presumption is that, at any shift change point, the amount of table inventory is unchanged and the amount of inventory fluctuation to be included in the computation win is zero. However, in actuality, a valuable check is provided by the practice of having inventory counts performed, regardless of the procedures to be used.

The second method of table inventory used is a floating system where the amount in any game inventory is allowed to change according to the circumstances. (These changes are generally within certain limits in an operational sense.) Under this system, the amount in any table inventory at the end of the shift varies considerably. Thus, the role of the end-of-shift inventory procedures and the documentation is particularly critical to the determination of the win on the table.

The choice of the system of table inventory procedure depends on a variety of factors. The most important is the ability of the pit supervisory personnel to accomplish the end-of-shift fills and credits. If the level of activity in the casino is high, then the floating system is usually used since it would be physically impossible to accomplish the end-of-shift fills and credits in a timely manner without disrupting the play and supervisory activities. However, in smaller casinos with a lower level of play activity, the par inventory method may be entirely workable. From a control standpoint, the par inventory system seems to be preferable since the table inventory should be a fixed amount at any shift end. With the fluctuations from end of shift to end of shift, the floating system may cause some errors since the ending amounts are never subject to review or comparison to established standards.

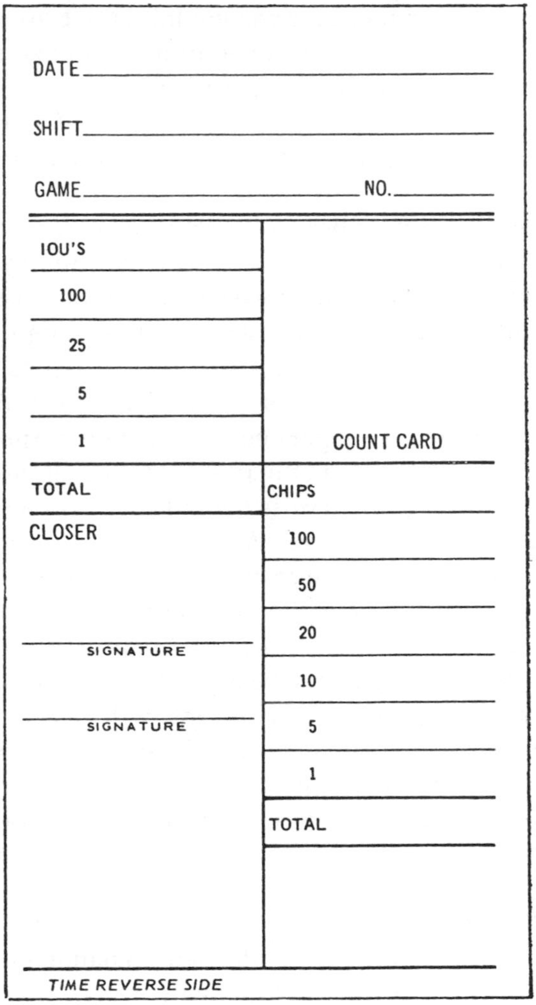

IOU'S		COUNT CARD
100		
25		
5		
1		COUNT CARD

DATE _____ —

SHIFT _____ —

GAME _____ NO. _____

IOU'S	
100	
25	
5	
1	COUNT CARD
TOTAL	CHIPS
CLOSER	100
	50
	20
_____ SIGNATURE	10
_____ SIGNATURE	5
	1
	TOTAL

TIME REVERSE SIDE

Fig. 6-6. Open/close inventory.

Table Inventory Procedures

The actual operating procedures used to take the table inventories are quite straightforward. The off-going and oncoming supervisory personnel usually count the inventory together by actually breaking down the chips on the table or, if the game is quite busy, by observing the chips on the tray. The two individuals then complete the inventory form and sign it. A sample game inventory form is shown in figure 6-6. It is customarily a two-part, color-coded form. In general, numeric control is not exercised over it. The form contains various items of information that must be completed. The essential information is identification: shift, game, and date and time; count of the amount units specified by denomination of chips; and signature verification of the persons performing the count.

At the end of audit periods, the determination of the amounts by denomination of chips is important, allowing the subsequent verification of the total amount of chips in all table inventories. This, in turn, is an important part of determining the amount of chips in the custody of the casino—and the chips outstanding, which will ultimately determine the chip liability of the casino.

The form is then separated into its two parts, and the top portion, either color-coded or marked as "original," is inserted into the drop box. This is to serve as the indication of the closing game inventory and is customarily referred to as the *closer*. The second copy, of a distinct color (the original is usually white, and the second copy is either pink or yellow), is held on the table temporarily until the new drop box is attached to the table. The first item that goes into the new drop box is the copy of the inventory count sheet that indicates the opening table inventory for the new shift. This part of the document is known as the table *opener*. In cases where the table is closed after a shift, the pink opener may stay locked in the table tray until the game is reactivated. At this point, the table inventory is put into the drop box for the next operating shift.

Table Fills

The second component in the determination of the table win in a casino operation is the accounting for fills and credits.

Table fills usually occur when the amount of inventory on the table tray has dropped below a certain amount. The limit below which the table inventory is not allowed to drop is usually a matter of informal procedure within the casino, modified by the judgment of the dealer and the supervisor in the casino pit. On a table with a standard inventory of $2,000 to $2,500, the working inventory is generally not allowed to drop below about $1,000. When an additional amount of chips must be added to the table tray inventory, the following procedures take place:

1. A request for fill form is completed. This is a two-part form, usually color-coded but not numerically controlled. The two-part request for fill is prepared and signed by the supervisory person-

nel in the pit. The copies are then separated, and the original is sent to the casino cage by a security runner who brings the fill or credit back to the pit. The copy of the signed request is kept in the pit area as confirmation of the request that is pending.

2. The security person carries the request slip to the cage area. The cage cashier then reviews the request for completeness, correctness, and the signature of the pit supervisor.

3. The cashier prepares the fill. This procedure consists of the cashier counting out the chips in the denominations and amount requested by the pit supervisor. The cashier then completes a fill slip. A sample fill slip is shown in figure 6-7. The fill slip usually consists of a three-part, prenumbered form—customarily a white original, a yellow second copy, and a pink third copy. In general, the procedure to be used with all forms in the casino operation is that the original copy always follows the money.

The fill slips are customarily housed in a locked dispensing machine. This machine allows only one fill slip to be completed at any one time. The cashier fills out and completes the fill slip while it is still in the locked dispensing machine and signs the document. The security person who is responsible for transporting the fill to the table also signs the fill slip while it is still in the machine. The cashier then advances the dispensing machine and removes the first two parts of the fill slip. The third copy remains in the locked dispenser in an unbroken numeric sequence in order to record all fill and credit activities without exception or interruption. Only the accounting department is allowed to remove those copies, usually storing them securely in an area separate from the casino cashier. When additional fill slips are required, it is the responsibility of the accounting department to open the locked dispenser and refill the machine. In this way, separate independent control is assured over all accounting records that evidence the issuance of money from the casino cage to the table.

The amount of the fill is then recorded by the cashier on a separate document that is a recap of all fill and credit activities. This recap sheet is kept in the cashier cage and is known as the *stiff sheet*. The term arises from the fact that it was customarily a heavier piece of paper stock, allowing the casino management to review a summary of the fill and credit activity during a shift on all tables in the casino. While the cashier's cage is completing the stiff sheet with the identification and the amount of the fill transaction, the security runner doublechecks the count of the amount

BOOMTOWN CASINO
VERDI, NEVADA
FILL SLIP

DATE		TIME	

SHIFT

☐ GRYD. ☐ DAY ☐ SWING

GAME	NUMBER	DENOMINATION	AMOUNT
"21"		.25	
CRAPS		.50	
		1.00	
BIG 6		5.00	
KENO		25.00	
		100.00	
		TOTAL ▶	

MEMO

CASHIER		
		RUNNER
FLOORMAN	DEALER - BOXMAN	

B 207179

Fig. 6-7A. Fill slip.

BOOMTOWN CASINO
VERDI, NEVADA

CREDIT SLIP

DATE			TIME	
SHIFT				
☐ GRYD.		☐ DAY	☐ SWING	
GAME	NUMBER	DENOMINATION	AMOUNT	
"21"		.25		
CRAPS		.50		
ROULETTE		1.00		
BIG 6		5.00		
KENO		25.00		
		TOTAL ▶		
MEMO				
CASHIER				
			RUNNER	
FLOORMAN		DEALER - BOXMAN		

C 15596

Fig. 6-7B. Credit slip.

of the fill. The number two copy of the fill slip is stapled to the original of the request for fill and is retained by the casino cashier in the cage to be recorded as a reconciling item when the total amount of cash at the end of the shift in the cashier's cage is accounted for.

4. Security then transports the original of the fill slip, the number one copy, and the chips that constitute the fill to the pit.

5. The pit supervisor matches the fill slip that accompanies the material transported by the security runner to the request for fill made out earlier. The supervisor counts the fill amount and then signs the original fill slip for that amount. At this point the shift boss may do one of two things. Some casinos may wish to preserve the request for fill forms. In this case, the request for fill is stapled to the original of the fill slip. Other casinos may not wish to retain this documentation and may allow the pit supervisor to destroy this copy of the request for fill. The pit supervisory personnel may also carry a record of the fill transactions to all the tables under their supervision. This is a stiff sheet similar to that kept by the casino cashier but applicable to only a limited number of tables in a specific pit area. In this way, the pit supervisor has a total summary of all fill activity in that area for a specific shift.

The fill, after being double-checked by the pit supervisor, is transported to the table. The dealer counts the amount of the fill, puts the chips on the table tray, and signs the fill slip. The fill slip (which may have the request for fill attached to it) is then dropped into the locked table game box.

The items of identification to be completed on the fill slip fall into three basic categories. First, there is the essential identification information, which includes the date, shift, time, and game to which the fill applies. Second, there is information regarding the denomination of the chips used to complete the fill, together with the total dollar value by denomination and total dollar value for the fill itself. Third, there is a required signature block, with spaces for the cashier, dealer, pit supervisor, and security person who is responsible for transporting the fill from the cashier to the pit area. In certain casinos, the floor supervisors may actually leave the pit area to get a fill from the casino cashier. In this case, only three signatures appear on the fill slip. Finally, there is a preprinted numeric sequence that serves to control the issuance of all fill and credit activity.

The apparent complexity and number of copies essential in

accounting for table fills arises for two distinct reasons. First, the general rule is that money should never move in a casino without having some paper documentation to accompany it. This documentation should include the amount of money and signature blocks to identify those responsible for each step of the handling. Second, the number of copies is essential to assure that the money reaches its final destination and then is accounted for properly back through the system and is reconciled with other copies coming together from the cage cashier system.

The essential control principle that applies to the table fill procedures is a rigorous separation of duties, with each independent system assuming responsibility for the money by signing all the documents. The second key control element is that the extensive documentation allows no improper transactions to be initiated without proper control reporting.

Subsequent discussions of the drop and count procedures of the casino show how the various copies of the fill slips are reunited with one another in a reconciliation procedure that assures completeness of reporting.

Table Credits

Table credits are the exact mirror image of a table fill. A table credit is required in the situation where the game is winning and the total amount of chips and tokens on the table is building. For security reasons, as well as for operational simplicity, those amounts should be removed from the table.

The following procedures take place with regard to a credit to the table.

1. The security runner is called to the pit area.

2. The dealer on the table and pit supervisor count the chips from the table and put them in a rack for transporting back to the casino cage. During this time, a request for credit is completed in the same two-part form used as a request for fill and is signed by the pit supervisor and dealer.

3. At this point, two essential controls must be established. First, a temporary marker button (known as a *lamer button*) is placed on the individual tables from which the money has been removed to signify the amount taken from the table. Second, the pit supervisor retains a copy of the request for credit as evidence that the money has left the pit area and is being transported to the casino cashier.

4. A security runner carries the money and the request for credit to the cage. The cage cashier reviews the request for completeness and correctness.

5. A security person counts the chips and reconciles the total amount to the request for credit. The cashier then completes and signs a three-part credit slip. This credit slip may be a separate form or may be exactly the same form used for a fill, and is merely completed on a different side or marked at the top as being a credit transaction. The cashier then removes the two copies of the credit slip from the locked dispensing machine and time- and date-stamps the two parts of the credit slip. As with a fill transaction, the third copy remains in the locked dispensing machine and forms a tamper-proof sequential record of the transaction being processed. It is customary for the casino cashier and the security runner who transports the money both to sign the credit slip before it is removed from the dispensing machine. At this point, the cashier updates the summary sheet (stiff sheet) with the amount of the table credit.

6. The original of the credit slip is attached to the request for credit and the original credit slip remains in the cashier's area, attached to the stiff sheet. Again, the original copy of the form follows the money back to the cashier's cage.

7. A security runner carries the second copy of the credit slip back to the pit.

8. The shift supervisor compares the amount and the denomination on the credit slip with the original of the request for credit, signs the credit slip, attaches the request for credit to it, and takes it to the individual table involved. The table dealer verifies the credit slip to the amount of the marker button on the table, removes the marker button, and puts the credit slip into the locked table game drop box.

Figure 6-8 shows a flowchart explanation of the systems, procedures, and internal controls over this fill and credit activity.

Other Table Transactions

Other table transactions of importance include even-money exchanges and the use of the marker and lamer buttons to indicate transactions. Even-money exchanges are periodically required in order to balance chips among several tables. Since these procedures allow the transporting of money from table to table without

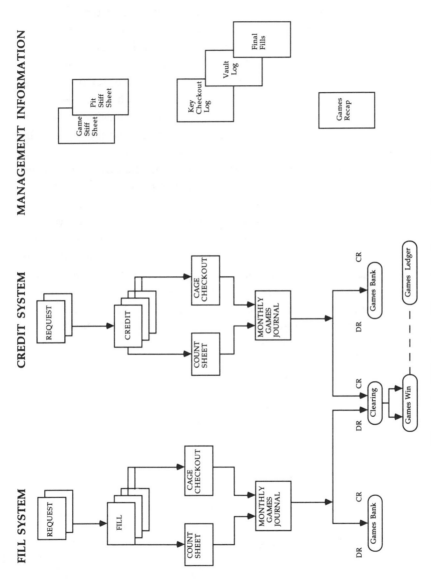

Fig. 6-8. Fill and credit system forms relationship.

an accounting document customarily accompanying them, they are strongly discouraged by gaming regulatory authorities on the basis that there should be no loose or floating money in the casino pit area. However, in order to simplify the transactions and to eliminate an excessive number of fill and credit transactions from the pit to the casino cage, some even-money exchanges usually occur. In order to control these transactions, there should be some method of accounting for the removal of money from the table. This accounting can be accomplished by a memorandum type of document such as an even-money exchange form or through the use of lamer buttons, which indicate that a transaction either is due back to the table or is going to be coming to that particular table.

Lamer buttons are generally small plastic chips or buttons approximately ½ inch to ⅝ inch in diameter with dollar denominations imprinted on them. They are used for what could be described as quick and dirty accounting records and are accepted only for temporary purposes. Their use is generally discouraged except in situations where temporary transactions have been initiated but the paperwork has not yet come back to the point of origin. They can be used in a variety of circumstances, such as in even-money exchanges or to indicate the temporary extension of credit before the credit has been formally signed at the table or at the casino cage.

Table Drop Procedures

Table drop procedures take place at the end of the shift. The general overall procedures have already been discussed in earlier sections of this chapter. The main element in the drop and count procedures at the end of the shift is the process of actually removing the table drop boxes and maintaining their custody back to the count area. The general procedures outlined here show what happens to the table drop boxes at the end of the shift.

The basic end-of-shift procedures cover the following general steps. The empty drop boxes are taken from their security storage to the pit, where the full drop boxes are removed and replaced with the empty boxes for each table. The empty boxes are taken back to the secure storage area and held until the count process can start.

Detailed Drop Procedures

The detailed procedures relating to the drop process outlined above are as follows.

1. The time at which the drop boxes are to be removed from the various table games must be specified in writing to the gaming regulatory agencies, and those drop times must be carefully adhered to. This requirement is based on the necessity of allowing regulatory supervisory personnel actually to observe the procedures of dropping table game boxes from the pit area should they wish to do so.

2. At the specified times at the end of each casino shift, the drop team, usually consisting of one or two security guards and a supervisory person, obtains keys to the storage area from the cashier or the vault.

3. The process of issuance of keys is documented by the recipient signing a key checkout log indicating name, time, and purpose for the removal of the key. This log is a vital record and must be maintained to indicate whenever these critical control keys are actually out of possession of the cage or vault. There is usually one key that allows the removal of the drop box physically from the table and a second key that opens a locked area from which the empty drop boxes are taken and to which the full drop boxes are returned to be held for safekeeping.

4. The drop team then goes to the vault area where the empty drop boxes are stored, unlocks the storage area, and removes the empty drop boxes for the oncoming shift. These drop boxes are put on a metal cart and are transported out to the pit area. During the time when the empty boxes are removed and the full boxes come back in, the storage area remains locked. The drop team then moves to the pit area; after the closing table inventory procedures have been completed, the table game drop box is physically removed from the table by unlocking the lock that attaches the box to the table. When the box is removed from the table, the slot closes in the drop box. This procedure assures that once the table game box is taken from the table, it is completely sealed and nothing can be put into it or removed. Once the full box has been taken, a corresponding new empty box is then placed on the table. The full box is placed on the transport and is moved through the pit area until all the full boxes have been removed and new empty boxes have been placed on the tables.

5. The full table boxes are transported back to the secure storage area that is usually located adjacent to the casino cage or vault. It is unlocked, and the full boxes are placed on the storage shelves. The storage area is then relocked and the drop procedures are completed.

6. The table game box key and the lock for the storage area are signed back into the cage area.

7. The full storage drop boxes remain in their storage areas securely locked until the appropriate time for the table count procedures.

Because of the necessity of removing the full drop boxes for each shift in the casino, it is usually necessary to have four complete sets of drop boxes. This allows the casino to keep one set of boxes for each shift to be held full until the following morning when the count actually begins, and still have a fourth set of boxes available for current use during the time the table count is being performed.

Table Count Procedures

The table count procedures are sometimes known as the *soft count* because the general contents of the table drop boxes are currency and paper, as distinguished from the count of coins usually associated with the slot drop procedures. The table count procedures involve two primary controls. The first is a specific control over the actual cash handling during the time that the drop boxes are being opened and the contents being counted. It is necessary to observe the count procedures to ensure that all the contents of the drop box actually find their way into the accounting records. The second control is to assure that all amounts of cash, currency, and other documents in the drop boxes are both accounted for and recorded on the summary recap records.

Physical Controls

The importance of physical control over the count procedures, the count area, and recording of the transaction must not be underestimated. Accounting control in a casino cannot and does not effectively exist until there has been some recording of the initial transaction. Therefore, in the absence of compensating accounting controls early in the revenue recognition process, it is essential that good physical control procedures supplement the accounting record-keeping procedures. The primary method by which physical control is achieved is through the use of careful step-by-step procedure matched with locks, surveillance, and the employment of independent and trustworthy personnel.

The first component of physical control is that the soft count area is generally separated from the vault, but is customarily located close by to ease the process of physically transferring money once the count has been completed. The second characteristic of the table count area is that it should be adjacent to the area in which the full drop boxes have been stored for safekeeping. This allows the physical handling of the boxes to be accomplished with a minimum of difficulty. Generally, the count room may be an area of the vault that is separated by some sort of glass or steel bars from the actual bulk money storage area. The third important characteristic of the table count area is the presence of surveillance cameras, TV cameras, and unique counting devices such as glass-top tables. In addition, it is customary during count procedures for count personnel to wear smocks, generally without pockets, while they are performing the count. In the New Jersey regulations, the count personnel are required to wear jumpsuits that have no pockets at all. The final control factor is that access to the count room is limited to those persons who are specifically authorized, usually in writing by management, to perform the count procedures. Owners and senior management personnel of the casino are not even allowed in the count area. The members of the count team must be specified in writing to the regulatory authorities, and any changes in the composition of the count team must also be communicated to the regulatory authorities. Finally, the specified times of the count must be observed without exception. This again is based upon the fact that regulatory authorities and auditors may wish to observe the count and must be able to know the exact time that it will occur.

Count Procedures

The following detailed count procedures take place.

1. At the identified time, the count team arrives at the count area. A second special key is signed out of the casino cage or vault to unlock the table boxes, so that they can be completely emptied. Another key is also signed out to unlock the storage area in which the table drop boxes are being held after being removed from the tables at the end of their shifts.

The same procedures of key control are followed for the count team. The person responsible signs out the key, with name, time, date, and purpose recorded in the key checkout log book.

2. The count team generally consists of three persons who are departmentally independent of each other. No one from the casino management group or the pit is allowed to participate in the count procedures.

    a. The three persons assigned to the count team usually separate the responsibilities of the count. First, one person is responsible for opening the drop boxes, assuring that all contents are removed, and then showing the box to another team member to ensure that the box was empty. This step usually includes putting the box in view of the television camera monitor to verify it is empty. That person then resets the sliding panel so that the top slot is open, and relocks the door on the side of the drop box and replaces it in the storage area.

    b. A second person on the count team usually has the responsibility for sorting and separating the different kinds of documents in the drop box and performing the initial count of the currency.

    c. The third person on the drop count team recounts the money and records on the proper forms the fill, credit, inventory open and close, and other bookkeeping information.

3. The actual cash count procedures involve a first count by one team member, followed by a reverification count by a second count team member.

4. After the currency count has been verified, the amount of drop is indicated on the game recap sheet. This is the point at which the first accounting recording takes place for the casino revenue. The game recap sheet summarizes the amount of currency (including foreign chips) in each of the drop boxes for each shift. Once the amount of currency is indicated in the drop column, the opening and closing inventories are recorded, along with the total amount of all fill and credit activity. These items are then summarized in order to determine the total win for that particular game and for that individual shift.

5. The count progresses through all games for a single shift. It then proceeds to the next shift, until the count for the entire day is completed.

6. After all the boxes have been opened and the currency separated from paper transactions, a summary for that shift is prepared. The shift summary includes counting the money, sorting it by denomination, and banding it into standard denomination bundles. The third member of the count team records the shift count and adds up the individual game results in order to verify the total shift result.

7. This process is then repeated for each of the other two shifts until the total amount of currency on hand has been counted, all fill and credit slips have been accounted for, and all opening and closing inventory transactions have been included in the count. The total amount of money and chips, together with the documentation, is then summarized, and the total amount of win is determined to correspond with the cash and fill and credit activities.

8. The members of the count team sign the games recap sheet, indicating agreement with the amounts.

9. A separate money transfer is prepared to account for the transfer of the currency and other documentation from the count room to the casino vault.

The count process is now complete. Figure 6-9 shows a pit recap and game recap or summary sheet used to report the results of the count activity.

Vault Count Procedures

The last link in the count process is the casino vault. The vault represents the point at which the accounting transactions are cross-checked and verified. On one hand, the money from the tables is coming into the vault through the count procedures. On the other hand, the paper accounting for the fill and credit activities has been transferred from the casino cage to the vault. A summary count sheet indicating the amounts of fill and credit activity previously transferred to the vault by the cashier's cage is now reconciled to the fill and credit slips contained in the table drop boxes.

All the fills and credits from the casino are matched with those of the count to assure that all are present, that the amounts agree, and that the recording of the game number, time, and shift is correct. This independent verification at the vault assures that no errors or omissions take place in the process of reporting game revenue.

GAMES DROP SUMMARY SHIFT _____ DATE _____

	BJ-1	BJ-2	BJ-3	BJ-4	BJ-5	BJ-6	BJ-7	BJ-8	BJ-9	BJ-10	WHEEL	CRAPS	TOTAL
Currency $100													
50													
20													
10													
5													
1													
CHIPS													
TOTAL													

CASINO GAMES COUNT REPORT

		(1)	(2)		(3)	(4)	(5)	(6)	(7)	(4 + 7)	
					CREDITS				DROP		
GAME		OPENING	FILLS	Fill and Credit Slip No.	Ret. Chips	Markers	CLOSING	(1+2-3-4-5) NET	SOFT	TOTAL HANDLE	-6 + SOFT RESULT
	1										
	2										
T	3										
W											
E	4										
N	5										
T											
Y	6										
	7										
O	8										
N											
E	9										
21	10										
"R"	1										
Craps	1										
Gr. Total											

Count Verification

DATE _____

SHIFT _____
C00032 (2M) 5/81

COUNT TEAM | COUNT TEAM | COUNT TEAM

Fig. 6-9. Shift count sheet.

The transfer of the drop count to the vault from the count room results in an increase in the total amount of money available in the casino. This usually is recorded in the form of vault transfer sheet and is attached to the daily game recap sheet. The vault cashier signs the transfer document, acknowledging responsibility for the money.

Unusual items such as foreign chips or mutilated currency from the count are segregated and accounted for in the vault. These foreign chips are held until periodically redeemed by other casinos, at which time the casino's own chips are returned by other casinos. This process of chip exchange is called a *chip run*.

All cashier reimbursements are made, including the fill and credit activity. All checks cashed are cleared from the cashier in exchange for currency and/or chips. The cashier's cash and chips are brought back up to their required standard bank amounts.

The cashier then takes the checks, together with any excess currency, and prepares the daily bank deposit.

Figure 6-10 shows a general flowchart of the procedures, indicating the transfer of currency in exchange for the paper that is being held by the casino cashier.

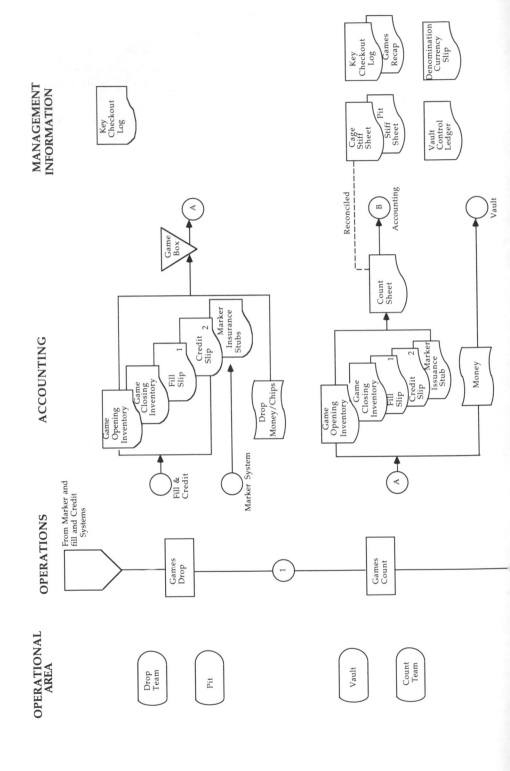

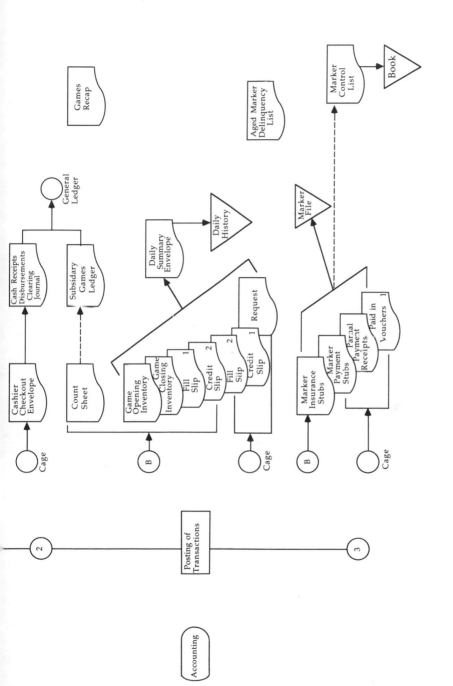

Fig. 6-10. Drop and count operation flow.

CHAPTER 7

Keno, Bingo, Card Room, and Sports and Race Book Accounting

Introduction

This chapter consists of a discussion of the accounting for other casino games, including keno, bingo, card room games (customarily including poker and other various derivative games), and sports and race book betting.

Traditionally, these games have constituted a small portion of the total gaming revenue for casinos; in fact, several of the areas of gaming activity are not even allowed in casinos outside of Nevada. The importance of these games is increasing, however, and astute gaming management recognizes the necessity of offering a broad range of gaming entertainment to the customer. These games also attract a type of customer who might not otherwise be a regular patron of the casino. In addition, the emergence of more widespread sports betting throughout the nation will undoubtedly lead to increased popularity of that activity within the confines of casinos.[1] The size of the revenue generated by these games is indicated in table 7-1.

Table 7-1. Keno, Poker, and Miscellaneous Revenue as a Percentage of Total Revenue (1984).

Size	L.V. Strip	Downtown L.V.	Reno-Sparks
$1–10 M	20.1%	8.1%	14.6%
10–20 M	8.6%	8.8%	10.2%
20–60 M	5.5%	10.5%	9.3%
over 60 M	6.4%	n/a	n/a

Table 7-2. Keno Median Win per Game (1984).

Size	L.V. Strip	Downtown L.V.	Reno-Sparks
$1–10 M	n/a	221,588	877,594
10–20 M	1,002,082	810,781	1,092,609
20–60 M	1,355,552	1,975,065	1,080,788
over 60 M	2,481,185	n/a	n/a

Keno Accounting

The origins of keno are ascribed to an ancient Chinese lottery game; it has been in existence for many years and has risen to new popularity levels following its broad reintroduction into Nevada gaming in 1948.[2]

Keno, as one of the principal miscellaneous games, has an interesting revenue pattern: revenues vary widely, depending upon the physical location of the casino in the state and, to some degree, upon the size of the casino. There are significant individual casino differences in keno revenue, depending largely upon the degree of internal promotion of the keno game in the club and the nature of the casino customers. These differences are shown in table 7-2.

It is interesting to note that, in the first two categories, the difference in win per game is relatively modest for the Las Vegas Strip casinos. Also, the differences between the Downtown Las Vegas win per unit and Reno-Sparks win per unit are fairly large. In the biggest casinos, there appears to be almost no significant difference in the win per keno game based solely upon the location of the casino.

Physical Layout

The keno game usually consists of a physically separate counter working area—a set of windows similar to a bank teller area—where several keno writers are seated. A supervisor and the various devices used to conduct the drawings of the keno balls are behind the counter area. The drawing of the balls is known as *calling the game*. A typical keno layout is shown in figure 7-1.

The result of the drawing of the balls is usually indicated on a large illuminated keno board. There are customarily a number of keno boards located throughout the casino, in bars, restaurant areas, and immediately behind the keno work area.

Keno is one game that requires a minimum of attention while it is being played. Because of this factor, it is ideally suited to be

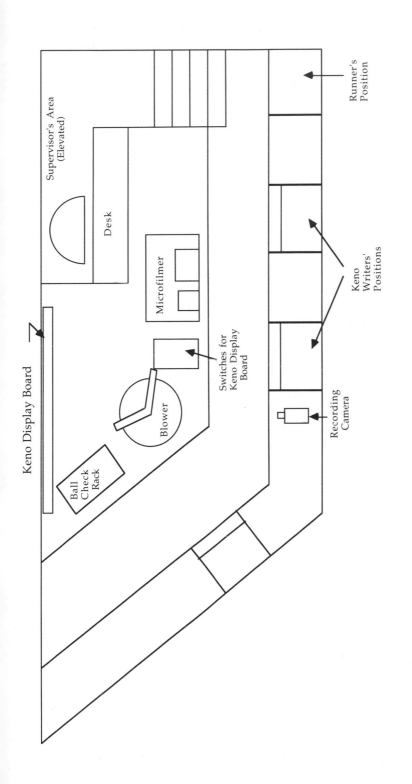

Fig. 7-1. Typical keno layout.

played while the casino customer is either eating or drinking in a restaurant or bar. It involves little concentration following the initial choice of numbers. Thus, the gaming activity can be carried to all persons in the casino without having them physically present in the keno gaming area.

Keno Employees

The second important factor in a keno game is the presence of a large number of personnel. As contrasted with pit games such as 21, there may be from three to eight persons involved in the conduct of a keno game. For this reason, its cost structure could be described as generally fixed, consisting largely of personnel costs. In order to keep a keno game open, minimum staffing costs must be incurred. There can be no partial or selective closing such as might occur in the pit. (Individual games or sections of the pit may be closed during slow periods, resulting in personnel cost savings.)

The customer's first contact with the keno game is through the keno writer. The keno writer is stationed at a tellerlike desk or counter that, depending upon the size of the casino, can vary from two to ten positions. The keno writer receives the marked copy of the keno ticket from the player, which is then duplicated, and the duplicate copy given to the player as evidence of the bet. The amount of the bet is recorded on the face of the original and duplicate ticket. The game number, time, and other identifying information is added to the original ticket and duplicated on the ticket given to the customer.

The original ticket submitted by the customer is retained by the casino and is known as the *inside ticket*. The duplicate ticket that is returned to the customer is known as the *outside ticket*.

The immediate supervisor of the keno writers is the keno supervisor or manager. There is at least one supervisor on hand at all times; during busy shifts, there may be two or more.

When the keno game is about to be called, the keno writers close their stations, stop taking wagers, and assume other responsibilities related to drawing the balls, marking the punched tickets, and illuminating the results on the keno board.

Keno runners are an important adjunct to the keno operation. These runners circulate throughout the casino, including the restaurant and bar areas. Their purpose is to pick up and deliver the keno tickets that are written by patrons in the restaurants and bars so they can continue to play in the keno game without leaving their eating or drinking. These runners pick up the money and the tickets with the appropriate markings from the customer. These tickets are then transmitted to the central keno game location where the duplicates are prepared. The duplicates are given to the keno runners, who return them to the players. The keno runners are also responsible for delivering the payoffs to the customers who are winners following the calling of the game.

Keno Payoff

Keno payoffs vary widely and often depend on a complex interaction of the number of spots chosen by the player and the total number of spots chosen or "hit" during the draw process. The simplest situation is when from one to fifteen spots are marked on a ticket. The customer generally is a winner if more than half of the total number of spots chosen were hit. This can be illustrated in the sample payout schedule in figure 7-2.

The monetary amount of the payoff depends on the amount wagered and the number of spots hit. At the halfway point, the payoff is approximately 1:1. As more and more spots are hit, the payoff rises dramatically.

Odds Structure

The odds structure for the keno game is determined by the total number of balls in the blower and the number of balls drawn from the total. Experiments conducted in the various keno games have added extra or bonus balls or have drawn twenty-two balls instead of the customary twenty balls. These alterations have been made in an attempt to make the odds more attractive to the player.

Given the customary choice of twenty balls from a group of eighty, the probability of choosing a specific number of balls can be computed using mathematical formulas for permutations and combinations. Once the probability of winning is determined for a given number of balls, these probabilities can be weighted by the dollar payoff schedule in order to determine the payoff percentage in dollar terms. In its simplest form, the probability of winning at keno is the probability of picking one ball out of twenty drawn from a group of eighty—approximately 12.5%.

As the number of spots chosen increases, the complexity of the payoff computation increases and can be more easily calculated

MARK 1 SPOT

Winning Spots	$1.00 Ticket Pays	$2.00 Ticket Pays	$5.00 Ticket Pays
1	3.00	6.00	15.00

MARK 2 SPOTS

Winning Spots	$1.00 Ticket Pays	$2.00 Ticket Pays	$5.00 Ticket Pays
2	12.00	24.00	60.00

MARK 3 SPOTS

Winning Spots	$1.00 Ticket Pays	$2.00 Ticket Pays	$5.00 Ticket Pays
2	1.00	2.00	5.00
3	40.00	80.00	200.00

MARK 4 SPOTS

Winning Spots	$1.00 Ticket Pays	$2.00 Ticket Pays	$5.00 Ticket Pays
2	1.00	2.00	5.00
3	3.00	6.00	15.00
4	115.00	230.00	575.00

MARK 5 SPOTS

Winning Spots	$1.00 Ticket Pays	$2.00 Ticket Pays	$5.00 Ticket Pays
3	1.00	2.00	5.00
4	9.00	18.00	45.00
5	720.00	1440.00	3600.00

MARK 6 SPOTS

Winning Spots	$1.00 Ticket Pays	$2.00 Ticket Pays	$5.00 Ticket Pays
3	1.00	2.00	5.00
4	3.00	6.00	15.00
5	80.00	160.00	400.00
6	1420.00	2840.00	7100.00

MARK 7 SPOTS

Winning Spots	$1.00 Ticket Pays	$2.00 Ticket Pays	$5.00 Ticket Pays
4	1.00	2.00	5.00
5	18.00	36.00	90.00
6	350.00	700.00	1750.00
7	7500.00	15,000.00	37,500.00

MARK 8 SPOTS

Winning Spots	$1.00 Ticket Pays	$2.00 Ticket Pays	$5.00 Ticket Pays
5	9.00	18.00	45.00
6	80.00	160.00	400.00
7	1400.00	2800.00	7000.00
8	17,500.00	35,000.00	50,000.00

MARK 9 SPOTS

Winning Spots	$1.00 Ticket Pays	$2.00 Ticket Pays	$5.00 Ticket Pays
5	3.00	6.00	15.00
6	40.00	80.00	200.00
7	325.00	650.00	1625.00
8	4000.00	8000.00	20,000.00
9	18,000.00	36,000.00	50,000.00

Fig. 7-2A. Keno payoff schedule.

MARK 10 SPOTS

Winning Spots	$1.00 Ticket Pays	$2.00 Ticket Pays	**$5.00 Ticket Pays**
5	2.00	4.00	**10.00**
6	18.00	36.00	**90.00**
7	120.00	240.00	**600.00**
8	750.00	1500.00	**3750.00**
9	4500.00	9000.00	**22,500.00**
10	20,000.00	40,000.00	**50,000.00**

MARK 11 SPOTS

Winning Spots	$2.00 Ticket Pays	$4.00 Ticket Pays
6	16.00	32.00
7	140.00	280.00
8	750.00	1500.00
9	3600.00	7200.00
10	25,000.00	50,000.00
11	50,000.00	50,000.00

MARK 12 SPOTS

Winning Spots	$2.00 Ticket Pays	$4.00 Ticket Pays
6	10.00	20.00
7	50.00	100.00
8	400.00	800.00
9	1700.00	3400.00
10	4500.00	9000.00
11	26,000.00	50,000.00
12	50,000.00	50,000.00

MARK 13 SPOTS

Winning Spots	$2.00 Ticket Pays	$4.00 Ticket Pays
6	5.00	10.00
7	20.00	40.00
8	150.00	300.00
9	1400.00	2800.00
10	4000 00	8000.00
11	18,000.00	36,000.00
12	30,000.00	50,000.00
13	50,000.00	50,000.00

MARK 14 SPOTS

Winning Spots	$2.00 Ticket Pays	$4.00 Ticket Pays
6	4.00	8 00
7	16.00	32.00
8	64.00	128.00
9	600.00	1200.00
10	1600.00	3200.00
11	5000.00	10,000.00
12	24,000.00	48,000.00
13	36,000.00	50,000.00
14	50,000.00	50,000.00

MARK 15 SPOTS

Winning Spots	$2.00 Ticket Pays	$4.00 Ticket Pays
6	2.00	4.00
7	14.00	28.00
8	42.00	84.00
9	200.00	400.00
10	800.00	1600.00
11	4000.00	8000.00
12	16,000.00	32,000.00
13	24,000.00	48,000.00
14	50,000.00	50,000.00
15	50,000.00	50,000.00

Fig. 7-2B. Keno payoff schedule.

on a computer. A sample calculation for a ten-spot ticket is indicated in table 7-3.

Keno Draw Procedures

When a keno game is about to be called (some old-timers refer to keno as race horse keno and insist that a keno game is run—in the jargon of racing), the following draw procedures occur.

The mechanism of drawing the balls and the necessity of controlling the placing of bets to eliminate the possibility of making a bet with the results already known are critical to the control of the keno game.

At the conclusion of the acceptance of keno bets, and prior to the calling of the game, all of the keno tickets from the various writer positions, as well as the tickets transmitted by the keno runners, are collected by a supervisor. That person delivers all the inside tickets to the microfilmer for copying prior to the calling of the game.

Table 7-3. 10 Spot Payoff Computation.

1. Total number of combinations of 10 balls that can be drawn from 80 balls = 1,646,492,110,120 (1 trillion, 646 billion, 492 million, 110 thousand, 120).

2. 10 spot payoff schedule (based on a $1 ticket):

10 hits pays	$25,000
9 hits pays	4,500
8 hits pays	725
7 hits pays	125
6 hits pays	20
5 hits pays	2

3. Number of possible winning ticket combinations from the 20 balls selected by the keno game:

Wins	Number Possible		Amount Won on Each		Total Possible $ Win
10	184,756	×	$25,000	=	4,618,900,000
9	10,077,600	×	$4,500	=	45,349,200,000
8	222,966,600	×	725	=	161,650,785,000
7	2,652,734,400	×	125	=	331,591,800,000
6	18,900,732,600	×	20	=	378,014,652,000
5	84,675,282,048	×	2	=	169,350,564,096
			Total payoff	=	$1,090,575,901,096

4. Computation of total win:

Total possible bet	$1,646,492,110,120	100.0%
Total possible win	$1,090,575,901,096	66.2%
Amount to casino	$555,916,209,024	33.8%

Microfilm Control Procedures

The primary risk of loss in a keno game arises in two areas. The first is that the draw of the game might not be conducted in a truly random manner. This risk can be minimized by periodically inspecting the balls, the blower mechanism, and other mechanical devices used to execute the draw. The second risk is more crucial—that a game ticket will be played after the numbers have been drawn and will be slipped into the payoff stack. This method of betting after the results are known is called *past posting* in horse racing and was the technique used in the movie *The Sting*.

A microfilm procedure is used to prevent this practice from occurring in keno. Generally, if the microfilm machinery is in good working condition and if it is designed properly, then the controls work. The microfilm process is repeated for each keno game run. After all the tickets have been microfilmed, they are given to the keno supervisor, who holds them until the payoffs are claimed after the game has been called.

The microfilm recording sequence from game to game is indicated below.

Microfilm Position	Situation Indicated
START	Closer of prior game pictured
#1	Clear space indicating a new game
#2	Opener of current game is shown. The opener is the punched copy of the results of the prior game
#3	All inside game tickets are copied
#4	Closer of present game
#5	Blank space indicating new game to start

The closer of the prior game is usually a distinctively marked copy of an inside ticket, with the time, date, and game number clearly indicated on it.

The key to control over the microfilmer is that, once the blank space between games has been made, the next section of the film should form an unbroken sequence of opener, game tickets, and closer. There should be no way, short of physically disturbing the microfilm camera, to slip a phony ticket into the microfilm process.

When the balls are going to be drawn, the customary control is dropping the balls from the prior game from the rabbit ears into the blower. This action triggers the microfilm machine to advance—thus creating a blank spot on the microfilm.

Care must be taken to be sure that the camera is not tampered with and that there can be no way to rewind and remicrofilm the tickets after the game has been called. The manufacturers of microfilm cameras have designed machinery to assure that this does not happen. However, care must be taken to ensure that the manufacturers' controls are operating properly and are still functioning.

The Keno Draw

After the microfilm process is completed, the next game is then called or drawn. The blower is activated, and the person operating the blower opens a gate to admit one ball at a time to the rabbit ears. First one rabbit ear is filled, then the opposite is filled. In all, twenty balls are drawn.

As the balls are drawn, it is customary to announce or call the results over a public address system. Also, the number drawn is illuminated on various keno boards throughout the casino—using the master control switch located in the keno area. Finally, five to ten master game tickets are punched with the drawn numbers. These tickets are used by writers to verify the window payoffs and by keno runners to check winning tickets and to serve to mark the beginning of the next game sequence on the microfilmer.

At this time, a videotape may be made of the actual draw process; at a minimum, a photograph is taken of the final draw results, with the rabbit ears filled. In addition, the photograph or videotape customarily includes in its line of view the number of the game, a copy of the punched game master ticket, and a lighted keno board.

Following the punching of the master game ticket, the keno supervisor or other responsible employee manually turns on the microfilmer again. This automatically spaces the film prior to acceptance of the game master ticket and serves to start the next microfilm sequence.

Payoff Supervision

The keno supervisor reviews all inside tickets and pulls all winning tickets, usually very soon after the draw is completed. The supervisor then calculates the payouts by tickets and enters the total payout on a game log that is maintained at the supervisor's desk.

Customers holding winning tickets generally present the ticket to the keno runner or directly to the keno writer's window in order to have the ticket paid. Several common procedural options exist at this point. For example, the player can elect to play the same ticket again, in which case the winnings of the prior game become the amount bet for the next game.

If the ticket is presented for payment, the keno writer matches the outside ticket presented by the patron to the game master ticket in order to verify that the ticket is a winning one. The game master ticket is usually punched with the winning numbers represented by holes. This facilitates the comparison of tickets presented to the game master ticket.

The review and supervision procedures depend directly upon the dollar amount of the payoff. If the payoff is relatively small, usually under $10, the keno writer is empowered to make the payoff directly to the player without further action. If the win exceeds $10, then the keno writer notifies the keno supervisor, who verifies that the inside ticket and the outside ticket agree. The supervisor then authorizes the writer to make the payoff. As a result of the review of the winning tickets that the keno supervisor has already performed, the supervisor is able to make the predetermination of large winnings quickly and easily. This notification is important in the case of larger wins, since review procedures can be started to assure the propriety of the win.

If the win is over $1,200, the Internal Revenue Service rules add another dimension to the payoff process. The $1,200 threshold is set as the minimum amount required to file the information return form W-2G with the IRS. The casino must complete that form. The customer is required to submit two valid pieces of identification, along with a social security number. The amount of the payoff, the time, the date, and other relevant information is then supplied to the customer, and the form is completed in three parts with one going to the customer. The other two copies are transmitted to the accounting department. One copy is retained by the casino, and the second copy is sent to the IRS.

If the win exceeds a larger amount, usually $2,500 or $3,000, then more careful casino review procedures are called into play. The dollar limit is usually set by the individual casino. In the case of these large payoffs, the winning tickets may be required to be verified against the microfilm copy of the inside ticket if the keno manager considers it necessary. If this is the case, the appropriate roll of microfilm is developed, and the microfilm is matched with the inside and outside copy prior to effecting the payoff of the winner. If videotape is used to record the tickets, the tape does not have to be developed but can be viewed directly.

In the case of large payoffs, several other verification steps may be required. The most common is a ball check. In this procedure, the balls are drawn out of the blower and placed in a special prenumbered ball rack to assure that there is only one ball of each number and that there is a ball for each of the eighty numbers. In addition, the ball check is also a physical check of the condition of the balls to assure that they are not cracked, damaged, or in any way altered so as to affect the randomness of the draw. In cases of larger payoffs, usually exceeding $10,000, the keno management, the shift manager of the casino, and the general manager may be required to sign the payoff documents.

Keno Banks

Accounting control is maintained over the keno operation through the use of fixed banks for each of the keno writers and keno runners, and a fixed master bank for the keno manager.

The accounting operation of the keno game is to start each of the writers at the beginning of the shift with a certain fixed amount in the cash drawer. The physical control over the cash drawers is maintained by the cashier in cooperation with the vault. The cashier sets up the banks and stores them. At the end of the shift, the vault takes responsibility for clearing the banks so that the proceeds (the win) can be included in the count of the win of the casino on a daily basis.

During the betting transactions, money is received by the writers; if there are winners, the amounts are paid out. The unique accounting aspect of the keno operation is that there is a complete paper record of all the income and paidout transactions through the use of the keno tickets themselves as revenue documents. At the end of the shift, the increase or decrease in the writer's window bank is the amount of the win or loss on that station for the keno game.

If, during the course of the shift, there is an excess of money built up in the window bank or if more money is needed to pay off a large winner, then an appropriate keno fill or credit is utilized. The fill or credit activity varies depending upon the amount. The first type is merely an exchange in the form of a paper transaction from the keno manager's bank to the window bank. The keno manager's bank is later reimbursed from the main casino cashier, and the amount of the fill is recorded as a charge against the window bank. This fill is considered in computing the amount of accountability, as well as the respective win or loss on the window and the keno game itself.

If the amount needed to pay off a winner is more substantial, a fill may be required from the central cashier. In this case, two documents should be used, similar to a pit fill. The first document is a request for fill, which is illustrated in figure 7-3.

This request for fill specifies the amount of the fill required and the reason for it—either accumulation of many small wins during the shift or a large payout of a single jackpot keno ticket.

The request for fill is signed by the keno manager and by the keno writer and is transmitted from the keno area to the central cashier. The central cashier then completes a customary fill slip, and the copy of the fill slip is kept with the request for fill in the main casino cage. The other copy of the request for fill is kept in the keno area until the actual fill is made. This enables the keno

REQUEST FOR FILL or CREDIT

KENO

Shift _____

Date _____

.25 _____

.50 _____

Ikes _____

$5 Chips _____

$25 Chips _____

Other _____

TOTAL _____

AUTHORIZATION

Fig. 7-3. Request for fill or credit.

manager to verify that the amount of the fill actually received is the same as the amount requested.

The keno fill slip is a standard fill form, with three parts. The third copy is kept in the issuing dispenser machine. The original and the first copy go with the money to the keno area. These two copies are signed; the original copy is kept in the keno area and is turned in with the keno manager's reconciliation of the shift activity. The second copy, after appropriate signatures, is returned to the casino cashier where it is attached to the request for fill and entered on the shift fill/credit summary sheet.

At the completion of the shift, the keno supervisor prepares a keno shift report indicating the total amount of the write, deducting the amount of payout made, and arriving at a net figure for the shift. This net is then added to the amount of the manager's bank and becomes the amount of the cash bank that is turned in to the vault for safekeeping.

Keno Revenue Audit Procedures

The keno audit procedures are an after-the-fact audit of all keno tickets. The task of keno auditing developed as a way to check the accuracy of various payoff tickets that could on occasion become very complex. The task is usually performed by trained casino personnel and is a key review to assure the accuracy and integrity of the keno game. It is an important component in ensuring the correctness of keno revenue.

The keno audit is also a key step in internal control, creating a second independent evaluation of the keno game and its operations. The complexity of the keno audit can vary from a simple checking of payouts to a complete re-creation of the game. The extent of the keno audit is largely a matter of choice by the casino management.

One step in the keno audit that is usually not performed is some form of statistical analysis of the randomness of the draw. The randomness of the draw is essential, since any alteration of the game, either naturally or by deliberate manipulation, could cause the results to be different and expose the casino to a potential fraud situation. The risk to the casino is significant if certain balls are always drawn in a game or certain balls are never drawn. A casino should develop a method of collecting the game results automatically and analyze the results using standard statistical tests to determine the randomness of the draw. If there is a problem, then the appropriate action can be taken by management to verify that the physical aspects of the game are correct or to improve the internal control procedures over the game.

The basic procedures of keno audit involve transmitting all inside keno tickets from the keno game area to the keno auditor. The tickets are usually separated and bundled by game number and by shift in order to identify the tickets accurately if more than one keno game is operating in the casino. The tickets are also separated by the appropriate writer or source of origin.

The keno auditor recomputes the total write (amount wagered) and deducts the total payouts. The total payouts are recomputed to verify that neither underpayments nor overpayments are being made. The amount of the payouts is then compared to the game summary sheets to see if a difference exists.

If there is a significant difference (a $10–$20 difference is usually considered significant), then the reason for the difference is investigated and the nature of the error is described in the keno audit report. The report is given to the keno manager, who is responsible for taking whatever action is deemed necessary to correct the problem.

Differences can occur in both the income (write) side and the expense (payout) side. Therefore, both sides of the keno operation are audited.

A more detailed keno audit procedure may be followed if one of the assigned duties of the keno auditor is to verify the payout procedures in detail. If a detailed audit of the payoff is required, then the microfilm may be developed to verify the accuracy of the draw and to assure that the integrity of the recording and draw has been maintained. Verification of proper adherence to other payoff procedures such as a ball check and the presence of all descriptions and signatures on the fill or credit slips could also be carried out as a part of the keno audit function.

Costs of a Keno Game

Keno is unusual in a financial sense in that the game is very expensive to establish and, once established, has certain minimum fixed costs of operation. A keno game requires a substantial initial investment in basic game equipment. It has been estimated that these costs are about $60,000–$75,000, depending on the complexity of the machinery.[3] In addition to the equipment, there is a substantial cost associated with bankrolling a keno game. Since the current Nevada Gaming Control Board requirement is between two to four times the maximum game payout, the bankroll amount could easily be between $100,000 and $200,000.

Given the three-shift, 24-hour nature of Nevada casino operation, a keno game also has a unique operating cost structure. First, since there is usually a minimum of one keno game in a casino, the game must be kept open constantly. Only if there are multiple games can some of them be closed during slow periods to save costs. Second, the nature of keno, which can be played while customers are eating or drinking, further reinforces the necessity for continuous operation. Third, a keno game requires a certain minimum number of people to operate. There must be at least one writer, one runner, and one supervisor. During busy periods, this staffing may increase substantially. These factors all contribute to the high fixed-cost nature of the keno game. In order to be financially successful, a keno operation must do two things:

1. Initial costs of investment must be controlled.

2. Value or volume of play must be maintained in order to exceed the break-even point in ongoing keno operations.

Complexity of Way Tickets

One of the serious problems of control in a keno game lies in the multitude of possible combinations in marking the number choices on keno tickets. Tickets with groupings or special patterns are called *way tickets*. These way tickets are the equivalent of playing multiple keno tickets but marking only one ticket.

Figure 7-4 shows various way tickets. The upper left ticket has four groups of two spots each, plus one group of eight spots marked.

1. The eight marks are considered one ticket.

2. Each of the groups of two is considered one ticket.

3. The total is five tickets at $1.00 per ticket, for a total ticket cost of $5.00.

The way ticket's appeal is based on the feeling that the chances to win are enhanced since more spots are marked. However, the odds structure remains unchanged, and most of the attraction is merely psychological.

Fig. 7-4. Keno way tickets.

Once the multiple concept of way tickets is understood, the process of evaluating the wins and losses on individual game tickets can be determined.

Concession Keno

Another area of concern to the keno operation is the accounting and internal controls over those keno operations that are run by individuals other than the owners of the casino.

In these situations, the operation is known as a *leased department* or a *concession keno operation*. The unique feature of this style of operation is that there is an independent third party involved in the operation, while the same controls must be adhered to in the conduct of the keno game. Differences exist in the areas of accounting controls over the payoff procedures, determination of profits and losses, and the ultimate division of those profits or losses.

During the conduct of the keno games, the concession operator is bound by the same rules and terms of conduct of the game as if the casino operation were operating it. There may be special concern about improper payouts being made to a confederate of the concessionaire, to the detriment of the lessor. In this case, special procedures should be followed to account for and document the payouts, and careful attention should be given to large payouts.

A second consideration is the ability of the lessor's accounting department to make the proper determination of the win or loss of the keno operation. This is essential in order to assure that there is a proper division of the profits. The typical division is patterned after slot machine operating agreements where 40% to 60% of the win goes to the operator and the remainder to the location or lessor. In general, the more desirable the location, the greater the "rent" or percentage that goes to the casino. Another consideration in the determination of the split is who provides the keno equipment. A heavy capital contribution by the operator would necessitate a larger portion of the winnings going to his or her account.

A minor but important point is that the split is always expressed in terms of the net win—that is, the win after all winners have been paid. Also, various concession agreements make specific provisions for adjustments of the split after the fact to take into account changes due to audits or tax assessments. Once again, as with slots, the concession agreement should also assign specific responsibility for the payment of gaming taxes and licenses.

Automatic Keno Machines

The advent of video keno machines has made a significant impact on the gaming industry in past years. In large part, these games are modified slot machines with a large video display of the typical eighty-number keno layout. The patrons select the numbers they wish to play with a light pen, and the game starts when the coins are inserted and the go button is pressed.

The elements of accounting and control for these machines are mainly patterned after the controls over slot machines, and not a regular keno game, due to their mechanical nature. The payoffs in these machines are substantially smaller than in a standard keno game. In all cases the payoffs are handled by slot machine payoff personnel, and they are documented and approved in the same manner as slot machine payoffs. The operations of these automatic keno machines are administratively controlled through the slot department as well.

Bingo Accounting and Controls

The basic accounting and internal control procedures relating to bingo operations could be categorized according to the main phases of the bingo game:

1. Controls over the "selling" of boards to customers.
2. Controls over the drawing of the balls during the bingo game.
3. Controls over the payoff of winnings.

Bingo is a game that has wide popularity outside of casinos.[4] However, as a casino game, it represents a very small amount of revenue and is offered merely to assure a full range of entertainment products to the casino customers. To some degree, bingo also appeals to a different class of customer than other games because it generally costs less to play. Because of the somewhat lower payoffs, it also has fewer major control problems.

On a structural and procedural basis, bingo games resemble keno in certain areas, particularly where the procedures for the draw of the game and the jackpot payoff processes are concerned. However, a major difference exists with respect to the revenue earning process.

Basic Procedures and Accounting

Card Control   The first area of concern is the control over the issuance of bingo cards in the game, as well as the collection of revenue from customers.

Typically, casino bingo earns its revenue by selling the use of a bingo card to a customer for a game or group of games. Bingo games in noncasino locations may occasionally charge an admission fee in addition to a fee for the use of the cards.

The principal revenue collection process is performed by floor personnel who circulate around the bingo parlor area and collect the fees for card use after each game and before the next game. In some bingo operations, the initial issuance of the bingo cards is done at a central cashierlike location so that the bingo cards can be controlled.

The bingo cards that are issued are usually permanent, with appropriate casino identification, as well as serial numbers and other marks that help to prevent counterfeiting. As patrons enter the bingo area, they purchase a game card from the vendor for a set fee. The amount of revenue is then tallied by the vendor and cross-referenced to the number of cards issued.

After the initial play, repeat plays are paid for on the floor of the bingo activity by having the floor person either pick up the bingo card after the customer has finished with it or else receive payment from the customer. There is usually some form of validation attached to the board for each of the games to be played to assure that any player has a validation sticker or mark indicating that he or she has paid for the game currently being called.

Other controls over the bingo revenue at this point include supervisor counts of the number of persons playing the game and reconciliation of these numbers with the revenue received by the floor persons. Also, standard operating procedures must be followed in order to ensure that irregularities do not occur and that floor persons are not diverting funds from the casino by indicating a card as inactive during a certain game.

After the shift is completed, each of the floor persons is required to check out. In this case, the validation slips are accounted for, and the number sold is multiplied by the fees to determine the amount of the required turn-in. The turn-in is calculated for each runner or floor person, and the bingo booth turn-in is also reconciled. These amounts are then transferred to the main casino cashier where the total amount of the win for the bingo game is determined.

Draw of the Game   The second key procedural control relates to the conduct of the draw of the numbered balls for the game. Again, the basic procedure is to draw one of seventy-five balls at random, each categorized into one of five groups by number, in a sequential manner until a winner is determined or a specified number of balls has been drawn.

The odds structure of the bingo game is such that as the number of balls approaches fifty, the odds of drawing twenty-four numbers (twenty-five spaces less the traditional center free play) are very small. After fifty numbers are called, the odds drop dramatically. To compensate for this, the amount of the award for a bingo with less than fifty numbers is very large, and the payoff drops dramatically for greater numbers. Most casino games are established with a minimum payoff, even if the number of balls counted is very high.

The odds structure can be modified somewhat for games that call for covering just a line of numbers, four corners, or other patterns of numbers selection.

The physical drawing process for the balls can be accomplished in much the same manner as for a keno game. The balls are housed in a cage or blower and are agitated in some manner and selected one at a time. Various types of devices exist to hold the balls that have been selected. Typically, they all have some way of assuring that the balls are categorized according to the B, I, N, G, and O groups. Also, there must be some way to indicate the balls that have been drawn. Usually this is done by lighting a large board, where each of the numbers is illuminated when it has been drawn.

The integrity of the draw process is important, and several alternative methods have been used. The simplest is to have an observer to assure that the balls that are drawn are the correct ones and that they are properly announced and the correct number is illuminated.

A more complex alternative involves keeping the balls sealed within a blower or selection machine and photographing or video recording the results of the draw of balls.

Once the draw has been completed and the winner of the

bingo game declared, secondary ball control procedures as a part of the payoff determination come into play.

Payoff Determination   The first step in the determination of the payoff is the verification of the correctness of the win by having a floor person read the numbers from the winning card back to the caller or ball draw person.

At this time, the card should also be carefully inspected by the floor person to assure that it is a valid casino card, and that serial numbers and other identifying marks are in place. Special care should be taken to ensure that the card numbers have not been altered in any way.

The next step in the payoff determination is a ball check, verifying that there are indeed seventy-five balls in the blower and that there are no duplicate, damaged, or otherwise improper balls.

At this point, the payoff of the winner should be processed. In general, a parallel set of procedures similar to those under the keno game system should be used. Small payouts require minimum documentation—including the time, the date, and an authorized signature on the paidout slip with the winning ticket attached. For more substantial payoffs, there may have to be supervisory or senior-level management approval. Also, as with keno, there are mandatory IRS information returns to be completed (Form W-2G) if the payoff exceeds $1,200.

Bingo Accounting

At the end of the shift, the floor persons and the main supervisor in the bingo area should turn in their individual banks. The floor persons check out and account for all game tickets sold and reconcile that with the total turn-in. In addition, any paidout documents are considered in arriving at the total amount for which they are accountable. The net amount of the turn-in constitutes the largest portion of the bingo revenue.

As with other games, if there are substantial winners, a specific fill to the bingo department may be required. In this case, the fill slip processing is the same as for any other game, and the fill slip copy is held by the main casino cashier while the original fill slip is turned in with the bank by the bingo supervisor at the end of the shift. The fill is deducted from the total cash turn-in amount in order to determine the win on the bingo operation for the shift and the day.

Card Room Accounting

Casino card room games include poker and other derivative card games. The casino's role in these games is unique; instead of being an active player, the casino acts only by providing the physical facilities to play and supplying the dealer to handle the cards and conduct the play.[5]

A traditional card room layout is shown in figure 7-5. The card rooms vary in popularity in Nevada casinos, generating 1.9% of the 1985 statewide gross gaming revenue. In Washoe County, they produce 1.4% of gross gaming revenue; in Clark County, 2.2% of total gaming revenue. Card rooms are frequently found in other areas of the country, and card rooms are legal under individual local laws in many states.

Revenue Accounting

The revenue to the casino from a card room operation is derived from the percentage that is taken from each hand, known as the *rake-off*. Other compensation programs for the casino may include a fixed commission rate or a rate charged for the time that the player is at the table.

Generally, the rates to play, if expressed as a percentage commission or as a time rental, are clearly posted in the game area. If the compensation method to the casino is a rake-off, then the minimum, the maximum, and the percentage rake-off amounts are specified and posted in the game area.

During the conduct of the games as the bets are being made, the dealer has the responsibility of estimating the amount of the

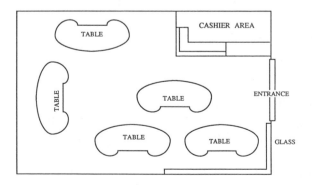

Fig. 7-5. Card room layout.

pots and taking the rake-off from the pot. The amount of the rake-off is usually set aside on the game table and held until the completion of the hand. This serves notice that the game is not being excessively raked and is an indication of good faith on the part of the casino. After the hand is completed, the rake-off is deposited in the table game box. Usually, only currency is deposited in the game box.

Accounting and Internal Controls

During the course of play, there are several key accounting control points that are of interest. The first is the point at which the dealer is responsible for changing currency and coin into chips. This cashiering function operates exactly the same as it does in other table games. The currency is deposited in the table drop box where it forms part of the computation of the table win that is determined during the overall casino game count procedures.

In addition to the dealer cashiering activity, there are usually small cashier booths located in the game room. These cashiers perform several functions. They replenish the working inventory on the tables during the shift, act as a turn-in location for the table inventories taken by each dealer from the game cashier to the table, and act to change currency to chips and back for customers. The cashiers also perform minor administrative chores, such as bookkeeping for the game room and ordering complimentary beverages for players at the instruction of the card room manager. In some casinos, the card cashier may also initiate some credit transactions.

If a dealer is in need of additional chips on the table, he or she indicates the need to a supervisor. A lamer button in the amount of the fill requested is then placed on the table by the dealer. The security guard goes to the card room cashier, who prepares a fill using a traditional three-part fill slip. The original fill slip and copy are transmitted to the table from the cashier, and the dealer and supervisor sign the fill slip. The fill slip is then deposited in the table drop box. The lamer button is removed when the formal fill slip is signed by the dealer and the chips are put on the table. The copy of the fill slip is then returned to the cashier where it is recorded as a fill to the table and is retained until the end of the shift.

At the end of the shift, the table tray is removed from the card table and returned to the card cashier. The card cashier records the opening and closing inventory. The cashier then forwards all the documents along with the copies of the fill slips and table inventories to the main casino cashier where the documents are cleared back to count rooms at the appropriate time.

The accountability of the card cashier is maintained as with other cashiers by the use of imprest balances. The balances account for all paidout items to the tables along with the chip, coin, and currency inventory in that location.

The overall conduct of the business in the card rooms is remarkably similar to that of other casino games. The accounting processes are very much the same—only the revenue-earning process is different. The house takes a rake-off or commission, rather than participating in the play of the game.

Sports and Race Book Accounting

This section discusses the basic accounting procedures to be followed in the conduct of a sports and race book in a casino or in a stand-alone location.[6]

The Odds

In order to take bets on a sports or race book event, odds must be posted. The odds are determined by professionals in a variety of fields. The oddsmakers are generally independent specialists, usually in sports or in racing, who provide information to others for a fee.[7] The providing of such information is subject to Nevada licensing requirements, and appropriate fees must be paid. Larger sports and race books may employ their own oddsmakers, but this is relatively rare.

Horse race odds come directly from the track, not as a result of the pari-mutuel betting, but from independent specialists. Some race books indicate that they pay track odds, which may vary slightly from the odds posted in the casino. In general, the casino odds are slightly less favorable than the track odds on the same race.

The basic odds are called the *line*. The line may be adjusted from time to time in order to balance the betting activity. Also, the casinos may make layoff bets to balance their own exposure. The basic concept of sports book betting is that the book should be balanced, with the casino earnings coming in the form of the difference between the true redistribution payoff and the payoff according to the odds posted in the casino. In general, there is never much deviation from the line by any one casino. Comparisons among casinos reveal little if any variation.

Betting Procedure

Once the odds have been set, the sports book can accept bets on an event. Not only must each bet be recorded, but the money bet on each event must be carefully controlled and recorded.

The bets are taken by the writers. Each writer is located in a station similar to a keno writer's location. The customer indicates the choice of bet and gives the writer money. The writer then fills out a three-part form indicating the nature of the bet, the amount of the bet, details such as win, place, or show, and other important information. The dispensing machine issues the ticket. The original is retained by the sports book, the first copy is given to the customer, and the second copy is retained in the machine, which is under lock and key. This third copy is a numeric sequence copy and is removed only by personnel from the accounting department.

The original of the ticket is kept by the sports book as evidence of the transaction. The tickets are periodically gathered by the supervisor and are sorted and filed according to the specific event. This sorting is also accompanied by a tabulation by the supervisor of the amount of money being bet on a particular event and serves as the basis for possible adjustment of the line if necessary.

Sports Book Payoff

Once the event has been concluded, the winner of the bet can be determined. The supervisor sorts through the tickets for that event from the file. Winning tickets are separated from losing ones and are priced so that the cashier knows at a glance how much to pay out.

The bettor presents his or her copy of the ticket to a central sports and race book cashier for payment. There is only one cashier in a sports book to pay bets, while there may be many writers to take the money from the bettor.

Upon presentation for payment, the cashier matches the copy submitted by the customer with the original ticket retained by the race and sports book. If all items agree, the bet is paid. This is the major control point in the sports book. Occasionally, a bet is presented long after the actual event has taken place. Various casinos have differing policies about the redemption of these bets and post them prominently in the sports and race book areas. In general, if a casino keeps the bet open for a period of time, there are procedures for the retention of the sleepers in a file for the specified amount of time.

Cash Handling and Controls

With the situation of many writers and only one cashier, there is often the need for additional amounts of cash to pay off the winners. If a fill is needed by the sports book cashier, it can be accomplished in several ways. The most straightforward is to provide a fill from the main casino cashier in the amount of currency needed. In this case, a request for fill is prepared, and the standard fill procedures are used. Appropriate signatures of all parties and the ultimate retention of the fill slip by the sports book cashier are evidence of the additional funds supplied. The main cashier clears the fill slip back to the vault and the count activity where it is considered in the determination of the sports book win for the shift and the day.

A second method of filling the sports book cashier is to transfer the necessary funds internally within the sports book, from the writer's cash drawers to the cashier's drawer. In this case, the transfer slip is completed by the sports book supervisor, with the writer, the cashier, and the supervisor all signing the transfer. One copy goes in the drawer of the writer to account for that turn-in amount, and the other goes in the cashier's drawer. The copy is retained by the supervisor and is sent to the accounting department.

Revenue Accounting

At the end of the shift, the respective writer banks are counted and turned in to the main casino cashier. The cashier also completes the same process. The amounts turned in are adjusted by any fills from the cashier, and the net amount of turn-in is calculated.

For the day's activity, the sports book turns in to the accounting department several types of documents. The first is the amount of write for the day, which is divided into amounts bet on events that took place that day and events that are to take place in the future. The total write, therefore, consists of two parts: earned revenue and deferred revenue. Bets on future events are transferred out of the deferred category and into the active revenue on the day of the event.

The accounting department reconciles the turn-in summary with its copies of the write for the day to determine the accuracy of the accounting.

Payoff transactions are summarized with the cashier turn-in. At this time, accounting verifies the propriety of all payoffs by comparing the details on the two matched copies of the original betting document. The betting documents are sorted and separated by the event to which the bet applied.

If a payoff transaction was for a previously unclaimed bet, the two copies are stapled together and sent to accounting. If the sports book copy of a ticket cannot be found, this is noted on the bettor's copy, and only a single copy is sent to the accounting department. The department then checks the second copy against the bettor's copy to verify the correctness of the payoff.

Detailed records are kept of the summary activities, particularly the status of various deferred items. The total sleepers cashed, the total future bets made, and the total of previous bets placed on that day's events are three items that are carefully tracked on a day-to-day basis. This is the only way that the win for the day can be related to the actual profit that is made—when consideration is given to these other items of future benefit and liability.

Some casinos, when faced with ever-increasing volumes of sports and race betting, together with the complexities of betting on future events, are adopting computers or are seriously considering such a move. This seems natural, since the creation of the betting record would enable the management to assure better control over the volumes being bet on various events, and it would also allow more accurate control over the cashiering activities. The process would also greatly simplify the count and reconciliation procedure for the sports and race book.

♠ ♡ ♣ ◇　CHAPTER 8

Central Cashiering

The Role of Central Cashiering

Central cashiering could be described as the nerve center of the casino cash flow and the operational center of the casino itself. Having the cashier as the central point of the operation also creates an atmosphere of control over the casino operation. If the controls over the cage cashier are strong, then the controls over the entire casino operations are typically strong.

The cashier's cage and its related back room storage and working areas are known as the *vault* and the *cage*. The cashier's cage is a common point of reference in the casino and is usually located in a central and prominent location.

Physical Layout

For persons new to the casino, or to customers who have only a "public" exposure to the casino operation, the cashiering function appears to be restricted to operations similar to a bank teller or cashier. In reality, however, the role of central cashiering is much greater. This complex role is clarified by a good understanding of the physical layout of the central cashiering facility.

In most circumstances, the public service functions of the cashiering department are located in those areas of the casino where the public can be most easily and readily accommodated. Thus, functions such as check cashing, credit advances, and purchase or redemption of casino chips can be accomplished in a highly convenient location. These locations help provide customer service and encourage the patron to begin play as quickly and easily as possible. A convenient cashier location is both a short distance from the casino entrance and in close proximity to the slots and games.

With the diversification of cashiering locations for customer convenience, there is an increase in the problems related to both physical and accounting control over the monies as they move from the central storage locations to the various outlying cashier locations. The physical control over money moving through a casino during a busy period can be a special security problem.

In other casinos, the cashiering locations are physically centralized, with the backup or storage locations being located nearby or physically connected to the cashier's cage.

Distinctions: The Cashier, the Vault, and the Cage

The cashiering function usually refers to the activity of the cashier, while the physical location where the cashiering takes place is the cashier's cage. The vault, on the other hand, is a physical location usually separate from the cashiering cage. It is a highly restricted area where the public is never allowed; only specified casino employees are allowed to enter.

There may be a single vault in the case of a small casino or many vaults, each with its own separate function. Examples include a coin vault for coin storage, a counting area within the vault for the hard and/or soft count, a working vault area, and a long-term storage or backup vault area.

In some locations, the slot booths located throughout the casino can also function as minivaults, or minicashiers, and can have monies that should be controlled in the same manner as in a regular vault.

Cashiering Functions

There are four main functions of cashiering. The first is public service in changing money from large denominations to smaller denominations or supplying coins or chips for paper money. This is the true cashiering function and is similar to a bank cashier.

The second function of the cashier is the cashing of checks for customers. This function may be restricted according to a variety of rules or procedures. For example, some casinos handle the cashing of traveler's checks like the cashing of a personal check, while other casinos have separate procedures for the cashing of payroll checks, and still a third set of procedures for cashing of personal checks.

The cashing of payroll checks and traveler's checks is usually simple and straightforward and may or may not involve checking to see if the checks are on a "hot list" or are otherwise irregular. This type of check cashing is relatively low risk; if the company payroll is from the local trading area and is known, the check can probably be negotiated by the casino without further problem.

Since the cashing of personal checks may involve the assumption of additional business risks by the casino, there tend to be additional procedures for verifying a personal check prior to cashing. These procedures are discussed in detail in chapter 9 in the section dealing with credit accounting.

The third function of the cashier at the cage is the processing of various transactions to reimburse the gaming tables for the chips that they need to conduct their gaming business. The table fills (chips transferred to the tables) and the table credits (chips transferred to the cage) are handled through the casino cashier. In small casinos, these transactions are handled by a single cashiering location and can be treated as a part of the overall cashiering responsibilities. However, in larger casinos where the number of games is larger—or the volume of public cashiering is such as to impede the flow of chips to the tables—a separate area or separate table cashier is established. In this situation, an area is set aside for table transactions. This also simplifies the accounting and control for the cashier since there should be no coins or currency in the table cashier area—only chips and tokens.

The fourth and final function of the cashier is casino credit extension. This process is often handled by the cashier, again as a part of the regular cashiering responsibilities. The credit extension responsibility at the cashier's cage is substantial and is usually vested with a senior casino executive; the cashier's role is merely to issue the proper chips or to conduct other credit paperwork at the request of the credit manager.

Depending upon the volume of the other cashiering transactions and the nature of the credit extension policies, there may be a separate credit cashier who has responsibility for: 1. the issuance of new credit and chips, and 2. the redemption of chips or other instruments that are issued for credit. Again, if the credit play in the casino is an important part of the casino operation and a part of the casino marketing, then the credit extension process may be centralized in one area where all credit decisions are made. The cashiering function from that point onward would merely be to issue chips or tokens based on the unused but approved credit limit for that individual. In this situation, the credit process becomes much the same as the public cashiering or check-cashing functions described earlier.

Accounting for Cashiering Activities

The primary accounting responsibility for the cashiering function is control over the amount of funds assigned to the cashier. This responsibility is reflected both individually within each cashier's drawer or working change fund, and for the amount of funds assigned to the cashiering location in total. The cashier accounting usually begins with the initial establishment of an imprest balance at the cashier. This balance is the amount that the cashier is responsible for and is regarded as a part of the overall casino bankroll. The cashier bankroll amount for control purposes includes the amount of both chips and tokens for which the cashier is responsible.

Another responsibility of the cashier is revenue clearing, which is particularly important in a small casino. The cashier gives out monies or takes in monies from the table games. These issues and redemptions must be cleared back to the count rooms so that these transactions can be considered in the computation of the win or loss on the gaming operations and the individual games. Thus, there is a substantial amount of revenue clearing that must take place in the cashier's cage at the end of the shift when the net transactions are transferred or "sold" back to the count room by the cashier.

A problem that must be considered is the physical flow of money within the cashier and vault. Checks from patrons must be transferred to the banks and cleared through the commercial banking system. In addition, there must be sufficient cash kept on hand for operations. Thus, the checks on hand at the end of a shift must be cleared to the vault where the bank deposit is prepared. Likewise, the cash deposited in the drop boxes must find its way back to the cashier to be recycled. These results are usually achieved by having the cash contents of the drop boxes sold back to the cashier in exchange for the amount of checks transferred from the cashier to the vault cashier. The excess cash is then deposited along with the checks in the bank account.

The situation is very similar with coin transfers from the count rooms. The coin is never deposited in the bank, but rather is sold to various cashiers or coin booths in exchange for the equivalent amount of cash. The cash is then added to the cashier's account in order to balance the checks cashed or deposited in the bank.

Accounting for the Vault Operation

The principal accounting operations of the vault are concerned with the safekeeping and custody aspects of the vault, and the role of the vault as a revenue repository following the completion of the count procedures for both the games and the slot machines.

The vault also operates on an imprest balance basis, which allows the shift-by-shift checkout or verification of money on hand. The amount of vault accountability consists of the total of coin, cash, chips, and tokens. The amount on hand is temporarily increased by transfers from the slot and table count results, decreased by the outflow to the cashiers for fill and credit slips, and finally decreased by the deposit to the bank of the win for the day.

Vault operations must also take into account the physical custody of various items such as foreign chips (which are being held temporarily pending exchange with other casinos), foreign currency pending exchange with the banks, or other odds and ends such as mutilated or foreign coins. Control of these items in the vault is maintained at their face value for ease of counting.

As this discussion shows, the functions of the cashier and vault both demand a high degree of accuracy and attention to detail. In addition, a cashier must be skilled in dealing with the public. For these reasons, special care should be taken in selection of cashiers. Training as a bank clerk or teller and an attitude of attention to detail and controls have proven to be good background experience for casino cashiers.

Other Cashiering Functions

Other functions of the cashiers are enumerated below. They include a diverse set of responsibilities:

1. Information and validation—providing information of a general nature to casino patrons, including such things as validating free parking tickets.

2. Redemption center—acting as a redemption center for various promotional items, including free nickels and presents, or exchanging types of coupons.

3. Control point—acting as a turn-in point for other cash items such as bar, restaurant, poker, or keno banks.

4. Safekeeping—serving as a safekeeping or safe deposit box location for both casino and hotel guests.

Function of the Vault

The central vault (or in New Jersey the main bank) is the part of the cashiering function that serves as the backup or secure storage for various cash items in the casino.

The principal characteristic of the vault is its location, away from the general public and subject to extremely tight security. Access to the vault area is generally very limited for both security and administrative control. Only certain people such as vault count personnel are allowed in the area. To prevent the problem of possible skimming, senior executives are generally not allowed in the vault area. In addition, those persons in the count area of the vault are subject to special procedural and administrative controls—for example, not being allowed to bring personal items such as purses or tote bags into the vault or to wear clothing that might easily conceal the theft of items from the vault.

The vault also has the primary custody of the casino bankroll. The bankroll is the working stock of money that is needed for operation. The amount of the bankroll may vary widely. Generally, the only time the bankroll becomes critical is during heavy play when the casino needs enough money to meet the demands of heavy check cashing or heavy credit play, or when a regulatory audit is being conducted. In these cases, the total amount of money on hand must be carefully accounted for. The amount of bankroll is considered the minimum amount of money that the casino should have on hand to operate. The minimum bankroll amount is determined during licensing, when the regulatory agencies must satisfy themselves that the casino operator has enough money to conduct operations.

Custody of Tokens

The use of gaming tokens in a casino presents an unusual accounting and control problem. The control of the tokens and gaming chips has three significant parts.

First, the tokens and chips must be accounted for inside the casino as if they were money, for in gaming and other related activities they are as good as money. The recent concern of the U.S. Treasury Department about the proliferation of a second currency in Nevada has led to a reduced acceptability of tokens and chips for purposes other than gaming, even within the casino. Also, the willingness of casinos to cash chips from other casinos has been reduced, unless they are played on the games or played in slot machines. These limitations are based on both the unwillingness of the casinos to participate in the possible redemption of stolen casino chips (which, after being stolen, have to be converted to cash), and a positive desire not to offend the U.S. Treasury Department, which might declare the chips and tokens illegal.

The second aspect of chip and token control is that it begins at the date the chips and tokens are ordered from the various casino equipment suppliers. The total amount of chips and tokens purchased must be recorded and must be kept up to date with subsequent purchases or disposals.

The third aspect of chip and token control is that those chips and tokens that are outstanding in the hands of the general public or other casinos are subject to redemption and must be accounted for as a liability for balance sheet purposes.

The casino is liable under most circumstances to redeem the chips at face value. In fact, many casinos pride themselves on the fact that they will redeem old casino chips without penalty. For example, Harolds Club in Reno redeems its old chips and immediately places them in its museum collection.

At certain times, the chips may be canceled. This is usually the practice when the casino is closed or if there is a change in ownership. The new owners or operator do not want to take responsibility for the control or lack of control over chips by the prior owners or operators. The obligation to redeem casino chips is usually not assumed by new purchasers of the casino. In these circumstances, notices are usually placed in the casino and in the newspapers to advertise the fact that chips will no longer be redeemed after a certain date. Such a notice is shown in figure 8-1, which indicates the general terms and conditions under which the chips will be accepted, prior to the name change at a casino.

The problem of actual physical disposal of the gaming chips can give rise to some unusual solutions. The chips are made of hard clay and are very difficult to destroy or dispose of. They cannot be shredded like paper and cannot simply be thrown in the garbage. Harrah's used a unique method of burying them in the concrete of the tenth floor of its new parking garage floor. Other casinos have smashed the chips prior to having them taken to a refuse burial site.

Notice:

After Jan. 14, 1987,
Bally's Reno
will no longer redeem
MGM Grand Hotel
gaming chips or tokens.

BALLYS

2500 East Second Street
702-789-2000

Fig. 8-1. Bally's token notice.

Count Rooms

Count rooms have a layout designed for two principal purposes: to ease the physical process of counting very large quantities of money and to assure the maximum amount of security over the money being counted.[1]

The physical layout usually includes some storage facility for the game drop boxes that have been removed after each shift from the various table games during the previous day. This means that there are three sets of drop boxes present, one for each shift. At the time the count is to take place, the necessary keys are checked out from the cashier, a key log is signed, and the keys are taken to the count room together with all necessary forms. Once the count has begun, there is usually no interruption, and no one on the count team is allowed to leave the area until the count is finished. The physical layout also includes a clear plastic or glass counting table that allows the security personnel, either personally or through closed-circuit TV monitor, to see that nothing improper is going on "under the table."

The counting activity usually proceeds in several major steps. The boxes are opened and the contents are emptied upon the table and separated into their functional types, such as paperwork, fill and credit slips, and currency. The currency is counted, and the fill and credit and currency amounts are entered on the count sheet. The currency is then recounted for accuracy and sorted and bundled into the various denominations for further counting and ease of handling. The bundling and recounting is usually assisted by physical bins that separate the currency by denominations, similar to a large cash register drawer with partitions. In addition, there is usually some form of writing surface with an adding machine used to record the results of the individual game count on the count and recap sheet.

The game count and recap sheet may be added up and the win determined by an adding machine, a small computer, or a computer terminal tied into a larger computer system. The use of computers eases the amount of work the count team must perform and eliminates some of the problems of human error in adding and reading the results of many games in a large casino. This process also improves the accuracy of subsequent data capture for accounting purposes by reducing the number of data entry items.

After all the counting activity is completed and the total amount of money is determined and counted, the count sheets are signed by the members of the count team; the money, together with the count sheets, is transferred to the vault. Here the results are entered on the daily activity of the vault as a transfer from the count room, and the various items such as fill and credit slips are reconciled.

The fill and credit activity from the cashier is reconciled with the fill and credit slips contained in the various game drop boxes and counted in the count room. Once all fill and credit slips are accounted for, and agreement between the cashier and the drop box copy is found, the net amount of the win per game is determined. The attention now turns to reconciling the turn-in amount from the cashier. The cashier's checks are exchanged for currency turned in by the count team to the vault. These transactions are usually evidenced by vault transfer slips showing the amount, the timing, and the parties responsible for the transaction. The excess currency and other items requiring special handling are then stored in the vault—as in the case of foreign chips—or the deposit is prepared by the vault cashier and taken to the bank.

The use of the daily bank deposit technique is favored because it gives the accounting a logical end point where the results of operations are independently verified by a third party. Over weekend periods, two to three deposits accumulate in the vault. These multiple deposits are then made on the next business day, and the bank records still indicate the separate daily deposits.

Other Special Vault Operations

The vault, as mentioned earlier, is the place where the drop boxes are stored pending the next day's count. It is necessary to have enough drop boxes and storage facilities to accommodate three sets of drop boxes. These drop boxes must be kept under lock and key at all times. This includes not only the times when the boxes are full and awaiting the count (to prevent anything being taken from the boxes) but also the times when the boxes are empty and awaiting use (to prevent anything being added to them).

There should also be a substantial physical separation of the vault and the count rooms from the public cashier areas. This is to ensure that there are no improper transactions between the point of public disbursement of the money—the cashier—and the point of first accounting for the revenue—the count room and vault.

There are two additional considerations in vault accounting. The first is that there should be some very secure storage for the money inventory that constitutes the backup bankroll. This is the safety stock of money as well as unused gaming chips and tokens that are held in secure storage. These items are not customarily counted each and every shift change, so a thief could take chips from boxes or currency from bundles without these items being immediately missed during the normal course of vault or cashier checkout.

Also, boxes of chips should be kept unopened and sealed if possible. This eliminates the necessity of examining the contents in detail and allows the count by box, thus speeding the casino audit and vault count procedures.

A final factor in the vault operation is the desirability of separating the vault functions according to the type of items being handled. There is commonly a separation among coin, currency, and chip vaults. The problem here is that the coin count and storage is physically demanding and requires special carts and machinery, as well as an extensive amount of physical space. Currency, on the other hand, can be stored fairly easily. But in some circumstances where large volumes of currency are being handled, there is a need for physical space for the specialized machinery used to count paper currency. It is common to have two separate vaults: one for coins, and one for currency, chips, and other items.

Cashiering Systems and Functions

The key concept of accounting control over the cashiering function is the use of various forms of accountability. That is, the cage and vault are charged with the responsibility for custody and maintaining balances in certain amounts. This accountability includes being responsible for currency, coin, chips, and tokens. The net amounts of received and paidout transactions of the cashier and the vault are taken into consideration when determining the new balance of the cashier or the vault.

There are two main systems of accounting for cashiers. The first is the imprest or static balance system, and the second is the utilization of a floating cage balance. Smaller casinos and small cages within larger casinos are ideally suited for the imprest balance system of control. Under this system, the balance in the cashier account must always be maintained at a fixed amount. If, for example, the cashier area is a slot change booth, then the balance in the slot booth may be set at $5,000. This balance is represented by coins of various denominations at the start of the shift and may include tokens for the slot machines as well. Upon assuming responsibility for the slot cage, the slot cashier counts all the coins and currency: the total should be $5,000. Then, during the course of the shift, various transactions result in selling coins in exchange for currency. In addition, payoffs for slot winnings may be made by the slot cashier. These transactions are evidenced by the various paidout slips.

At the end of the shift, the slot cashier tallies up all of the slot payout slips and other items that should be reimbursed and transfers or sells the items to the main cashier. In exchange, the slot booth receives either currency or coin, depending upon the needs of the cage. Thus, after reimbursing the slot cage, the balance should return to $5,000. If the slot paidouts are not cleared back to the main cashier, then the reconciliation of the slot bank consists of some cash, some coin, plus the aggregate amount of the paidouts, which again totals $5,000.

The disadvantage of the imprest balance system is that it is inflexible. If the needs of the cashier are heavier during the shift, the only method to reimburse the coin in the bank is to make a preliminary clearing of the slot paidouts and currency back to the main cashier or cage.

The second method, the floating cage, works in roughly the

same manner as the imprest system, but changes in the balance of the cage can be made from time to time to meet the anticipated needs of the cashier. Thus, a temporary increase in the cashier balance may be made early on Friday evening and be reduced during the day on Saturday, again increased Saturday night, and reduced on Sunday morning. These variations take place as temporary changes in the overall vault accountability, with the cashier portion increasing or decreasing as appropriate.

The floating system allows the greatest flexibility in providing adequate amounts of money and coin on hand for the cashier in order to provide maximum customer service. It also forces a more careful accounting by the cashier, since the amount of effective balance in the cashier's cage is not always known or can vary from time to time. This makes cheating or other manipulation difficult.

Either of these two methods could be used for vaults. If the imprest system is used, then the amount transferred to the bank at the end of the day brings the balance in the vault back to the imprest balance.

In general, smaller casinos use the imprest balance system, while the volume of transactions coupled with the irregularity of transactions has led to the use of floating systems in most larger casinos.

Cashier Balance Procedures

At the beginning of the shift, the oncoming cashier counts the balances in the cashier area. The off-going cashier has usually counted the area prior to the arrival of the new cashier and has written down the amounts on a count sheet. The second count assures the propriety of the amounts; the oncoming cashier indicates agreement and accepts responsibility for the amount by signing the checkout sheet. To avoid an interruption of service to the customers during the shift change, there are usually two drawers used by the cashiers. The first drawer is closed out and counted and then locked until the oncoming cashier has counted it. During the period when the oncoming cashier is counting the cage area, the off-going cashier is working out of a second small drawer. When the primary cashier area and the first drawer are finished being counted, then the second small drawer is counted, and the transfer is completed to the new cashier.

The end-of-shift count sheet is then signed, usually in ink for

MAIN CASHIER CHECKOUT

DATE _____

ONCOMING CASHIER _____
(Signature)

GOING OFF CASHIER _____
(Signature)

SHIFT _____

CURRENCY BUNDLED - $50 & $100			CHECKS		
20					
10					
5					
2					
1					
CURRENCY IN DRAWER $50 & $100					
20					
10					
5					
2					
1					
COIN HALVES			COUPONS		
FULL CANS QUARTERS			CASH REFUNDS		
LONG DIMES					
LONG NICKELS					
SHORT NICKELS					
PENNIES					
COIN QUARTERS					
PARTIAL CANS LONG DIMES					
LONG NICKELS			FILLS - DAY		
SHORT NICKELS			SWING		
PENNIES			GRAVEYARD		
SILVER DOLLARS RACKED			MACHINE P.O.		
SILVER DOLLARS BAGGED			BALLY P.O.		
LOOSE COIN IN DRAWER			MISC. P.O.		
CHIPS AND TOKENS $25					
$ 5			LATE ITEMS		
$ 1			VAULT FILL		
CUPS					
BAGGED COIN					
FOREIGN CHIPS			CAGE VARIATION		
FOREIGN CURRENCY & COIN			SUBTOTAL		
PAIDOUTS					
I.O.U.'S			CAGE BANKROLL		
CAGE BANK					
CHANGE BANKS			SHIFT VARIATION		
RESTAURANT BANKS					
BAR BANKS					

Fig. 8-2. Main cashier checkout.

a permanent record, and the off-going cashier leaves the area. Figure 8-2 shows a sample of the cashier checkout sheet.

Cashier accountability includes cash, currency, chips, and tokens. Also included in the count are all paidouts, all fill and credit slips, and all other items that may affect the balance in the cashier's cage.

Periodically, the cage cashier is reimbursed for the amount of various items that are contained in the cage. This includes the clearing of all fill and credit slips back to the vault, where they are verified and checked back to the copies of the fills and credits that are removed from the game drop boxes. All promotional and other paidout items are also cleared. These are exchanged with the vault for the necessary cash, coin, or chips. Typically, unless the balances in the cashier's working bank are getting low, the transfer is accomplished just prior to the end of the shift. Thus, the oncoming cashier is counting coins and currency and not many other items of paper. This also assures that any errors or irregularities can be traced back to the appropriate individual and that the mistakes of one cashier cannot be transferred to another cashier, either deliberately or inadvertently.

Cashier Recording of Fills and Credits

The cashier is responsible for keeping track of one side of the fill and credit activity that takes place between the cage and a variety of places. The most common destination is the table games, but the cashier could also be responsible for reimbursing or filling the keno game or issuing funds to various bar and restaurant banks as well. In the nongaming situation, the addition of funds to the bank is accomplished with an ordinary paidout document. However, if a casino game such as 21, craps, or keno is filled, then the transaction is processed differently. The fill or credit is completed as described in chapter 6. In addition, the cashier notes the transaction on a separate record. This summary record is usually called the *stiff sheet* and is used to record the fill (money given to a game) and credit (money taken back from a game) to various tables. The stiff sheet is totaled at the end of the shift and gives a quick recap during the shift of the amount and frequency of these transactions, as well as which tables are involved. This alone can be an effective control device, since the pit boss or other supervisory personnel can tell by glancing at the stiff sheet what amount has been necessary to keep the games going (if they are losing) and what has been taken off the games (if they are winning). The copies of the fill and credit are attached to the stiff sheet and are thus kept track of in a reasonable manner. The stiff sheet is cleared back to the

DATE _____   SHIFT _____

CRAP 1		CRAP 2		CRAP 3		CHEMIN DE FER	
FILLS	CREDITS	FILLS	CREDITS	FILLS	CREDITS	FILLS	CREDITS

TWENTY ONE 1		TWENTY ONE 2		TWENTY ONE 3		TWENTY ONE 4	
FILLS	CREDITS	FILLS	CREDITS	FILLS	CREDITS	FILLS	CREDITS

TWENTY ONE 5		TWENTY ONE 6		TWENTY ONE 7		TWENTY ONE 8	
FILLS	CREDITS	FILLS	CREDITS	FILLS	CREDITS	FILLS	CREDITS

TWENTY ONE 9		TWENTY ONE 10					
FILLS	CREDITS	FILLS	CREDITS				

WHEEL 1		WHEEL 2					
FILLS	CREDITS	FILLS	CREDITS				

Fig. 8-3. Stiff sheet.

vault on a shift basis. Figure 8-3 shows a typical stiff sheet.

Other frequent paidout transactions are also recapped in a similar manner to assure both that the accounting for these items can be accomplished in an expeditious manner and that the controls over the amounts have been maintained. Checks cashed may also be posted to a summary record, including individual customer records, to assure that a customer does not cash more checks than his or her limit might allow. The cashier might also prepare a summary list of checks by bank routing number to assist the preparation of the bank deposit by the vault cashier.

Vault Systems and Functions

The key to the operation of the vault is the extensive physical security that this money storage area is subjected to. The weakest link in the vault system is the paidouts. These items represent evidence that money has gone out of the system, either to a customer or to a game. As long as transactions are just a cash-to-cash transfer, such as customers' checks in exchange for currency or chips, then the problems are few. However, there are many cases where money paidout slips have been processed by the cashier or the vault cashier in order to cover thefts. Two procedures are used to prevent this possibility. The first is to match all fill and credit slips to the tables or games with the copies that are taken from the drop boxes during the count procedures. The second method is to make arrangements to assure that the drop boxes are secured in some area and that the contents cannot be tampered with once they leave the table area. Other paidouts must be manually scrutinized to verify the accuracy of the amount paid.

Vault Transfers

The transfers from the vault to another working area of the casino are a critical aspect of internal control. In most of the areas, the transfers are merely cash-for-cash transactions, evidenced by some form of accounting control document created at the time of the transfer and signed and acknowledged by the persons doing the transfer. Figure 8-4 shows a sample vault transfer document.

Transfers from the coin vault to the cashier are more difficult to understand. First, it is critical that the coins do not ever leave the casino physically. (When the theft of $7 million in slot revenue was first uncovered at the Stardust Hotel, it was considered to be physically impossible, since the theft of that amount of money would be equivalent to stealing truckloads of coins. As indicated below, there is no necessity of moving the coins—the mere translation of the coins into currency would accommodate the theft.)

The transactions between the coin vault and the cashier are accomplished in the following manner. Once the total amount of the coin wrap and count has been determined, the amount is recorded as the win of the particular time period. As explained

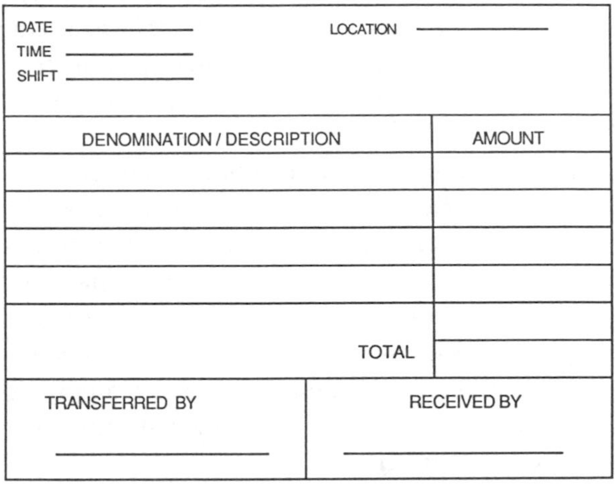

DATE
TIME
SHIFT
LOCATION

DENOMINATION / DESCRIPTION	AMOUNT
TOTAL	

TRANSFERRED BY	RECEIVED BY

Fig. 8-4. Vault transfer.

above, the drop frequency could be weekly, biweekly, or daily. Once the actual amount of the coins is determined by the count procedures, the coins are physically transferred to the custody of the coin vault or, if there is not a separate coin vault, to the central vault. At this point, the vault takes both accounting and physical control over the coin. The amount of the coin win is entered into the deposit activity for that day, the bank deposit is prepared, and the necessary statistical information is forwarded to accounting and data-processing departments.

In order to avoid the physical transfer of coins to the bank, the coins are stored in the vault, and the win amount is made up of currency or checks already in the vault or transferred from the cashier. The coins are then either stored in the vault or, upon demand, transferred to the various slot change booths.

The transfer from the vault to the cashier and from the cashier to the slot booth is recorded. Accompanying the physical transfer is usually a vault transfer slip. This is merely a tracing document that indicates the items, the amount, the denomination, and the parties responsible for the transfer. The document is then recorded on a memo basis for both the vault and the cashier. The transfer is recorded on both sets of records, and the imprest balance of both records is maintained.

The actual physical transfer of the coins is accomplished at the same time. The cash on hand and vault accountability are reduced by the coin amount transferred, and the cash (currency) accountability is increased. The currency to coin transfer maintains the balance in accountability of the vault. The accountability of the cashier is maintained by reducing the currency (cash) accountability of the cashier and increasing the coin accountability.

In the Stardust slot theft situation, the amount of coin transferred to the slot booths was understated. This understatement was possible because the coins were underweighed to determine the count. When the coins were resold, the extra cash was deposited into a special place where $100 bills were periodically removed by a casino executive. Thus, the balance was maintained, and the slot coin theft was converted into currency that could be more readily removed from the casino.[2]

Reconciliation of Fill Slips

One of the key steps in the process of verifying the integrity of the cashier and the vault process is reconciliation of the fill and credit slips.

The fill slips are the evidence of the most common type of payout made by the cashier and are also an integral part of the determination of the game performance—the game win or loss. The correct physical handling of the fill slips is important. The fill slip copies, together with the summary stiff sheet, are usually cleared from the cashier to the vault at the end of the shift or may occasionally be held in the cashier's area and included as an item on the cashier accountability report. When the fill slips are transferred to the vault, the same fill slips constitute a paidout item for the vault until they have been integrated with the game revenue computation.

Vault processing of the fill slips includes the following steps:

1. The copies of the fill slips transferred from the cashier to the vault are matched against the fill slips that are removed from the table game drop boxes. They are examined and matched for:

    a. Numeric sequence.

    b. Agreement of date, time, shift, and other data.

    c. Amount of fill or credit.

    d. Verification that all proper signatures are on all appropriate copies (the cashier copy should have the security runner signature, but only the drop box copy should have the pit supervisor and dealer or boxman signatures).

e. Agreement with all elements on a request for fill.

2. The fill slips are then included in the computation of the game win or loss for the shift and the day. The win or loss is computed for the entire day. The net amount of win is determined to be the net addition to the vault amount.

The win for the day is included as a vault increase. This increase is then decreased by the amount of the deposit to the bank. Once again, the balance in the vault is restored to the imprest balance amount.

There is an additional reconciliation step that takes place within the fill slip procedures: verification that the third copy— locked in the machine—is in agreement with the other two copies of the fill slip that are eventually transferred to the accounting department together with the bank deposit slip. This is to assure the integrity of the revenue reporting system.

Vault Security

The large volume of cash, chips, and currency handled by the vault requires that the area be physically very secure. There are also additional security procedures:

1. Limiting the access to the vault storage areas to certain key vault personnel during each shift.

2. Having the count areas in the casino separate from the vault working and storage areas, keeping in mind that the areas cannot be widely separated since there is a security and physical problem associated with moving money or coin over long distances.

3. Having firm arrangements regarding standardized count procedures, count room organization, and standards of employment and conduct of count personnel.

Examples of special vault security include the maintenance of closed-circuit video or one-way mirror observation areas, the use of glass partitions in the vault itself, and the extensive use of unannounced inspections and counts by auditors and security personnel. Other desirable procedures include the periodic counting and balancing of the vault areas, including periodic count of the secure long-term storage areas.

Personnel controls over the vault operation include limiting access to the vault to only three or four persons outside of the vault personnel. Senior executives are definitely not included in this group. Other controls also include the use of counting personnel who are not associated with the casino operations in any way.

Bank Deposits

The deposit to the bank is the final accounting step in the flow of funds in the casino. The bank deposit is prepared in order to document the amount either won or lost by the casino in the accounting period—usually a day. The bank deposit is prepared by the vault cashier after the compilation and verification of the win or loss for the day.

The bank deposit is usually transmitted to the bank physically by a representative of the accounting department accompanied by a security guard. The deposit is receipted by the bank (an independent third party), and the deposit slip is returned to the accounting department where the win is recorded in the general books of account.

The bank deposit serves as an ultimate control over the integrity of the revenue reporting process. It allows the casino to be sure that no diversion of funds could occur between the count room and the final deposit of the funds. If the deposit agrees with the results of the count activity and all other areas are in balance, then the consistency and integrity of the accounting system are assured.

Temporary Vault Increases

At certain times, and as a result of certain transactions, the vault and the cashier may experience temporary increases in the amount of the vault or cashier balances. These temporary increases usually occur if a large payoff of a keno ticket or slot jackpot takes place. Under these circumstances, the general accounting office prepares a check for the amount of the large special payoff. This check is then transferred to the vault as a temporary increase in the vault accountability. The vault transfers the check to the cashier, as a special short-term item. The cash or check is given to the customer in exchange for the properly completed documentation of the paidout—either the keno win ticket or a slot paidout document. Then the paidout is transferred back to the vault, and the cashier's accountability is reduced. The slot or keno win is included in the win or loss for the day, and the bank deposit is adjusted accordingly. At the end of the count process, the paid out item has been properly considered and has been accounted for in the daily overall win or loss of the casino, and the temporary increase to the vault has also been accounted for.

CHAPTER 9

Credit Accounting

Introduction

A recognition of the role that credit extension plays in casino operations is important in developing a proper understanding and appreciation of the necessary internal controls and procedures for credit accounting.

The availability of casino credit is a crucial element of a casino's marketing and operating strategy. While the importance of credit is indisputable, the necessity of maintaining controls over the credit procedures is equally important. This chapter discusses the accounting and procedural controls over casino credit.[1]

Credit in the casino has been most commonly called *marker credit*. Other minor forms of credit include deposits in advance of playing in the casino, the use of casino scrip or other restricted types of casino chips, and unlimited or generally loose check-cashing policies.

Credit Control and Abuses

The need to control the losses incurred, as well as to prevent improper writeoff or the use of credit extension as a method to steal from the casino, has given credit control a very large and important role in modern casino operations.

The actual process of credit extension and the skills and talents necessary to evaluate casino credit are more properly discussed elsewhere.[2] The present concern is the accounting and financially related controls over credit.

Credit extension in a casino is essential to effective marketing. The availability of credit, as in traditional retail or other consumer markets, results in more widespread purchase or consumption of the product. Thus, the availability of credit invariably results in higher betting activity on the part of casino customers.

There are several interesting trends in casino credit today. The most significant is the advent of the New Jersey rules, whereby credit extension can be accomplished only in the presence of a signed negotiable instrument—a check, which can only be held for a very short period of time.[3] This trend has also been noticed in Nevada, where the casino credit instrument—the marker—has become virtually a counter check.

Credit Personnel

The credit manager of the casino is responsible for all credit granting and collection. In some smaller casinos, senior management or other casino personnel may be involved in the process. In this case, they perform these credit tasks in addition to their other regular managerial activities. Casino hosts, pit personnel, and the owners or senior management also participate in credit activities.

The prudent management procedure is to vest control over all aspects of the credit function in one person.[4] This responsibility includes the accounting and supervision of the issuance of credit, the evaluation of the credit-worthiness of the customer, and the final collection of the debt. The only functions that should be organizationally separate for good accounting and internal control are the actual custody of the casino markers themselves, and the processing of the payments received on the markers.

A related area that often involves the granting of casino credit is the *junket*,[5] a tour conducted to the casino primarily for the purpose of gambling. Junkets typically are arranged for good gambling customers: transportation, food, and rooms are provided free of charge. This special treatment is in exchange for the customer spending a relatively large amount in gaming activities. Controls over the granting of junket credit—and collection afterward—are especially critical because of the large volume of credit that even a small and limited-term junket can generate, coupled with a long-distance credit collection problem.

Credit Procedures

The credit-granting and control procedures can be divided into four main steps:
1. Credit Investigation and Approval.
2. Cashier Credit Issuance.

3. Table Credit Issuance.
4. Payment and Collection Administration.

Credit Investigation and Approval

The process of granting credit can be divided into two distinct phases: granting credit to new customers and granting credit to established customers. Some of the more detailed procedures associated with granting credit to new customers should periodically be repeated for established customers to assure that good controls are maintained over the changes in credit-worthiness.

The credit approval process is initiated when the customer asks for credit. The basic procedure is to have the customer fill out a credit application and bank reference form. The application also asks for the estimated amount that the customer would like to have for credit extension purposes. A limit of a certain amount of credit per day or per visit to the casino is usually suggested to the customer. This control is intended to prevent the casino from extending more credit than it wants to or than the customer has requested. Another reason for this limit is to allow cooler heads to prevail during a period when the customer may wish additional credit. If the customer is given additional unauthorized credit during a losing streak and the losses increase, the customer is frequently upset that more than the basic amount was extended. If the limit is exceeded, the casino may have a difficult time collecting the full amount.

After the credit application has been completed and the authorization has been secured to have the casino contact the customer's bank (usually to confirm the amount of money flowing through the customer's account), a first-time courtesy credit amount may be extended or else the customer is asked to wait until the next business day for verification of credit.

Because of the 24-hour nature of the gaming business in Nevada and the widespread availability of credit privileges, several services have developed that allow the verification of credit at any time of day or night. This independent service is provided by Central Credit, Inc., which is a private credit reporting facility for the gaming industry only. It has records on customers of all casinos, and the information is generally shared throughout the credit reporting process. If a customer is known to Central Credit, and it is able to provide a positive credit history, then the credit can be extended fairly quickly. If there is no casino credit history, then the conservative procedure is to grant a nominal amount of credit and then to verify the credit directly with traditional sources such as lending institutions and banks on the next business day.

Issuance of Credit

Once the credit has been approved, issuance of the credit is the next step. The recording of the credit issuance at the cashier's cage is fairly simple: usually the customer signs a document resembling a check or a marker that is given in exchange for casino chips. The extension of credit at the table is somewhat more complex.

There is widespread discussion of the most appropriate payment in exchange for the marker. Some clubs give ordinary casino chips; some give unique chips that cannot be readily exchanged for cash. Other casinos issue special scriplike coupons in exchange for casino credit. The reason for the issuance of these special types of "money" to the credit customers is to avoid an obvious problem where the casino customer is granted credit, gets the chips, plays very little, then converts the remaining chips back into cash and departs from the casino with the money. The customer may then refuse to pay the marker debt and has essentially stolen the amount of the marker—in cash—from the casino. A variation of that process is that the customer merely pockets the chips, moves to another casino, and cashes the chips—away from the scrutiny of the issuing casino.

The issuance of credit at the cashier's cage may be accomplished through the regular cashier or, in some cases, may be handled through a special cashier whose responsibility is only to handle various credit transactions.

The documents created by the issuance of the marker by the cashier include the original copy of the marker, which becomes a negotiable instrument (a check) with the addition of the magnetic ink coding on the bottom, and a second and possibly third copy, which are retained by the cashier in order to provide a record of the paidout amount. This enables the cashier to maintain the proper balance in the cash accountability account. This copy is typically detached from the marker itself immediately after issuance, and is retained in the cashier's cage.

Other copies of the marker include a copy used to record when and if the repayment is made and the numeric record copy. The numeric copy is typically separated from the original at the time the marker is issued and is retained in a numeric control file.

The recording of the issuance of the marker by the cashier is somewhat simpler than issuance at the table, since the money is taken out in a true cashiering situation and the addition or reduction of the money does not affect game win statistics.

An operational benefit is that the casino credit can be more easily controlled through a central location that issues all the credit. (If the credit is issued at the tables, the customer can move from table to table or from pit to pit and gain more credit in total than should be allowed, if the communication between the pits is poor.) However, restricting the credit issuance in this way can have a negative impact on convenience to the customer and the smoothness of the game flow in the pit.

A second key step that the cashier should accomplish, besides basic identification, is to assure that the customer to whom the credit is being extended is indeed the person who is qualified for the credit. The third step is to record in some manner the amount of credit extended. This type of record is essential to assure that the cumulative amount of the credit does not exceed the amount authorized and that the records of the borrowing transactions have been made for future reference. This also serves to create a record of the borrowing transactions, which can be vital to the evaluations and extension of future credit amounts. The recording of the credit extension may be a manual record, usually on the individual's record sheet, or may be performed by a modified accounts receivable system within a computerized system.

The issuance of credit to a customer may also be recorded on a master sheet that serves to summarize the credit transactions for a particular shift. This type of record is a parallel to the fill and credit summary that the cashier prepares for other casino operations when money is transferred to the tables. This master credit sheet acts as a quick and convenient summary of credit activity during the day and can be used by the casino management to verify the activity, to whom the credit is being extended, and with what frequency.

Where the volume of credit extension is expected to be very substantial, such as in the case of large junkets arriving at the casino, it is customary to provide for preauthorization of the junket credit. In this case, all that might be required is the signature of the customer on forms that are already filled out, with the amounts of chips set aside, ready to be picked up.

Preauthorization procedures also help to build the goodwill of hotel guests or other visitors to the casino.

From an accounting standpoint, the issuing of credit by the cashier is a fairly simple process of recording the paidout amount and creating a memo record of the total outstanding credit at any time.

The cashier must also be mindful of the situation where the previously extended credit together with a new request may exceed the limit on the customer's account or be close to that limit. In this case, the cashier should bring the matter to the attention of the relevant credit person who decides whether to extend additional credit or to refuse the credit. The cashier's prime responsibility is to identify the situation and to abide by the rules specified.

Credit Rules   The basic credit rules of the casino, including the procedure for handling over-limit customers, must be decided on initially and specified in writing very carefully. The reasons for this care are twofold. The first is that the casino must have credit policies specified in some detail. This allows the management to make decisions on granting credit that avoid either indiscriminately loose credit that would create collection problems or restrictively tight credit that would limit the effectiveness of the casino marketing policy.

The second reason for these controls is that the regulatory authorities insist that credit extended in violation of the casino's own established policies is not allowed as a deduction from the gross gaming revenue and is therefore subject to tax. The improper extension of credit has been limited somewhat by applying this type of penalty taxation.

Ideal Credit Marker Systems   The basic operating goal for the ideal marker control system would be ease of issuance of the credit instrument as well as ease of repayment. In addition, the system should have the ability to record the transactions of issuance and repayment, provide status reports for the various credit customers, and account for full or partial repayment.

The system should also have the ability to identify the impact of the credit extension on the games accounting and should assure that no distortions result from the issuance of credit or the repayment of credit on the table.

In addition, the system should ensure the smooth paperwork flow from pit to pit as the credit customer moves from one area to another. Finally, there should be a smooth flow of the credit instrument from the pit to the cage. Typical controls over the casino credit instruments should include:

1. Providing numeric control over all markers issued.

2. Preventing deliberate or inadvertent destruction of the credit instrument.

3. Ensuring accurate and complete recording of the marker and summary update information.

4. Controlling the overall credit extension procedures and recording the total amount of dollars extended in casino credit.

5. Assuring proper custody over individual customer subsidiary ledger accounts and accurate summarization of the total amounts of casino credit outstanding.

Care should be taken that all these controls are operating properly and that their costs are reasonable. The controls must be both effective and efficient.

Credit Extension at the Tables

A major difference in the handling of the credit recording and credit extension occurs when the location shifts from the cashier to the table game.

There are two major ways the credit extension is handled at the pit location. The first is to allow the extension of credit at the pit, but to have the accounting and record-keeping centralized at one location within the pit, such as the pit clerk's stand. The second method is to have the credit transactions handled entirely at the gaming table.

The main problem is accounting for the markers that are paid or repaid at the table. These credit extension transactions at the game are large cashiering transactions that can severely distort the results of the game operation, while the repayment of a marker at the pit game can make the game appear to be a large winner when this may not be the case. Also, the inclusion of the documents in the table game drop box tends to make the accounting for the game results—the win or loss—considerably more complex. It adds numerous paper items to the drop box that in turn can cause operational difficulties when the boxes are emptied and counted.

The communication between various pits and between the pit

and the cage can also be difficult and may result in erroneous credit extension or overextended credit when this is clearly not the intention of the casino.

The first step in credit extension at the table is the establishment of certain preissuance procedures for the casino. If the customer is going to be requesting the credit at the gaming tables, then the customer should be preauthorized to receive the credit.

In addition to preauthorization, the table inventories for games where credit is to be extended should be increased in anticipation of the greater volume of cashiering activity expected to take place on the table.

Finally, some clerical arrangements should be made in order to assure that there is timely completion of the credit requests at the tables and that the extension process is handled smoothly.

Credit Preauthorization   Before preauthorization takes place, the basic credit information has to be gathered, processed, and evaluated. If it is satisfactory, then a credit approval is made prior to the customer's request. There are two important additional steps to be taken to prevent credit problems.

1. Steps must be taken to assure that the person receiving the credit is the person for whom the credit has been approved.

2. Steps must be taken to control the extension of credit, including granting new credit only to those customers who have fully repaid previous credit extension.

A form of preauthorization might include the posting of "front money" by the casino customer. In this situation, the front money is played first; if the pattern of play and other operational aspects of the gaming activity appear proper, then the credit may be extended at that time.

Credit Extension Procedures   Typically, when a customer requests credit at the table, the request is transmitted by the dealer or boxman in charge of the game to a pit boss or floor supervisor. The floor person then verifies the propriety of the request by asking the pit bookkeeper if the customer, who is known or identified to the pit boss, has a line of credit authorized.

The customers who are expected to request credit are usually indicated in a master pit record book if they have preauthorized credit. Also, the amount of the total credit is indicated, and the credit previously extended is recorded. In this way, the pit boss can make the credit-granting decision very quickly, without keeping the customer waiting. If the customer's credit standing is not indicated in the pit clerk's records, or if the customer is over the limit, then it is the responsibility of the pit boss to refer the customer to the casino cage to discuss the limit with the credit manager or to establish or reopen a line of credit.

In some circumstances, if the customer is known to the casino and if there are no current problems, it may be possible to activate a credit record for a customer from the pit, with the pit clerk adding the new customer to the files of active credit players after receiving approval from the central credit cashier.

If the credit request is granted, then the pit boss authorizes the issuance of the credit at this point. The pit boss or floor person instructs the dealer on the table to give the customer the appropriate amount of chips. Marker buttons are usually used temporarily to indicate the amount of the chips advanced to the customer. The use of these marker or lamer buttons helps to speed the process of credit extension. The chips can be given to the customer immediately after the credit approval. The paperwork can then be completed, and the customer can sign the marker a short time later.

The floor person receives from the pit clerk a blank marker to which the following information is added:

1. Amount of the transaction.
2. Date and shift.
3. Table number.
4. Customer's name and other identifying information such as tour group or junket representative.
5. Customer's signature.

At the same time, the pit records are updated to indicate the customer's name and the amount of the transaction. The responsible floor person and pit clerk sign or initial the records. The master record is up to date with the credit information.

The marker is then given to the customer, who signs the document. The marker button is now removed, indicating that the formal credit extension is complete.

Control must be maintained over the lamer or marker buttons to ensure that they are only removed after the marker has been properly signed by the customer. If a marker button is removed before the marker is completed, the granting of credit may not be properly recorded. In general, only senior pit personnel are allowed to touch the marker buttons, and only marker buttons of a particular color, shape, or type are used for credit extension. In this way, control is exercised over this critical temporary period of credit.

The marker is then returned to the pit clerk, who examines it for completeness and accuracy, checking to assure that:

1. The marker is completed properly with the time and date stamped.

2. The amount of the marker is entered in the pit book as well as added to the game record.

3. The signature matches the credit application of the customer. This is accomplished in some casinos by showing the marker on a TV camera connected to the main credit cashier where the signature is compared to other credit records.

4. The issuance stub is removed from the marker and put into the locked box used to control the markers from that particular pit.

5. The marker is attached to a customer's ledger card or else filed in sequence by name in the pit.

The pit book, maintained by the pit bookkeeper, functions as an overall control over the total amount of credit extended to a customer, and the table game record ensures that the amount of credit issued or repaid to a particular table is properly recorded so that the table inventory fluctuations are later counted properly in computing the win on the table.

The flowchart in figure 9-1 shows the basic document flow in the marker system. The actual casino marker is shown in figure 9-2, which illustrates the principal parts of the marker and their uses. The marker typically consists of four parts and is prenumbered, in most respects appearing to be the same as a check. The parts are:

1. The original, which ultimately is kept in the credit office. This original is temporarily held in the casino pit until the end of the shift, then it is transmitted or transferred to the credit control file.

2. A copy, which is usually kept in the accounting department as a control copy. These control copies are usually filed in numeric sequence.

3. An issuance transaction copy, which may be either a complete copy of the marker or a stub at one end of the marker that is used to record the original issuance of the credit. Depending upon the system used, the issuance copy either goes into the drop box of the game from which the chips were issued, or else it goes into the central pit bookkeeper's box. It is later included in the count

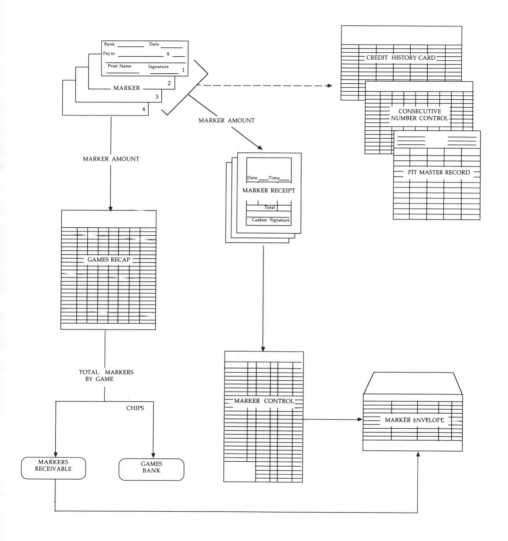

Fig. 9-1. Marker system.

TO ______ ABA NO. ______ CASHIER ______

NAME OF BANK

______ AUTH. ______ Nº

NAME OF BRANCH

______ DATE ______ 19 ___ T# ___ TIME ___

CITY STATE ZIP

PAY TO THE
ORDER OF ______ $ ______

For value received, I represent that amount is on deposit in said bank subject to this check and is hereby assigned to payee, and I guarantee payment with exchange and costs in collecting.

STREET ADDRESS ______ SIGNED ______

CITY & STATE ______

PHONE ( ) ______ PRINT NAME ______

C00017 (1M) 07/82 BANK ACCOUNT NO. ______

Fig. 9-2. Customer check (marker).

procedures in order to maintain control over the fluctuations of the table inventory resulting from issuing chips from the table for credit.

4. The repayment transaction copy is used to record the repayment of the marker made at the table. The repayment transaction copy is used only if repayment is made prior to the transfer of the marker to the credit cashier. If during the shift the customer wins or otherwise wishes to repay the marker, then the table inventory is increased, and some document is necessary to record that transaction. The repayment copy is used for this purpose; upon completion, depending upon the system used, it is put either in the game drop box or in the locked pit marker box.

Repayment Procedures   If the customer wishes to make a repayment of the marker, the control procedures followed are outlined below. The procedures vary depending on whether or not the marker is still in the pit area or has been transmitted back to the cage.

If the repayment is less than the full amount of the marker, the amount of the repayment is indicated on the face of the marker and on the repayment copy. The marker, if paid in full, is usually canceled by the bookkeeper, the repayment is recorded on the master game and pit sheet, and the marker is returned to the customer. If the marker is only repaid in part, it is retained by the pit clerk.

It is increasingly common practice to cancel the old marker if a portion of the marker is repaid and to prepare a new marker for the amount of the remaining balance. This simplifies the subsequent collection, where a single document can be presented for payment rather than a document that may have been altered in some way to reflect the partial repayments.

In all of these repayment transactions, the dealer and the floor person both sign the repayment copy of the marker indicating that the amount of money, either in currency or in chips, has been added back to the table. Cash and currency are dropped into the table drop box, and the chips are added to the table inventory.

Repayment of Markers at the Cage   If the markers are not paid at the pit, as usually occurs if the customer is gambling over a longer period of time, the markers are transferred to the credit cashier and the repayment of the marker must be made at the cashier's cage.

The transfer of the markers to the credit cashier is offset by the issuance of credit slips in the amount of the markers transferred. The credit is issued to the respective tables that issued the chips for the marker in the first place. Any repayments are also taken into account in completing these credit slips. The amount of the credit slip is actually for the net marker activity for the table during a particular shift.

A second way to achieve this proper control and accounting is merely to include the issuance copy and repayment copies, if any, in the soft count routine where they are considered to be either fill or credit slips in the determination of the game win or loss.

When the markers arrive at the credit cashier, they are recorded on a master sheet, and the total amount of accountability is updated.

Marker Control and Collections

The control over the markers that are outstanding in the casino, as well as the procedural control over the collection process, can be very critical to a casino.

The first key issue is the necessity for safekeeping of the credit obligations, including markers and other similar instruments. In general, hold checks (bank drafts that have a future presentation date), as well as true markers, must be controlled both individually for credit collection purposes and for aggregate accounting purposes as well. The same types of controls should be exercised over ordinary checks that may have been returned from the bank for other reasons.

The first element of control is to assure that the respective accounting files are properly updated and that the current credit status is recorded. This can be particularly critical if the credit customer is close to the credit limit. Thus, at the end of each shift, the total credit outstanding to a particular individual should be updated to ensure that any subsequent credit decisions are based on current information. This avoids the potential problem of extending credit to a customer in excess of agreed maximum amounts and the related problem of subsequent collections.

The second element of control is the necessity of assuring that the procedures for both the original issuance and subsequent collection efforts are in line with various regulatory requirements. In this situation, in order to avoid having to pay the gross gaming revenue tax on uncollected markers, all appropriate steps must be taken to ensure that credit was extended in good faith and that an effort has been made to collect the marker. Simply losing the marker does not satisfy the requirement.

A third element of control over markers is the need to maintain accurate and complete records for financial reporting purposes. This is reinforced by the necessity of being able to provide independent, governmental, and regulatory auditors with adequate detailed information that will allow them to perform necessary testing of the receivables.

A fourth and final control element regarding markers is the problem of assuring that adequate controls exist over the collection process so that the amounts actually extended in credit are collected by the casino. Various controls over these procedures can be implemented by the casino. For example, in New Jersey, state rules call for the automatic presentation of all counter checks within three banking days of the original granting of credit. This effectively means that the credit on the books cannot become old, either through management delay or through mere neglect.

Credit Collection Procedures

The practices and procedures of casino credit are largely the same as the collection of any other form of debt. The general principles of timeliness of presentation of the bill, together with adequate communication of the responsibilities of the customer to make the repayment, parallel standard commercial collection practices. Strong-arm collection tactics have long since ceased to be good management practice.

One area of importance in collection is the control that must be placed on persons visiting the casino in an organized group such as junket. As a matter of course, most junkets or groups of gamblers will have markers outstanding at the end of the visit. Arrangements must be made to aggregate these markers and to collect the amounts due from the various customers.

The actual practice varies; in some cases, the junket master or another party assumes responsibility for the payment of all the debts of the individuals on the tour and arranges to pay off all outstanding markers with his or her own money. The junket master then assumes the responsibility for the collection of the markers, independent of the casino. This process has resulted in some instances of improper or particularly aggressive collection efforts on the part of the junket master that have in turn hurt the reputation of the casino that was visited. In some casinos, the practice of the junket master assuming the debts of individuals has been discontinued. Instead, the junket master serves as a commission collection agent on behalf of and in the service of the casino. This allows more control by the casino over the collection process and removes the financial burden and responsibility from the junket master.

Marker Control Systems

The markers that are on file with the credit cashier are usually stored in individual envelopes, with a record on the outside of the envelope of the amounts of credit markers contained. If a marker is paid, then the balance on the envelope is reduced. The envelope may also contain other key information that could be used in contacting the customer or in notifying casino personnel if some problem exists.

In addition to the individual marker envelopes, there are also systems of control over the aggregate amount of markers receivable. These controls parallel a standard accounts receivable system with controls over the age of the receivable, records of adjustments and credits, and, most importantly, records of the payment program and the total amount outstanding.

Another element in the marker control system is the updating of the individual customer credit record. The timely updating of this record is important in the extension of credit. There must be an accurate indication of the total amount of credit issued, the terms, the timeliness of repayment, and other factors so that future credit decisions can be based on good historical information.

A difficult situation for accounting control exists in cases of partial payment or redemption of a marker. If the partial payment occurs after the customer has left the casino, then the customary practice is to leave the marker in the envelope and to indicate the payments on the outside. Only after the entire marker amount has been paid is the marker returned to the customer. Proper adjustment of the amounts of aggregate casino markers must also be made to reflect these partial payments.

Another serious issue of accounting control is partial payment made while the customer is still in the casino. In most of these situations, the old marker in the higher dollar amount is returned to the customer in exchange for a new marker executed in the amount of the remaining obligation. This enables the casino to clean up its bookkeeping; should the need arise, a bank draft may be negotiated for the smaller amount with less difficulty than for a larger draft.

Off-Site Credit Collections

There are key accounting controls over the collection of casino markers away from the casino itself. In this case, several important procedural controls should be followed. First, it is often necessary to have the original marker on hand at the location of the customer in order to secure payment. If a substantial marker is to be paid, then the customer almost always wants to have the marker returned at the time the payment is made. In this case, the original copy of the marker must be taken out of the control area and transmitted to the customer representative in that town or else carried by a casino collection representative directly to the customer. In these situations, a copy of the marker is retained in the marker envelope during the time that the marker is out of the casino, along with an explanation for the absence of the original document. This copy of the marker is either destroyed or canceled if the payment is made. The payment is also recorded on the outside of the marker envelope.

Other alternatives may be used if the customer does not immediately desire the return of the original marker. In these situations, a copy of the marker is sent to the customer or taken in person by a sales or collection representative, and the original is retained by the credit cashier. After complete payment is made, the original marker is indicated as paid and returned to the customer.

If the off-site collection is to be handled by a person other than a casino employee, some form of responsibility for the markers that are taken from the casino must be secured. In this case, a simple statement acknowledging the responsibility of the collection individual such as the junket master is sufficient. This individual's obligation is primarily for the custody of the markers; should they be lost or payment not be made, payment to the casino may be enforced.

Settlements

In some situations, the credit manager or collection representative may deem it wise to settle a marker debt for an amount less than the face value. The power to accept less than full payment gives the collection personnel a very great opportunity to manipulate the collection procedures. For example, this could result in the reduction of a marker from $76,000 to $50,000 when in reality the customer paid $60,000, allowing the collection representative to pocket the extra $10,000.

To avoid this potential problem, various casinos have implemented administrative procedures to assure that the amounts of writeoffs, including settlements for less than face value of the obligation, are subjected to fairly extensive management review. In general, a top-level committee of the credit manager, the casino manager, and the senior financial staff must approve the writeoff or settlement of casino markers for less than face value. This review assures that individual collection representatives properly use the power they have to negotiate the settlements in order to collect the bills promptly and still be responsible for the full amount of markers assigned to them for collection.

Collection Methods

Marker collections present some unique problems, which are attributable to the larger size of casino markers when compared to traditional consumer debt obligations. The first collection method is to have the casino debt replaced by other debt that can be paid off in installments by the customer. A second procedure is to arrange to have the casino customer pay off the entire amount. This may be facilitated by the liquidation of other assets or by special payment from a source such as a closely held corporation, partnership, trust, or other entity.

Finally, casinos may reluctantly accept programs of installments for the payment of the casino debt. This alternative is somewhat undesirable for reasons that are both financial and managerial. First, the casino is not set up to handle installment payment obligations efficiently, and the cost in administrative time is very high. Second, the casino does not customarily charge interest on markers, and the time payment plan costs the casino in terms of not having the cash available for other purposes. Finally, the casino customer is usually not granted any additional credit while paying off an obligation and is therefore emotionally unwilling to return to the same casino to gamble again. Thus, with the installment payments, the customer is lost for a substantial period of time and is likely to go to another casino, which might result in the permanent loss of that customer.

Collection Services

Some casinos have used outside collection services for the markers in the past. These services must be handled with great care. Problems arise from several sources. The first is that the collection service requires a substantial percentage of the amount collected. This results in a smaller realization to the casino than if the debt were compromised or settled by the casino in the first instance. Second, the conduct of the collection service must be consistent with the desire of the casino to have appropriate collection methods. For example, if the casino believes in using less rigorous methods of collection, then the utilization of a strong-arm collection service merely harms the image of the casino.

The accounting for items sent to outside collection services and the administrative controls over these assignments are as follows. The first control is the accounting for delivery of the markers and other supporting documents to the collection service. In this case, the credit cashier accountability must be reduced with a transfer to the accounting department. At this point, a memorandum record is created of the accounts transmitted and the dollar amount. Most casinos choose to write off the receivables at the time they are transmitted to the collection service. Then, if any recovery is occasioned in the future, the amounts are restored and indicated as paid at that time. The recording of the writeoff resulting from the assignment to the collection agency must be subjected to the same controls and administrative review as direct writeoffs, reductions, and settlements. The aggregate amount of casino receivables must also be adjusted by the amount of the writeoff at this time.

Credit Reporting

In some instances, special forms of management-oriented financial reporting are required of the credit transactions. First, it is in the best interest of the casino carefully to monitor the efforts of all its collection representatives. If one person has a consistently high or low collection ratio or a high rate of settlement or other adjustments and reductions, that information should be brought to the attention of senior management. There may also be special regulatory requirements that necessitate the recording of the amounts and the persons for whom the writeoffs are made. This allows the regulatory auditors to guard against a consistent pattern of writeoffs being made to a single person or group. Finally, there may be special reporting requirements for writeoffs for certain categories, such as junket representatives.

Conclusion

The careful maintenance of a casino credit system can be of major benefit to the marketing and profitable operation of a casino. However, the credit system is a volatile area and must be subjected to the most careful procedural, accounting, and internal systems control in order to be effective. This chapter has outlined some of the major requirements for effective accounting and operational control over the credit system.

♠ ♡ ♣ ◇ III

Auditing, Taxation, and Financial Management Issues

♠ ♡ ♣ ◇ CHAPTER 10

Casino Auditing, Accounting, and Financial Reporting

Introduction

This chapter describes the current practice and principal problems in the auditing of casino operations, the status of accounting principles as they apply to unique casino balance sheet and income statement items, and current problems regarding the financial reporting and disclosure requirements for the industry. Many of the issues that are discussed in this chapter have been either introduced or discussed in some detail in other chapters.

Other ongoing efforts regarding casino accounting and auditing are also discussed. The American Institute of Certified Public Accountants has issued an audit guide covering the casino industry.[1] The study task force was first constituted in 1979 and worked through late 1983. The audit guide, officially published in 1984, constitutes the basis of authoritative accounting principles and auditing procedures for casino operations in the United States.

The Casino Auditing Environment

The modern environment of casino auditing is a result of a unique partnership among:

1. Casino Management, including the casino internal audit department.

2. Government Gaming Control Agencies.

3. Independent Certified Public Accountants, including traditional SEC reporting and regulatory reporting.

Each of these groups has a unique interest in the integrity of the auditing process. The commonality of interests in financial reporting that is the natural result of the auditing process expected in other industries is quite disparate in the casino industry. This tends to lead to considerable differences in the audit objective and procedure used by the different groups indicated above. Also, even within the independent CPA group, the concern with SEC reporting is a fairly new phenomenon; in some cases, the auditing and reporting for small privately held casinos is felt to be significantly different from the auditing procedures and reporting for large publicly traded and corporately owned casinos.

Casino Management and Internal Audit

The maintenance of an effective system of internal controls is of paramount importance to the profitable operation of the casino. The complex operations of the casino, together with the large amounts of cash and chips in use, create a situation where ironclad controls are essential. Comprehensive systems of checks and balances are required to safeguard the assets of the casino, to assure accurate financial reporting, and ultimately to preserve the goodwill of the customers by maintaining an atmosphere of fair dealing within the casino. This public perception is also vitally important to the marketing success of the casino, since no one wants to patronize an establishment that cheats.

A second important dimension is that the regulatory authorities continue to allow the casino to operate and that the granting of authority to operate or of a gaming license not be placed in jeopardy. The shortest and easiest way to lose a gaming license is to be accused of cheating and to have it proven. Beyond the regulatory control, the overall public perception of the integrity of the casino operation is important in assuring that casino operations continue to be socially tolerated by the large majority of the public. Without this public acceptability, the image of the industry will be degraded, and the continued legalization of gaming could be challenged.

It is the responsibility of the internal audit departments of the various casinos to act as top management's first line of defense in maintaining the integrity of casino operations. They are responsible for ensuring that:
1. Designed internal control procedures are followed.
2. Customers do not cheat.
3. Employees do not cheat.
4. Efficiency of operation is maintained.

It could be said that these objectives are the traditional objectives of good internal control. While this may seem trite, in such a volatile control atmosphere as a casino, the recognition of the importance of the various roles of the internal audit staff and the respect that top management, as well as regulatory authorities, have for the internal audit staff speak very eloquently of their importance.

As a corporation becomes more and more diverse—including, for example, operations involving both Nevada and New Jersey casinos—the importance of casino internal audit is even greater. In this case, there are often corporate-level internal audit staffs that are independent of the local casino operation and help to assure not only the integrity of the operation, but also the accuracy of the reporting by various levels of management within the internal managerial information systems of the corporation. Holiday Inns is a prime example of this type of structure: a corporate internal audit staff in Tennessee is a key feature of managerial control over the diverse operations in Nevada and New Jersey. Both these locations have their own internal audit staffs, but it is the corporate-level internal audit staff that maintains control over the reporting of subsidiary management to the head office.

Governmental Gaming Control Authorities

The gaming control agencies in Nevada and New Jersey have been described in considerable detail in the sections dealing with licensing and regulation of the gaming activities in their states.[2]

The auditing focus of these governmental control agencies is somewhat unusual. The regulatory agencies are first and foremost concerned with the proper reporting of casino revenues. A secondary objective is proper reporting of the amount of gaming taxes levied on this revenue. Since the overwhelming dollar amount of taxes comes from this gross revenue taxation, the primary focus of tax collection is on the accuracy of the revenue reported from casino operations.[3]

Another important objective of the state regulatory audit procedures is monitoring the extent to which the systems, procedures, and policies specified in the internal control system of the casino are followed in actual practice. In Nevada, the concern is the degree of adherence of the system—as submitted to the regulators by the casino—to the actual operation. In New Jersey, the primary concern is how closely the internal control operations of the casino fit with the largely prescribed statutory procedures for internal control. From this secondary objective, two benefits are derived.

The first is that there is some indication of how well the casino is being controlled. The second is that, if there is a high degree of adherence in the internal control systems, then there is a high degree of reliability of the financial statements generated as a result of the accounting system operations. Thus, the first objective, the integrity and propriety of the gross revenue figures, is enhanced.

Certified Public Accountants

A third element in the audit environment of a casino is the role of the certified public accountants—the traditional group most closely involved with auditing and financial reporting.

The role of certified public accountants (CPAs) has emerged over a period of years in the state of Nevada, and the relationships fostered there have had a significant effect on the legislation regarding CPAs in New Jersey. CPAs are presently involved in the following areas:

1. Traditional Financial Audits, conducted on an annual basis.
2. Submissions to the Securities and Exchange Commission.
   a. Annual Audits.
   b. Special Audits.
   c. Quarterly Reviews.
3. Submissions to Regulatory Agencies.
   a. Annual Financial Audits.
   b. Annual Internal Control Evaluations.

These three basic areas of auditing vary slightly depending upon the type of organization that owns and conducts the casino business. For most of the larger casino operations, there is a recognition of the necessity of an annual financial audit; even without the mandatory regulatory auditing, these operations would be audited.

However, it appears that the overall force driving the casino auditing business, particularly for many of the smaller casinos located in Nevada, is the regulatory requirements of annual financial audits and annual internal control evaluations.[4] Clearly, many casinos would not voluntarily have annual financial audits if they were not required.

The same generalization regarding the size of the casino is applicable to those casinos that have publicly traded stock. These organizations, which are typically the largest casinos, understand the necessity of regular reporting in line with traditional SEC requirements, and the auditing of these types of organizations has been going on for many years in the state of Nevada.

It is of considerable significance that the CPA was first required to attest to the adequacy of the internal control system in Nevada in 1975. This requirement was viewed with considerable enthusiasm by the public accounting profession. The adoption of these internal control reporting requirements predated the broader application of similar certifications under the Foreign and Corrupt Practices Act by at least three years.[5]

The importance of internal control evaluations together with the standards for conducting such audits and the reporting standards for such activities are discussed in detail later in the chapter.

Scope of Audit Responsibility and Types of Audits

This section outlines the various types of audits performed on casinos by persons other than the regulatory agencies and briefly describes the scope of the audits typically encountered.

Financial Audit

The traditional objective of an examination of a casino's financial statements by an independent CPA has been the expression of an opinion as to the fairness of presentation of financial position, results of operations, and changes in financial position. This objective is still the predominant factor in most casino financial audits. However, several major changes or special factors in the financial audit that can have a significant impact on the audit scope should be recognized.

The first issue involves the entity that is being audited. For most publicly traded corporations, all operating units, including subsidiaries, clearly must be included in the financial audit. This can cause some monumental headaches, since the casino operations may be just one part of a larger enterprise. In these cases, the casino operations must be audited and the results presented in some manner so that the regulatory authorities have the necessary information. This means that a separate set of audited financial statements must be made available for the gaming operation alone, which are then submitted to the appropriate regulatory authorities. In addition, the overall corporate financial information also must be submitted to the regulatory bodies.

If more than one operating entity is involved in the casino operations, then the propriety of cost allocations, cost division, or cost-sharing arrangements must also be considered part of the overall audit scope and subjected to appropriate audit tests.

For smaller casino operations, where only one operating entity is involved, the casino operator may wish to have supplementary information provided in order to determine department-by-department profit or loss. In this case, the audit scope must be clearly defined in order to decide if the audit procedures are to include just the overall financial statements, with supplementary information not being subjected to full audit scrutiny, or if all statements, including departmental information, are to be audited.

Another concern is the consideration of whether or not a hotel-casino operation is considered to be a single line of business (or segment) with supporting hotel, food, and beverage operations or several separate lines of business, each requiring separate disclosure. The majority of practicing CPAs regard the casino operation, with its typical support facilities, as a single line of business that should be reported as such.[6]

The second major determinant of the audit scope is the time period under audit and the related issue of other auditors who may or may not have performed audit services for the casino client. In general, the audit period is a calendar or fiscal year. During changes in ownership or when opening a new casino, a short accounting period may be used.

Some problems may arise if the auditor is appointed after the end of the fiscal year, or if a change in auditors has been made. In general, due to the requirement of having casino financial statements audited, reliable prior years' information is usually available upon which to base comparable financial statements, eliminating most of the time-related scope problems. Existing procedures relating to predecessor auditors in the professional literature appear sufficient to guide the casino auditor in most other areas when a change of casino auditors has taken place. As long as the new auditor can make reasonable determinations of the accuracy of inventories and year-end cash counts, then the appointment of auditors after the year's end should not present any significant problem. If there are some reservations, then the appropriate scope limitations should be outlined in the auditor's opinion.[7]

Other scope issues regarding the examination of specific items, accounts, or the general limitations on material items should be taken into consideration in the initial specification of audit scope or in the determination of appropriate wording of the final audit opinion. For example, failure to obtain satisfaction with regard to casino receivables would cause a scope limitation in a casino audit, just as it would in the audit of any other firm. For good client relations, however, these potential scope problems should be anticipated and critical areas subjected to some review and discussed with the client prior to accepting the engagement.

Regulatory Filings

There are two different types of regulatory filings that must be made with the gaming control agencies. The first are those reports that are unique and must be made only to the gaming control agencies. The second type are those reports that are generally given to owners, managers, or other regulatory bodies, copies of which must also be filed with the gaming regulators. The first group of reports is fairly small, while the second group is considerably larger. The primary concern of this discussion is the first area, the filings with the gaming regulators that are unique to those agencies.

There are two unique regulatory filings. The first is the filing of standardized financial statements.[8] These financial statements utilize standard definitions of revenue sources and standard formats and allow the compilation of statistical information for analytic purposes. These statements are also key elements in the regulatory review of casino profitability and financial health by the gaming regulatory groups. The second filing is the submission of the CPA's evaluation of the system of internal controls for the casino.[9] This document is discussed in detail in later sections of the chapter.

The process of completion of the standard financial statements is a fairly simple clerical task. These statements do not require the auditor's opinion and are usually prepared by casino personnel rather than by the independent auditor. The standard financial statements consist of four main parts: 1. balance sheet; 2. income statement—with details for each of the major operating divisions, including casino, rooms, food and beverage, and other departments; 3. detailed revenue produced by different games and gaming devices; and 4. various items of statistical information such as hotel room occupancy. The process of providing this information can be fairly difficult if the accounting system of the casino is not designed in a manner to make the information from the basic financial statement compatible with the standard financial statement format. The simplest solution that most of the casinos have adopted is to use a chart of accounts or general ledger that closely approximates the structure of the accounts necessary to provide the regulatory disclosure.

The Nevada report is required to be filed on a June 30 fiscal year-end basis, regardless of when the casino's financial fiscal year end actually is. New Jersey requires its annual report to be filed on a December 31 year-end basis, again regardless of the actual casino year end.

Internal Control Filings

Both Nevada and New Jersey require regulatory filings of the CPA's review and opinion on the system of internal controls in place in the casino. These reports must be attested to by a certified public accountant or public accountant licensed to practice in the respective state. The specific statutory requirements are set out in Nevada Gaming Control Board Regulation 6.050 (6) and New Jersey Gaming Regulation 19:45.7.

The internal control reports that are required to be filed vary somewhat between Nevada and New Jersey. The Nevada regulation has two significant requirements that are not found in New Jersey. First, the independent accountant's report in Nevada must include references to *all* instances and procedures discovered by or brought to the attention of the independent accountant that he or she believes are not in conformity with the systems of internal control relative to gaming operations that have been submitted to the Gaming Control Board. This disclosure must be made *regardless of the materiality or nonmateriality of the exception*. This same standard applies to both the internal control over gross revenue and casino entertainment receipts and the corresponding tax liability.

This standard of reporting, regardless of the materiality of the transaction, is not found in the New Jersey regulation, where the traditional auditing standard wording "in all material respects" is retained. If, however, there are material weaknesses in the system of internal control, then a trigger mechanism comes into play and the accountant *must report all weaknesses* discovered, regardless of the individual materiality.

These differing materiality standards, particularly the requirement in Nevada, are somewhat counter to the present professional standards and are one of the most significant differences between regulatory reporting requirements and the reporting required under generally accepted auditing standards.

A second requirement in the Nevada internal control evaluation is an affirmative statement by the independent accountant as to the "continuing effectiveness and adequacy of the systems."[10] This not only puts the accountant on notice for the evaluation of prior transactions under the internal control system, but, as some people have suggested, also calls for a professional judgment as to the quality of internal control expected in the future accounting periods. The New Jersey regulation merely specifies that the internal control system be evaluated "during the period covered by his examination" (of the financial statements).[11]

These internal control filings must clearly meet the letter of the law. However, they can often contain wording that exposes management and independent auditors to burdensome reporting requirements as well as substantially increased risks of legal action.

Other Reports Required

Another group of reporting requirements generated in the course of a regular financial audit in turn are required to be filed with the appropriate gaming control agencies. These are briefly described here.

Independent accountants commonly supply letters and recommendations to management, pointing out problems of internal control, operating areas needing improvement, and ways to increase overall efficiency or to improve the effectiveness of certain tasks. As mentioned above, those items pertaining to internal control problems must be disclosed in a separate report to the gaming control authorities. In addition, the complete management letter or list of recommendations to management must also be forwarded to the gaming control authorities.[12]

Other notifications that are required to be sent to the gaming authorities include copies of all SEC-filed documents (including 10-K and 8-K reporting forms), details of all loans, borrowing, and leases. Also required to be reported are all installment purchase contracts, as well as all changes in the capital structure, including dividends, withdrawals, or additions of capital.[13]

The purpose of these miscellaneous regulatory filings is to assure that the gaming control agencies are well informed of any significant or material changes or problems in the casino operations. The broad-ranging disclosure requirements are a significant administrative burden for both management and independent casino accountants.

Internal Control Evaluations

In addition to evaluating the casino's system of internal control for financial statement purposes, the independent auditor is also required to report on the system of internal control itself. This separate reporting requirement demands an evaluation that goes beyond the scope of the traditional internal control evaluation used in other industries.

Reliance on Internal Control

The importance of the evaluation of internal control in the casino operating environment cannot be overemphasized. The internal controls are the only way that the integrity of the operation and the financial statements can be assured. While this seems like a truism for many industries, the nature of the revenue-generation process—the physical aspect of games and the various coin-operated gaming devices—together with the volatility of the coin, currency, and chips in the casino makes extremely tight controls mandatory.

In addition, accountants may be called upon to perform a variety of services with respect to internal control systems. Typically, they will be asked: 1. to help in the design of the original internal control systems for a new casino; 2. to attest to the adequacy of the internal control systems as a part of the annual regulatory reporting requirements; or 3. to assist in the redesign or improvement of elements of the internal control systems. Given the large amount of involvement of accountants in the internal control system and the system's overall importance in casino operations, it is necessary that every casino accountant have a comprehensive understanding of the system of internal control.

Submitted System of Internal Control

The key to the internal control evaluation process is the use of the concept of the "submitted system." In both Nevada and New Jersey, all casinos, whether new or existing operations, are required to file a documented system of internal controls with the respective regulatory agencies. These narrative and diagrammatic descriptions should contain the following basic components.

The system of accounting control relative to gaming operations shall provide a plan of organization and a description of the procedures and records that are designed to provide reasonable assurance that the following objectives will be obtained:

1. That the assets are safeguarded
2. That the financial records are reliable
3. That transactions are executed in accordance with management's general or specific authorization
4. That transactions are recorded as necessary to
   (a) permit proper recording of gaming revenue, and
   (b) maintain accountability of assets
5. That access to assets is permitted only in accordance with management's authorization
6. That the recorded accountability for assets is compared with existing assets at reasonable intervals, and appropriate action is taken with respect to any differences.[14]

These documented systems give the gaming control agencies, as well as the independent and internal auditors, a basic document against which to make their internal control evaluations. The idea behind the system is that the casino should say what its system of internal control is and follow it. This method allows considerable latitude for innovation in control procedures, which in turn allows acknowledgment of the differences between various casinos, a problem that is particularly significant in Nevada.

These control systems, which are required to be submitted to the control agencies, are then evaluated by the regulatory authorities; where weaknesses are encountered, changes are made by the casinos. The process of evaluation of these submitted systems can take a very long time following the initial submission. The variety of forms used, extent of procedures, and complexity of the submissions make the evaluation process by the gaming control authorities very difficult.

The key in Nevada is that each of the submitted systems has to meet the minimum standards as specified in the gaming legislation, regulations, or internal evaluation policies of the Gaming Control Board. Due to the attitude in Nevada of allowing each casino to design its own internal control system to meet its unique needs, there is tremendous variation in the systems described and submitted. This variety calls for a very high level of understanding on the part of the gaming control evaluation personnel; thus, the control evaluation takes a long time to complete.

The New Jersey system, on the other hand, has specified a very strict and uniform system of internal controls for virtually all aspects of the casino operations. Although submissions of the internal control systems are also required for New Jersey casinos, the differences among casinos are very minor. This high level of consistency allows only slight changes or innovations in controls, but does simplify the job of evaluation of the adequacy of the internal control system, as well as simplifying the job of casino oversight and regulation. Given the restrictive nature of the casino industry in New Jersey, this approach is very satisfactory, but it would not be expected to work in Nevada.

Limitations of Casino Internal Control Systems

The internal control systems present in the casino have several severe structural limitations that must be recognized and discussed. These limitations, once recognized, lead quite naturally to consideration of various alternative types of controls that are commonly found in a casino operation and are unique to that industry. These nontraditional internal controls are then available to augment the more traditional methods of assuring good internal control.

The first problem of casino operations is that the revenue-generation process is very open and not easily adaptable to using some type of documentation for the transactions. Quite simply, you cannot put a cash register on the gaming table to record the betting, payoff, or house win transaction. Some considerable strides have been made in newer slot machines to allow the automatic recording of transactions, but for the immediate future, the uncertain nature of revenue documentation will continue. The earliest point at which the revenue is documented is during the daily count of table drop boxes and slot machine drop. Once the count has been performed, there are adequate documents that form the basis for future controls.

A second problem is that the revenue-generation process is the result of rendering an intangible service, and there are no ancillary records of the sale of goods or services to which the revenues can be meaningfully compared.

Because of the uncertainty of documentation in the revenue areas, and also because of the volatility of the casino cash and chips, various types of nontraditional controls have developed that are used to assure good internal control in the casino. Some of these are listed below. In general, these controls must also be tested in the process of assessing the adequacy of the overall internal control systems of the casino.

1. Eye in the sky, including both observation platforms and various types of electronic surveillance of the casino floor, cashier cages, count rooms, and other sensitive areas.

2. Extensive supervision of all aspects of operations, including such apparent redundancies as numerous pit supervisors, security guards, cashier supervisors, and duplicate count room personnel.

3. Extensive separation of duties, accompanied by the necessity of multiple signatures on documents and multiple check and counting of transactions between separate casino operating departments.

4. Complete access and key controls, as indicated by the nearly universal use of locks on all parts of the casino, coupled with very restrictive policies limiting the access of personnel to more than one sensitive area.

5. Extensive use of highly standardized and regular procedures for critical casino operations.

Other Casino Internal Control Concerns

In addition to these unique casino control procedures, casino internal control evaluations must be mindful of the traditional areas of internal controls that are documented in other forms of professional literature relating to generally accepted auditing standards and accounting principles. A primary example is the necessity of evaluating the internal controls over computer operations in the casino, just as must be done in a regular industrial corporation.

Scope of Internal Control Evaluations

The requirement of a separate report on internal controls has resulted in the Nevada Society of CPAs specifying to its members that additional work will generally be required beyond that necessary to express an opinion on the financial statements.[15] This recommendation is consistent with the additional requirements contained in SAS 30, which was designed to provide guidance for internal control evaluations relative to the Foreign and Corrupt Practices Act.

In general, when the universal requirement of a regulatory internal control evaluation is coupled with the traditional financial audit, most accountants merely extend the testing of the internal control procedures to a degree sufficient to meet the higher standard and utilize the results of examination to determine the subsequent scope of the substantive testing of the other financial records.

A second major issue of significance for the scope of the internal control evaluation process is the recognition of the critical nature of time in the process of internal control: the quality of internal control may vary considerably over the period of a year, or possibly even over a quarter or month, depending on many factors. Thus, the internal control procedures in a casino may be very good for the off-season, but fail to meet the requirements of a high-volume transaction period such as the summer. It is therefore recommended that the auditor be aware of the possibility of these types of problems and consider the use of multiple testing periods during the year in order to validate the internal control evaluation.

Finally, the concept of materiality of the exceptions noted in the process of testing the internal control is a long-standing professional concept that has been radically changed by the regulatory requirements in Nevada and to a lesser degree in New Jersey. Careful consideration should be given to procedures to identify all exceptions for regulatory reporting by the accountant, while the collection of these exceptions, and the overall materiality judgments within the traditional financial auditing framework, should also be documented adequately during the evaluation of the internal control system.

Critical Internal Control Areas

Another issue related to the scope of the internal control evaluation is the recognition of the importance of certain specific areas as being of critical concern to the overall casino operations. Thus, when the internal control for the areas listed below is being evaluated, a somewhat higher standard of performance should be expected and fewer exceptions allowed. An important element in the materiality decision is a recognition that the performance of systems in these critical areas has a significant impact on the accuracy and integrity of casino operations and overall financial statements. Some of the particularly critical areas in a casino are:

1. Credit or marker play procedures, including credit and collection activity.

2. Revenue accounting, including drop, count, and all cashier cage to table activity, such as fill and credit procedures.

3. Cage and vault procedures, including bankroll control.

Internal Control Evaluation Procedures

The process of evaluating the internal control procedures has been substantially eased by the existence of documented systems of internal control that are required by the gaming control agencies. The practical benefit of this regulatory requirement is to provide any auditor (whether it be the regulatory agency auditor or the independent auditor) with a documented system of internal controls. This leads to substantial savings of audit time and improved audit results. In prior years, a substantial amount of time was spent preparing documentation of the internal control system. In the casino audit area, under ideal circumstances today, all that has to be done is to review the internal control documentation and, in subsequent time periods, review the changes that have been filed with the regulatory authorities. The evaluation of the system documentation is the key first step in the process of evaluation of internal control.

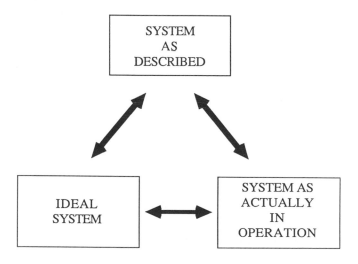

Fig. 10-1. Internal control system evaluation.

The second step in the evaluation involves a three-way comparison of the system of internal control. The components of this comparison are indicated in figure 10-1 and outlined below:

1. Between the system as it is described and the minimum statutory requirements. This assures that the casino systems are not in violation of statutory requirements.

2. Between the system as it is described and the ideal requirements for a casino of this type. This leads to improvements in the system as the nature of casino operations changes over time.

3. Between the system as it is described and the system as it is actually operating in the casino. This assures that the controls are not merely window dressing, but are actually operating effectively.

At each comparison step, the weaknesses in the internal control systems should be noted, with examples properly documented and gathered together in order to determine, for financial statement purposes only, the overall materiality of the errors found.

In order to facilitate the comparison between the internal control system described and the minimum specified in the control statutes and regulations, the following steps are suggested:

1. The auditor should become familiar with the current requirements for internal control. Updates and changes regarding requirements must also be considered, to assure that all essential controls are being used, while unnecessary controls are avoided.

2. If available, questionnaires, checklists, or other documents from the respective regulatory agencies should be used to evaluate the system of internal control. This allows the independent auditor to ensure that the key statutory or regulatory requirements have been met. These documents are generally available in Nevada, but the New Jersey control agencies have not made their internal control documents widely available.[16]

3. Differences uncovered should be investigated carefully to determine if a weakness exists or if some alternative procedure is adequate to meet the control objective.

4. Where control weaknesses exist, they should be documented, and the nature of the problem should be discussed fully with the client. If changes in procedures or new procedures are recommended, then those changes should be made to the system of internal control and the regulatory authorities should be informed.

In the review of the differences between the internal control system as described and some measure of an ideal casino control system, a few audit procedures are suggested.

1. Internal control procedures should be evaluated by reference to checklists, questionnaires, or other documents that may contain highly sophisticated control procedures. A typical source of these "ideal" questionnaires for a smaller casino operation would be a larger casino. Some aspects of New Jersey control procedures could also form the basis for improved procedures in a Nevada casino, and vice versa.

2. Consideration should be given to a careful analysis of hypothetical procedures or transactions that may deliberately try to stress or cheat the system. In this way, possible effects of these procedures could be used to suggest ways to strengthen the controls.

3. If applicable, internal control procedures from other industries could be used to provide guidance for suggested new procedures or the adequacy of existing procedures. For example, commercial bank operational practices for tellers and vaults are relevant to controls in the cages and vaults of a casino.

If any suggestions are made for the improvement of the casino systems, they are generally presented in the recommendations to management. Since they represent changes toward an ideal system, they are not considered to be departures from the present system and do not require specific disclosure to the regulatory authorities. However, these proposed changes should be fully evaluated for their costs and benefits to the client and discussed with appropriate personnel; if adopted, the changes should be communicated to the regulatory agencies.

Finally, with regard to the comparison between the described system and the internal control procedures as actually operating, some traditional audit procedures are suggested.

1. The audit program should select those areas to be tested, including the scope of the procedural testing.

2. Audit samples should be selected, using criteria such as anticipated error rates, time period coverage, critical nature of specific transactions, prior audit results, number of transactions, and client size and sophistication.

3. Specific criteria should be set to differentiate between errors that are considered material and those that are considered im-

material in an audit sense. Procedures should be in place to ensure the reporting of *all* errors, should the regulatory reporting require that standard.

4. Traditional procedural tests should be established to evaluate all the critical areas of the casino operation:

    a. All steps, supporting documents, and procedures in the revenue flow must be tested in considerable detail for accuracy and completeness.

    b. Adherence to control procedures in all areas must be verified.

    c. All signatures and approvals of transactions must be verified.

The primary objective of procedural testing is to review a group of transactions in an extremely detailed manner and to examine each procedural step to assure that the transactions were generated correctly, summarized properly, classified correctly, and eventually posted accurately to the general ledger. The effect of the procedural test is virtually to duplicate the transaction and to review every aspect of its impact on the accounting system.

The next step of the procedural testing is to complete the testing of the nontraditional internal controls that are mentioned above. This includes verifying that the eye in the sky or television surveillance has been performed and that the results of the observations have been documented. Procedural tests of access and key controls should also be conducted to ensure not only that the sensitive areas are locked properly, but also that the issuance and use of keys is in accordance with written procedures and guidelines.

Finally, tests should be made of the effectiveness of supervision, separation of duties, and the use of standardized operating procedures by direct observation by the auditor. Only by observing the operation of these types of person-to-person controls can their effectiveness be determined.

Internal Control Assessment

The last step in the internal control testing procedure for the casino operations is to make an assessment of the results of this procedural testing. This assessment is a critical step in determining if the conditions of control have been met and whether or not any further action is necessary. In general, there are several actions to be taken at this point.

1. If errors occur, a decision must be made regarding the ma-

teriality of the errors. At a minimum, the errors may cause the traditional scope of the financial audit substantive tests to be expanded.

2. A decision must be made regarding the disclosure to regulatory authorities. Depending upon the jurisdiction, the problems encountered must be enumerated in the proper manner.

3. If errors are not significant, then the financial audit should proceed, using the scope for substantial tests originally planned.

At this point, the procedural testing phase of the audit, encompassing both the requirements of traditional financial audit and the regulatory internal control review, is complete.

Casino Substantive Auditing Procedures and Financial Reporting

Introduction

This section outlines the basic substantive audit procedures and financial reporting principles applicable to a casino operation. Many areas of casino accounting have been discussed earlier, when the various types of operational accounting procedures were outlined. This section discusses the overall issues of financial statement presentation, substantive audit approaches, and techniques applicable to casinos.

It must be recognized that a casino has many items of similarity with other businesses in terms of financial presentation. In the present discussion, only those items in which the casino business presents a unique set of problems of financial disclosure and of auditing are discussed.

Analytic Reviews

An important preliminary step in the discussion of areas of audit importance is the necessity of understanding the nature of the casino operations and what accounts may be of significant audit interest. Analytic reviews, as called for under SAS 23,[17] serve as one method of focusing attention on various accounts. In the area of casino auditing, however, there are both some significant advantages and disadvantages associated with the use of analytic reviews.

The most significant benefit arising from an analytic review is that there may be working relationships among accounts and among the various components of the overall hotel-casino operation that can explain significant differences in financial results or behavior. For example, increases in hotel occupancy have a direct impact on the levels of restaurant and bar income, as well as having a direct relationship to gaming income levels.

However, some relationships may not be well understood, and misuse of the information can cause improper managerial or audit decisions to be made. For example, the shift of marketing emphasis from a high roller to a middle market player can result in significantly lower levels of casino receivables. While this might seem beneficial, the shift in emphasis may result in the casino being less attractive to other high rollers, leading to poorer collection rates among the remaining casino receivables. In this case, the apparently desirable impact of less receivables could lead to an improper audit decision of devoting less time and attention to the valuation issues of casino receivables.

A second major limitation of the analytic reviews is the fact that various items of numeric or statistical behavior are very dependent upon the assumptions that go into the development of the data. For example, merely redefining what items should be counted in the drop box can substantially alter the drop figures from one month to another and can distort previously stable figures. Comparisons between casinos cannot accurately be made for this reason. Also, comparison of casino performance to the *Gaming Abstract* figures may not be accurate because of these definitional problems.

One type of analytic review that may have a high degree of validity is trend analysis. Using this method, the trends in certain selected measures over time—and for the same casino—can present an informative picture of various aspects of financial performance of the casino. The key issue here is that there must be a set of stable assumptions regarding the operation of the casino financial structure over the periods of comparison.[18]

Overall Casino Financial Structure

In trying to understand the key issues of casino financial presentation and auditing, it is informative to analyze the overall casino financial structure based on a percentage distribution of revenues, expenses, assets, liabilities, and owner's equity. Based on the 1984 *Nevada Gaming Abstract*, a casino operation could be characterized in the following manner.

Casinos generate about 95% of their revenue from table games and slots, with the percentages statewide being about 45% pit games and 50% slot machines.

The expenses of the casino operations are quite simple. The largest expense is payroll and related items, which amount to 23.5% of revenue. The next two items of expense are promotional allowances or complimentaries, at 10% of revenue, and gaming taxes, at 8% of revenue. Miscellaneous expenses amount to just 2%, for total expenses of about 50% of revenues. These figures do not include administrative costs or capital costs, which must be deducted from the casino net revenue figures.

On the balance sheet side of the casino operations, current assets constitute 15% of the balance sheet, divided into cash 6.6%, receivables 4.0%, prepaid items 1.4%, and other items 3.0%. Fixed assets make up 68.1% of the total assets, with other assets, mainly deferred items, constituting 16.9% of the assets.

The liabilities in total are 57.5% of the total assets, with owner's equity being 42.3%. Within the liability section, long-term liabilities are 41.4%, while the current liabilities are 16.3% of total assets. Within the current liability area, accounts payable and the current portion of long-term debt each account for 3.6% of the total, and accrued expenses and other liability items constitute 5.4% and 3.6%, respectively.

Long-term debt makes up 34.4% of the total, and other long-term liabilities, mainly deferred taxes, constitute 7.0%.

It is clear from this analysis that, in either a revenue and expense or a balance sheet approach, the process of casino auditing can be focused on several key accounts or account groups in which most of the financial resources of the casino are concentrated.

Specific Audit Areas

Each of the key audit areas for a casino operation is discussed in detail below, dealing with audit functions as well as key issues relating to the financial presentation and disclosure for that account.

Cash

The operating environment of a casino necessitates having large amounts of cash on hand at any time. This type of cash is in addition to numerous bank accounts that would be typical of any large commercial enterprise. In a very real sense, cash is the working inventory of a casino. The principal audit and financial presentation issues of cash are:

1. Assurance of a proper cutoff to provide accurate cash counts.

2. Physical verification of all cash in all areas of the casino.

3. Proper classification of cash, chips, and tokens, including recognition of the number of chips and tokens outstanding.

4. Evaluation of cash balances relative to casino bankroll requirements.

Cash Cutoff and Verification   The foremost problem of cash auditing is to assure a proper cutoff so that an exact accounting of all monies in the casino can be made. This problem is particularly acute in the 24-hour-a-day operating environment of casinos. The first step in a good cash audit is to ensure that an attempt is made to freeze the cash count at the end of the last shift of the last day of the fiscal period. In this way an accurate determination of the cash account can be made. Certain specific cash audit procedures are suggested.

1. To the maximum extent possible, all cash on hand should be counted at the same time.

2. If a simultaneous count is not possible, a sequential count should be planned, starting from each area of the casino floor, timed to coincide with the respective end of shift for each functional area. The next step is to proceed backward to the casino cage, and on the next morning to the count rooms and finally to the vault. (This procedure is equivalent to following the flow of cash through the casino.)

3. All cash-on-hand areas must be counted completely. This includes table trays, table drop boxes, cashier banks, slot machine loads, slot drop buckets, slot change banks, slot change aprons, keno banks, bingo or poker banks, and, most importantly, the central vault.

4. For all cash counts, careful records must be kept of the denominations of all cash, coin, chips, and tokens. Attention to this step simplifies the later determination and reclassification of chips and tokens outstanding.

Proper Classification of Cash   The proper classification of cash is necessary to avoid a misstatement by simply counting chips and tokens as cash. It is common practice within the casino to regard these items as money and to maintain various change banks or funds with balances that include the chips and tokens as if they were cash. The amounts of chips and tokens must be removed from the final cash count in order to arrive at the proper cash figure for external financial statement reporting purposes.

A second minor classification problem may arise in the area of participation slot machines. In these cases, a machine is owned by someone outside the casino, who shares the revenue generated by the machine with the casino owner. Thus, a portion of the slot machine load, the amount of coins actually contained in the machine, together with a portion of the slot drop, may belong to another business. The amounts of cash actually belonging to others must also be removed from the cash-on-hand figures. An alternative treatment would be to establish an account payable or other liability account to recognize the obligation to the owner of the participation slot machine, while maintaining the cash in the accounts of the casino. This treatment may result in some overstatement of casino cash, which may affect the testing of available cash to meet bankroll requirements.

Imprest Balance Accounts   Many casinos prefer to maintain virtually all of the operating banks, petty cash, and change funds on an imprest balance basis. This procedure generally simplifies the counting and auditing procedures by establishing a certain balance that should be met in all cases after checkout. It also serves as a powerful management tool, by clearly indicating to the employee responsible for the bank that the amount is not correct. This usually allows the employee to begin an immediate search for items that have caused the difference. This method also allows the audit procedures to be executed more quickly by simplifying the count procedures for audit personnel, facilitates test checking, and eases the reconciliation process for larger banks.

Cash Count Procedures   Due to the large volume of cash and coin in a casino, automatic count equipment or devices are often used, ranging from the simplest of devices, such as a container calibrated to hold a certain amount of coin, to a complex coin-weighing machine.

Where automatic equipment is used, it is an important internal control procedure, as well as an important part of the substantive testing, to calibrate and test the accuracy of the equipment. One of the major thefts of funds from a casino was accomplished by altering automatic coin-weighing equipment deliberately to undervalue the coins. The mechanical accuracy of these machines must always be tested and verified by the auditor.

Bankrolls   In order for the casino to operate, it must have sufficient cash on hand. The cash on hand must equal or exceed certain minimums set by the gaming regulatory agencies. The specification of the minimum bankroll requirements is indicated by the informal gaming guidelines in Nevada. This minimum bankroll requirement is necessary to assure that the casino can pay its winners in a proper manner. A test of the minimum bankroll is a key cash auditing procedure. Figure 10-2 shows the formula used by the Ne-

---

REQUIREMENTS :
GAMES: CRAPS, 21, AND ROULETTE

    NUMBER OF GAMES X TABLE LIMIT X 100   =   _____

SLOTS:
   NON PROGRESSIVE:
     NUMBER OF MACHINES X $50 =
   PROGRESSIVE: _____
     TOTAL OF ALL PROGRESSIVE JACKPOTS =   _____
KENO:
   NUMBER OF GAMES X $25,000 (or game limit,
     whichever is smaller) =   _____
OTHER:
   OPERATING ACCOUNTS PAYABLE (Amount equal
    to 2 weeks payables) =   _____
   PAYROLL FOR 2 WEEKS =   _____
   DEBT SERVICE FOR ONE MONTH =   _____

  TOTAL REQUIREMENTS: =========

BANKROLL COMPRISED OF
   CASH IN CAGE =   _____
   CASH IN BANKS, TCD, SAVINGS, etc. =   _____
   CASINO CASH ON HAND (Do not include
    slot machine bucket cash)=   _____
   Less: SAFEKEEPING MONIES =   (_____)
  TOTAL BANKROLL AVAILABLE: =========

Fig. 10-2. Bankroll requirements.

vada authorities in determining the adequacy of the cash on hand for bankroll purposes.

Casino Receivables

Perhaps the most unique accounting item in a casino is casino receivables. Casino receivables result from the extensive use of credit for casino play. Receivables are also known as markers, hold checks, or IOUs. Although not formally acknowledged, liberal check-cashing policies that are inevitably accompanied by a number of checks that do not have sufficient funds or are deficient in other ways result in informal credit being extended by some smaller casinos. However, the amounts involved are generally quite small when compared to the transactions of credit departments in larger casinos. For present purposes, returned checks are regarded as miscellaneous receivables and are not the main concern of this section.

There are extensive procedures involving checks and balances built into the systems relating to the issuance, collection, and administration of casino credit. These have already been discussed in some detail in the chapter on credit accounting.

From an audit and financial presentation standpoint, the primary audit objectives are:

1. Valuation of receivables.
   a. Specification of proper amounts of receivables, including proper accounting for the markers and any payment made against the total balance.
   b. Recognition of the bona fide nature of the debt, through traditional procedures of confirmation.
   c. Adequacy of valuation reserves, including those for uncollectibles, as well as provisions for foreign exchange losses on markers denominated in a foreign currency.
2. Consistent methods of revenue recognition from the credit play.

Legal Status of Markers   The common law status of gaming debts is that they are legal debts, but are not legally enforceable with respect to collection. This status has been modified somewhat by New Jersey statutes, which state that an unredeemed check issued to a casino is a debt upon which collection can be legally enforced within the state of New Jersey. Nevada case law has taken the opposite tack, maintaining the unenforceability of the collection of gaming debts until 1983. Legislative changes in that year legalized the collection of gaming debts provided certain conditions are met.[19]

Confirmations The traditionally accepted method of evaluating accounts receivable has been to perform various confirmation procedures. In casino receivables, confirmations have not been widely used. There are several reasons for this. In the early days of casino credit granting, there often was very loose control over the debt, and it was extended in a highly personal manner. Thus, many casino receivables did not even have a proper name or address. The absence of even this rudimentary information led to a dead end in the process of traditional mail confirmation. A second factor in lack of confirmation was the reputation of casino gaming during the early years. Many persons did not want their gaming obligation to be a matter of public disclosure, including even the delivery of mail bearing a casino return address. Also, many individuals did not want friends or family members to be aware of their gaming debts. Finally, the casinos themselves did not want to draw undue attention to the amount of gaming debts of some customers.

Faced with the possibility of embarrassing a valued customer as a result of any or all of the above circumstances, casinos did not press for confirmation of casino receivables. Under these circumstances, a number of important alternative confirmation procedures were developed and used. The most common technique is the use of subsequent collections or payment as evidence of the debt. Other alternative confirmation methods include telephone confirmation and personal contact with the customer. These methods, if handled discreetly, minimize the risk of embarrassment to the customer and of customer loss to the casino. A third alternative method is to verify the customer's credit-worthiness by consulting banks or other financial or credit institutions.

The recent trend in corporate gaming has resulted in the increasing formalization of the entire credit procedures, from credit approval, which is now evidenced by traditional plastic credit cards, to the collection methods, which are regularized and include monthly statements. Under these circumstances, the procedures are becoming more like traditional accounts receivable, and the process of confirmation, both positive and negative where appropriate, is finding increasing use in the auditing of casinos.

Allowances for Doubtful Accounts The methods used to estimate the allowances for doubtful accounts have traditionally been a combination of statistical analysis of past payment and collection activity and detailed analysis of large individual accounts. This hybrid system of determination of the allowance amounts also recognizes the relatively immature nature of the industry and the presence of only a few long-standing guidelines dealing with the evaluation of casino receivables. One of the few guidelines applicable to general business that also applies to the casino business is that casino receivables after four to six months rapidly lose their value and after six months are virtually uncollectible.

Major changes in economic events, ownership of the casino, or other environmental factors can also tend to result in the necessity of large writeoffs of receivables. This is particularly the case when a change of ownership occurs. In most of these circumstances, payment rates on markers plummet.

From an audit standpoint, there should be an extensive examination of the procedures used to estimate the uncollectible amounts, as well as full and proper testing of the procedures used to declare amounts uncollectible and remove them from the books. Estimates of uncollectible balances should be discussed with knowledgeable casino credit executives and should be tested by reference to industry norms, past individual casino experience, general economic conditions, and individual account evaluations.

Foreign Exchange Losses With an increasing amount of credit play being used by foreign nationals, some casinos are issuing credit instruments denominated in foreign currency. Given the fluctuations of these currencies relative to the U.S. dollar, the actual value of the debt can change as the foreign currency value changes. Major Las Vegas casinos experienced substantial losses on Mexican peso markers during the recent currency devaluations. A minor area of foreign exchange loss can also result from the casino's handling of amounts of foreign coin or currency that cannot be negotiated through correspondent banks at a rate equal to what the casino paid for the currency. In order to protect themselves from these losses, most casinos are recording their casino receivables in U.S. dollars. In this way, the casino is protected from significant foreign exchange losses, although the payment experience may be substantially poorer following a violent shift in currency relations such as occurs following a devaluation.

Adequate audit procedures should be executed to examine the amount of foreign denominated casino receivables, and appropriate adjustments should be made to the allowance for accounts that are expected to result in substantial impairment of value.

Revenue Recognition   The use of the accrual basis for revenue recognition arising from gaming operations is discussed in considerable detail in the following sections of this chapter.

Prepaid Taxes and Fees

The taxes that a casino pays are numerous and substantial in dollar amount. Earlier chapters have described in detail the taxes, their structure, and their application. In general, the taxes that are subject to prepayment are those gaming taxes and fees levied by the federal, state, and local jurisdictions against the gaming operation. Virtually all of the taxes are prepaid, and the casino auditor must be prepared to deal with a very large and complex accounting for prepaid taxes.

The audit procedures to determine the proper amounts and classification for these prepaid taxes, licenses, and fees are the same as would be followed for any prepaid expense. The primary difference between prepaid expenses in other industries and prepaid expenses in a casino lies in the very significant amounts of money involved. Therefore, these items should be subjected to considerable audit scrutiny.

The basic audit objectives should be the following:

1. Valuation of prepaid amounts.

2. Anticipated realization of prepaid amounts (with special attention given to the limited transferability of many fees and the long-term nature of the prepayment).

3. Tests of proper amortization of prepaid amounts during the year and expense computation.

4. Proper cutoff testing of prepaid amounts during first-year operations.

The auditor must also be concerned that the proper amounts of taxes are being paid. This verification can be most effectively performed during the time that the validity of the prepaid taxes and fees is being audited. The basic audit procedures are outlined below for the prepaid taxes and fees.

1. Verify the beginning balances for prepaid taxes, including

a detailed breakdown of all of the taxes, fees, and other license amounts that have been paid.

2. Verify the period of time to which the taxes and fees apply, in order to determine the proper amortization period.

3. Verify by reference to tax computation schedules and forms filed with the taxing authorities the following:

a. The accuracy of the computation of taxes paid, including assuring that the base upon which the taxes is paid is correctly stated.

b. The amount of taxes paid, by reference to paid checks.

c. The accuracy of the amortization calculation.

There should also be some detailed testing, either here or in the procedural testing area, of the accuracy of computation of tax payment and expense amounts. Given the certainty of audit scrutiny by the gaming authorities and the heavy penalty provisions, the auditors should satisfy themselves that all tax payment amounts have been properly interpreted, computed, and paid on a timely basis.

Where there may be questions about the realization of the prepaid amounts, due to an anticipated change in ownership or the discontinuance of the operation, special analysis of the amounts realizable from the prepaid taxes should be considered.

There should be a client-prepared amortization schedule that indicates the amortization of prepaid tax amounts for either the quarter or the year, depending on the payment schedule for the tax. The amortization of the prepaid amounts should be tested for numerical accuracy and traced to the appropriate expense account to assure correct categorization and accuracy of the posting.

Finally, where participation of shared revenue exists, the payment of all taxes and fees should be tested to ensure that:

1. All fees that are the responsibility of the casino have been paid.

2. Where the sharing or participation agreements call for the division of the taxes, the machine owner has been billed for his or her share of the fees and taxes.

In addition to these detailed audit tests, the auditor should also endeavor to test the reasonableness of the various prepaid amounts, as well as the tax expense amounts.

Given the high likelihood of tax assessments from the regulatory authorities, there should also be some special consideration given to footnote disclosure of possible future liabilities for taxes, either assessed and under dispute, or for assessments likely to be made but as yet unasserted if the amounts are thought to be material.

Accrued Tax Liability   A related area of the accruals of tax liability for gaming taxes and license fees could also be dealt with at the same time that the prepaid taxes are being analyzed. A few of the taxes are due in arrears; in such circumstances, the above audit steps could be repeated in order to assure that the accrual calculation of the taxes due is correct as of the financial statement date.

Other Prepaid and Deferred Items   Other significant prepaid items may exist on the casino's balance sheet that require audit investigation. Typically, these other prepaid items arise from the deferral of various expenses, such as pre-opening expenses, gaming licensing fees paid and expenses incurred, and, in some cases, the front-end costs associated with the establishment of a major entertainment program in the casino.

In these areas, the traditional audit tests that are used for the testing of the adequacy of noncasino prepaid items should be followed. These tests typically include:

1. Verification of amounts of payment to assure the proper computation of the amount of the prepayment.

2. Verification of estimates of future benefits, including assessment of the likelihood of future benefit.

   a. Determination of time periods of estimated benefit.

   b. Estimation of the ultimate benefit of the prepayment.

3. Verification of the computation and method of amortization of the prepaid items.

These accounts are typically included in prepaid or deferred items of a noncasino business. However, the existence of the deferred expenses and prepayment of the casino entertainment expenses can be an unusual as well as significant dollar item. In this area, careful estimates of the future utility or value of the expenditures must be made. The auditor may want to consult either prior experience of the same casino, prior experience of the show producer, or independent experts in the entertainment field to assure the propriety of the deferral and prepayment classification.

Fixed Assets

The audit concern for the fixed asset segment of the balance sheet again is based not on any unusual nature of the asset, but only on the very substantial capital investment in building, equipment, and furnishings that a casino operation requires. Typically, a casino has about 68.1% or in excess of two-thirds of the value of the total assets committed to fixed assets. The determination of the accuracy of additions and deletions and the amortization and depreciation calculations are critical to the proper determination of the casino financial position and results of operation.

Liabilities and Owner's Equity

The audit procedures for the liability and owner's equity section of the balance sheet are focused on traditional items of liability. As a matter of fact, the liability structure of a casino balance sheet has a very regular commercial structure, with substantial amounts of current liabilities, which are mostly trade accounts payable, together with fairly substantial amounts of long-term debt. As with many businesses, casinos also have a substantial deferred income tax liability and a few other deferred items such as deposits on hand.

The only two unique accounts that exist on the liability section of the balance sheet are those associated with progressive slot machine payout liability and chip and token liability. Each of these is discussed in detail below.

Progressive Slot Liability Progressive slot machines commonly used in a casino have a series of meters located immediately above the machine.[20] These meters indicate a jackpot amount that increases or progresses at a fixed rate based on the number of plays of the machine. For example, a $1.00 slot machine progressive jackpot may increase $1.00 for every $5.00 played on the machine. As the meter reading amounts increase, the amount of the jackpot to be paid increases.

As the amounts in these progressive meter readings increase over time with a corresponding increase in unpaid jackpots, it is common practice in casinos to provide for a liability equal to the amount of the unpaid jackpots. This provision is then increased or decreased to bring the account balance into agreement with the detailed meter readings. The amount of increase or decrease in the progressive slot liability is accompanied by an offsetting entry to reported slot machine income. This most commonly results in a reduction of the slot revenue.

The audit procedures to ascertain the proper progressive slot liability are outlined below:

1. Verification of client-taken progressive slot machine meter readings or direct observation by the auditor to assure the accuracy of the meter readings.

2. Testing of the progression of the slot machine readings by comparison to readings for a broad period of time.

3. Testing of the computation of the dollar amount of progressive slot liability.

4. Tracing of the adjustment of progressive slot liability to the general ledger.

Although a single progressive slot machine may not have a material jackpot payoff indicated, the increasing use of the "super jackpot" machine, together with larger-denomination slot machines, has created a significant liability for the casinos and a significant audit procedure.

Chip and Token Liability   A second unique issue of casino liability is the existence and nature of chip and/or gaming token liability. Virtually all casinos have issued various denominations of gaming chips for use in their casino operations.

Following the introduction of the Susan B. Anthony dollar and the limitations on the availability of the larger $1.00 Eisenhower coins, most Nevada casinos sought and secured permission from the U.S. Treasury to issue their own gaming coins or tokens for use in slot machines and in gaming operations within their casinos. The introduction of these tokens has avoided the cost of refitting all the $1.00 slot machines to handle the new coins.

From an operational standpoint, the chips and tokens that a casino has outstanding must be redeemed by the club upon presentation by a patron or another casino. At any time, the amount of liability (or chip float, as it is informally known) is the difference between the total amount of chips and tokens issued by the casino and the amount actually on hand within the casino. Over a period of years, the amount of chip liability generally tends to increase, as the club has more and more of its chips and tokens outstanding in circulation.

The primary reason for this increase over time is not merely transaction float in the immediate casino trading areas, but also the propensity for customers to keep chips and tokens for souvenirs. A second factor is that the redemption of the $1.00 tokens from casino to casino is lagging, since the physical separation of tokens is very difficult and time consuming. There are currently a large number of $1.00 gaming tokens outstanding in Nevada casinos. The reasons for this are not well known; however, the most likely reason for this large token float is the attractiveness of these tokens as souvenirs with minimal expenditure by the customer.

The determination of the chip liability is a complex task, and the audit is also difficult. The basic procedures are outlined in the chapter dealing with game accounting. Also, some of the audit procedures involving the counts of chips and tokens are included in the cash count audit procedures discussed earlier.

1. As outlined in the cash count areas, an accurate count of the amount of chips and tokens on hand must be conducted. This includes chips and tokens in all public cashier or gaming areas, as well as a very accurate count of chips in storage.

 a. Chips in storage are not often used. Therefore, there is some opportunity for theft from this reserve stock. Careful evaluation of storage access procedures as well as the counting of storage chips and tokens is an essential part of the cash count procedures.

 b. In order to reconcile the chips and tokens counts more easily, there should be a careful listing on the cash count sheets of each denomination of chips and tokens in possession of the casino. When the final chip liability is determined, it is very helpful to the auditor to be able to reconcile each denomination of chips in use in the casino, rather than merely reconciling the entire chip liability as a single amount.

2. An accurate compilation of the amount of chips and tokens purchased must be maintained. This purchase inventory may be a carry-forward schedule from year to year since casino purchases of chips are irregular and uncommon.

 a. The amount of purchase of chips reported should be verified by the auditor by confirmation directly with the chip supplier.

 b. Any purchases during the current fiscal period

should be tested in detail. Prior years' purchases should be accepted by reference to prior years' working papers.

3. Any removals from the chip inventory should be recorded. This includes use of chips and tokens for promotional giveaways or those withdrawn for display or direct souvenir sale.

4. If any cancellations or bulk disposal of chips were made during the year, these should be included in the computation of total chips purchased and in use.

5. The amount of chips and tokens on hand should be computed from the various cash counts. Again, the counts should be separated by denominations for ease of reconciliation.

6. The difference between the amount of chips on hand and the amount of chips in use (purchases less cancellations) is the amount of the casino liability for unredeemed chips and tokens.

7. An adjustment is made to the chip liability account to recognize the increase or decrease in chip float during the accounting period. The adjustment is offset by either a decrease or an increase to the casino revenue account. The reason for this revenue adjustment treatment is to recognize that the cash received for the chip or token has not yet been earned and represents a future liability. The revenue cannot be recognized until that liability has been met.

Other Liabilities   Other deferred liabilities for a casino operation are relatively minor amounts that arise in the normal course of business. Typical transactions here include the classification of customer deposits of money to be used in future gaming as a liability, either current or long-term, depending upon the time horizon of the customer's anticipated visit.

A second type of liability is that of long-term sports or race book bets made on various events well in the future. The standard operating procedure is to hold these bets in a suspense liability account until the actual sports event takes place or, in the case of some bets, until the sporting season is over. At this time, the bets on a particular event or season are then moved into the revenue stream.

The only audit procedure involved in this area is the determination of the amount and propriety of these various deposit accounts. Of particular concern is the propriety, amount, and classification of various customer deposits that are the property of the customer and not the casino and should not be included as casino revenue.

Deferred Income Taxes

Casino deferred income taxes operate in much the same manner as deferred taxes in other business entities. The deferred tax liability arises from the use of differing methods of revenue recognition for tax purposes and for financial reporting purposes. Two other sources of deferred taxes for casinos are the use of expense deferrals for financial reporting and the current expensing for tax purposes and the use of accelerated depreciation methods for taxes and more conventional straight-line methods for financial reporting.

Audit procedures for the deferred income tax account for a casino should be exactly the same as for other businesses. This includes the examination of tax returns, the verification or recalculation of the amounts of the deferred taxes, and the development of appropriate information for footnote disclosure.

Revenue and Expense Accounts

The next area of audit significance is the measurement and presentation of various revenue and expense accounts. In general, the revenue and expense accounts in a casino are treated in a manner very similar to that of any commercial enterprise. The unique needs of revenue control over games and slot machines have been discussed fully in their respective chapters. Expense accounting is much more traditional, with only one area of uniqueness, that of promotional allowance or complimentary services. Traditional audit review procedures for key expense accounts are usually sufficient in a casino audit.

Revenue Recognition

An overall issue of casino accounting is the apparent difference in presentation of the results of operations and which method of revenue recognition to use.

The controversy arises because there are two taxing authorities that allow the use of a modified cash basis for the revenue reports for tax purposes. The gross revenue taxation reported to the Nevada authorities is always on a cash basis, with the issuance and collections of casino receivables being either added or subtracted from the aggregate reported revenue figures. In larger casinos where there is a substantial amount of credit play, the differences between the accrual basis income and the actual cash income reported for gross revenue taxation purposes can be substantial. The second allowable cash method of revenue reporting is for federal income tax purposes. Again, for casinos with substantial credit play, the differences between the financial reporting revenue and tax basis revenue can be substantial. These revenue differences constitute the bulk of deferred income tax liability found on casino balance sheets.

Smaller casinos, with little or no credit play, will find that the differences in revenue reporting are nonexistent. Since virtually 100% of the casino activity is conducted in cash, coin, or chips, all of the smaller casinos report their revenue on a cash basis that is identical to the amounts reported on a full accrual basis.

Presentation of Casino Revenue Figures

Casino revenue, measured on either a cash or accrual basis, can be presented as a single figure, usually described as casino win, or by indicating the gross receipts (drop) less the fills, in order to arrive at the net casino win. Common industry practice regarding the presentation of revenue is to use only the single revenue figure for the primary financial statements and to present the drop, fill, and win figures only for the supplementary departmental financial information.

Promotional Allowances or Complimentary Expenses

A major issue regarding the classification of various promotional allowances or complimentary items arises in the discussion of this unique casino expense.[21]

It is customary industry practice to provide many customers with free rooms, food, beverages, and other amenities without cost. These free services are known as complimentaries or promotional allowances in the industry. From a practical standpoint, the services are usually rendered by the support departments of the casino such as the hotel or food and beverage operation in order to encourage customers to play in the casino.

The standard financial reporting rules for the Nevada Gaming Control Board require the inclusion of these complimentary services at full retail value in the reported revenues of the appropriate department (rooms, restaurant, or bar). This requirement follows the widespread hotel industry practice of valuing these items at retail value. Although there may be many different ideas of what constitutes retail, most casinos have established standard charge rates, usually slightly below premium prices for the valuation of complimentary services. The primary use of including these services at retail is to avoid distorting the operating ratios and performance measures in these support areas, particularly in the food and beverage area.

The treatment of the costs of these complimentary services is much less uniform. In some cases, the retail value is merely subtracted from the total sales to arrive at a net sales figure. This presentation then usually labels the deductions as promotional allowances and has become known as the *promotional allowance method*. The rationale behind this treatment is that the revenue is shown as being received, even though it was not really received, and should be immediately removed from further consideration. Also, its prominent location in the income statement clearly points out the amount and overall significance of that item to the operation of a casino. This approach is the method approved by the American Institute of Certified Public Accountants in the casino audit guide.

The second method, known as the *complimentary expense method*, treats the retail amount of the complimentary service either as a cost of operation of the department providing the service or, by using some form of transfer allocation, as a cost of business for the casino department. In some cases, the complimentary expenses are merely regarded as overall administrative expense, and the retail value of the goods and services is included in this area of expense.

In either method of reporting, the actual cost of the food, beverage, or support services for the room is contained in the individual department operating expenses.

From an audit standpoint, the promotional allowance method of presentation is preferred and results in the correct statement of the net income of the casino operation. Care must be taken to assure that the treatment of the promotional allowances or complimentaries is consistent from accounting period to accounting period. Also, steps should be taken to ensure that the casino revenues have not been improperly overstated when the complimentary services are considered.

Other Mandatory Accounting Disclosures

A final area of concern in financial reporting for casinos is the use of other supplementary information that constitutes the necessary full disclosure of the casino operations.[22]

Mandatory disclosure generally focuses on those items that constitute one of the following categories:

1. Description of the basis of accounting and significant accounting policies used by the casino.

2. Explanation of individual items on the balance sheet or income statement that require some form of supplementary disclosure.

3. Explanatory items of a general nature, which are needed to inform the reader of various conditions, problems, or contingencies that may have an impact on the casino.

The first two categories of items have been dealt with in traditional accounting and financial reporting literature for a number of years. Basically, the first footnote to the financial statements should contain a fairly full explanation of the unique accounting treatments of various items on the balance sheet and in the income statement.

Typical disclosures of this nature include:

1. Basis of revenue recognition.

2. Treatment of complimentary expenses.

3. General policies on capitalization and depreciation of assets, treatment of leases and methods, and limitation of deferral of certain items.

The second major area of footnote disclosure deals with providing additional information on material items contained within the basic financial statements. Examples include disclosures of some of the following:

1. The amounts and breakdown of accounts receivable and allowances for doubtful accounts arising from the casino and those arising from other operational areas.

2. Disclosure of the amounts of complimentary expenses.

3. Disclosure of detailed information on the value of assets, together with information on the accumulated depreciation of each class of assets.

4. Detailed information regarding terms, conditions, monthly payment, and collateral for various contracts, notes, and leases, both payable and receivable.

5. Detailed information on the components that make up the deferred taxes for the casino operation.

The third category of disclosure contains those items that are unique to the casino industry or do not specifically relate to an item on the financial statements but are still necessary in order to inform the reader of the financial statements more fully. Some examples of these types of disclosures are:

1. Discussion of material legal actions, with appropriate levels of disclosure or financial provision if amounts are known and the outcomes reasonably certain.

2. Discussion of material commitment made by the organization, including purchase commitments, new construction underway or planned, or other major limitation on future financial flexibility.

3. Description of the casino's major locations, gaming facilities, or gaming activities, in order to inform the reader of the extent of the casino activities in addition to more customary hotel and food and beverage activities. This is particularly important if the casino has operations in more than one geographic location.

4. Description of the terms and conditions under which gaming licenses are issued and the stringent regulatory environment that the casino is operating in. This serves to recognize the value of the gaming license and the permission to operate, which are factors that can affect the overall financial risk of the operation.

CHAPTER 11

Income Taxation of Casino Operations

Introduction

With the growth in the popularity and size of the casino industry, there is increasing concern regarding the income taxation issues arising from casino operation. There is a desire on the part of accountants to provide services to casino clients, but the industry practices and operating policies are not well known. This chapter discusses a number of taxation issues that are unique to casino operations, as well as examining more traditional issues that are of significance or are applied in a unique manner in the casino industry.[1]

A method of describing the basic issues facing the casino industry with respect to income taxation can be achieved by dividing them into three areas:

1. Issues of Casino Revenue.
2. Issues of Casino Liabilities.
3. Other Casino Expense Items.

Using this broad categorization of topics, this chapter focuses attention on some of the detailed issues of income taxation for casinos.

Issues of Casino Revenue

Unreported Income and Estimation Procedures

The main problem of income taxation in casinos during the past thirty years has revolved around the issue of unreported income, skimming, diversion of revenues, or outright theft of funds. However, modern accounting controls as implemented by all major casinos, reviewed by state regulatory agencies, and attested to by CPAs create a financial reporting framework that virtually assures that revenues do not go unreported. This regulatory and control framework, while intended to provide adequate controls, should not be considered absolute.

From the standpoint of income taxation, the status of unreported revenue is clear—it is taxable. In an effort to arrive at estimates of revenue for other businesses, it is common for the Internal Revenue Service (IRS) to use various estimation methods in order to develop and sustain estimates of unreported income. Due to a number of factors, however, casino revenue cannot be reliably estimated by indirect methods. Statistics presented by the Nevada Gaming Control Board in the annual *Gaming Abstract* point to differences in revenue even for the same game or machine depending upon the size of the casino and its geographic location. Table 11-1 indicates some of that wide range of variation. For example, for statewide hotel-casinos there is over a 50% difference in the spread between the lower quartile and the upper quartile in the reported win per game for 1985.

Based on these data, an estimate of annual gross revenue for a small casino (assuming six 21 tables, one crap table, 150 slot machines, and a keno game) would vary from $5,586,667 to $10,516,233 in annual revenue. This represents a variation of over 88.2%.

Another issue that prevents the accurate estimation of casino revenue is that the majority of casino operations are conducted on a cash or cash equivalent basis using chips or tokens. Therefore, the ability to measure business activity in the casino through indirect measures such as bank clearings can be severely limited. Finally, the patterns of business activity in a casino may be subject

Table 11-1. Comparative Estimates of Revenue.
Annual Win per Unit—Fiscal Year Ended June 30, 1983.
Publicly Owned Hotel-Casinos.

Game	Lower Quartile	Median	Upper Quartile
21	$165,292	$245,461	$392,785
Craps	559,128	833,970	1,404,176
$.05 Slot	7,726	9,369	10,709
.10 Slot	7,607	11,199	14,243
.25 Slot	16,993	18,640	25,305
.50 Slot	13,440	20,406	30,945
1.00 Slot	34,359	47,217	53,47
Keno	899,213	1,392,246	1,904,109

to extreme fluctuations, both by days of the week and by seasons. This factor makes statistical analysis and projection extremely difficult and generally unreliable.

What Is Casino Revenue?

The term generally accepted for casino gross revenue is *win*. This concept is documented in various state legislative enactments and is defined as the amount won by the casino after all wagers have been paid to winning customers. Win for the most part is the result of betting activity carried on within the casino on table games, in slot machines, and on games such as keno or bingo.

Rake-offs, commissions, or time buy-ins on poker games are other types of revenues to the casino that do not fit neatly into the category of win. Although the issue has been debated between casinos and regulatory authorities for gross revenue taxation purposes, all amounts, regardless of their character, are included in revenue for income taxation purposes.

Credit Play and Revenue Determination

The computation of the win or casino revenue for a cash operation is fairly straightforward. It is the total amount of cash won by the casino. However, once casino credit play is introduced, the accounting treatment of these receivable items (commonly known as markers) and the computation of casino win becomes more complex.

Part of the complexity lies in the very high loss ratios on casino credit. Estimates of uncollectible amounts range from 30 to 45% of the outstanding balances at year end. This creates a situation where a substantial amount of the casino revenue may never be collected. For state gross revenue taxation, markers are not considered part of the casino win until they have been collected.

The exclusion of credit play earnings as taxable income for the casino has no basis in regulation, law, or court decision. It is the sole result of casino operating tradition, enhanced by years of accepted practice within the industry. This practice has been sanctioned by the current Nevada Gaming Control Board rules and accepted to a limited degree by the New Jersey Casino Control Commission reporting rules. The current rules exclude all uncollected casino receivables from casino gross revenue for Nevada taxation and limit the exclusion amount to 4% of gross receipts in New Jersey.

This "when collected" method of regulatory accounting for revenues has had the effect of limiting the IRS to revenue recognition methods that are consistent with state-sanctioned accounting practices.

Since almost all casinos exclude most, if not all, of their markers from revenue for state gross revenue purposes, the same form of revenue reporting is widely practiced for income taxation purposes. This puts most larger casinos on a form of modified accrual accounting for tax purposes. The revenue is reported on a cash basis, and there is full accrual accounting for expense items. This often conflicts with the full accrual accounting method widely used for financial reporting and creates a substantial amount of deferred income taxes for the casino operations.

This accounting treatment of revenue has its roots in the English civil law concept of the uncollectability of gambling debts.[2] Since a debt of this nature is deemed not to be legally enforceable and collectible, the substantial uncertainty of collection seems to be a reasonable basis for excluding marker win from the taxable revenue of the casino until and unless it is collected.

Recent legislative enactments in New Jersey and Nevada providing for the legal collection of gaming debts may have had an impact on the tax treatment of these winnings. The related issue of interstate collection of gaming debts from New Jersey and Nevada to other jurisdictions has not been tested or adjudicated.

A curious offshoot of the issue of taxability of these credit winnings in a casino recently occurred in Carson City, Nevada. The Ormsby House casino (*Herman* v. *Sea-Air Support*, Nevada Supreme Court, 1980), in an effort to enforce collection of a gaming debt, sought to have the debt declared a legal obligation. Much to the surprise of observers in the gaming industry, other Nevada casinos filed *amicus curiae* (friend of the court) briefs that sought to sustain the position of the debtor—*not the casino*. The speculation was that the major Las Vegas casinos, where credit is a significant financial factor, might be faced with a major change in collection philosophy. They felt that with such a change in the legal status of collectability, changes in state gross revenue taxation and federal income taxation would follow closely behind. This decision would have led to the taxability of enormous amounts of uncollected gaming debts and a significant increase in the tax liability of the casinos. The Ormsby House case was resolved in favor of the debtor. Subsequent legislative enactments that have made the collection of markers legal in Nevada have not yet resulted in any significant change in the attitude toward income taxability of uncollected markers.[3]

Recent court cases in Nevada regarding gross gaming revenue assessments have narrowed the basis for not including markers in gross revenue. The regulatory bodies have disallowed the deduction for any marker that was issued without due care or in such an irregular manner as to render it virtually uncollectible.[4]

Two cases regarding the federal income taxability of markers have not settled the issue either. In *Desert Palace, Inc., v. Commissioner*, 72 TC. No. 1033 (September 11, 1979), the court held that markers do not represent taxable income until collected. In *Flamingo Resort, Inc., v. United States*, 485 F. Supp. 926 (D. Nev. 1980), the court determined that markers represent taxable income upon their accrual.

A final problem is that a major shift in the taxable status of markers in Nevada for gross revenue purposes may cause new calls for the consistent treatment of markers for federal income tax purposes. It appears, however, that the current practice of excluding these amounts from taxable income will be continued.[5]

Revenue Reductions—Bad Debts

A third issue of casino revenue relates to the reductions of revenue allowed through writeoffs of bad debts. Generally, through the operation of the modified accrual basis for income taxation previously mentioned, large amounts of uncollected casino receivables or markers are not yet in the revenue stream and are not subject to income taxation. If in the future the markers are subjected to accrual income recognition, it is reasonable to assume that appropriate revenue reductions through traditional bad debt writeoffs or allowances will be allowed. Consistent treatment of the revenue and the valuation of the receivable is essential to rational tax policy.

However, the issue of bad debts is still present where a casino may have a substantial amount of check cashing (either payroll or personal checks). The checks cashed are assumed to be used to wager in casinos. If the check of the customer is returned by the bank and remains unpaid, then the casino is forced to write off the bad check. These writeoffs are considered a reduction of revenue for both state gross revenue taxation and federal income taxation purposes.

The casinos in Nevada and New Jersey are required by law to specify in writing their procedures for check cashing and credit granting.[6] Included in these procedures must be a way of evaluating a bad debt, assessing the collectability, and approving the writeoff. In a casino operation, there may be various departures from the stated procedures at any point in the check cashing or credit extension. Often the violation in procedure has resulted in the disallowance of the bad debt as a reduction of casino win for state gross revenue taxation purposes. This disallowance takes place regardless of the lack of credit-worthiness of the debt instrument. It is based on the failure to follow the stated procedure. This policy of disallowance appears to be highly arbitrary; while it may lead to new challenges to the bad debt writeoffs for income tax purposes, it does not appear to be a reasonable or prudent practice.

Slot Hopper Loads and Table Loads

The fourth revenue issue of casinos is the problem revolving around the monies actually stored within a slot machine or on the table inventory of a pit game. Typically, slot hopper loads are required when the casino is first opened or if a new slot machine is added. At that time, a sum of money is placed into the slot hopper so that during the period of initial play of the machine, it is able to pay the jackpots that occur automatically. The coins deposited into the machine can go directly into the drop bucket located under the slot machine (and be included in revenue), or they can be diverted into the slot hopper in order to replenish the hopper (which may be at too low a level to meet normal operating requirements). In this case, some of the coins that are won by the slot machine are not placed in the drop bucket, and the revenue has been diverted and is underreported.

This problem has never been significant in the past. When the average slot hopper load for a $0.05 slot machine was only $50 to $60, the possible revenue error was very small. However, with the increasing popularity of $1.00 slot machines, slot hopper loads are typically $300 to $500 per machine. The problem now has become significant from two standpoints. First, when the new slot machine is put on the floor, the process of filling the slot hopper must be considered a capital transaction, funded from cash on hand and not merely accounted for as another kind of jackpot or payout—which are revenue reduction transactions. The improper use of jackpot fills for a new machine results in the increase in the amounts paid out by the casino (with a consequent reduction in casino slot win) and the understatement of taxable income.

A second problem is that the slot machine may be underfilled at the time of opening the casino. In a new casino with a minimum of cash on hand, this situation is not as unusual as might be expected. Over time, the gradual buildup of slot hopper loads from their original fill to the full amount (for example, from a minimum fill of $100 to a normal $400) can result in a significant understatement of slot win. This understatement of income arises because the winnings of the slot machines are not reflected in the slot drop, but rather remain in the slot hopper where they are not reported.

The procedure to avoid this underreporting of income is periodically to count the machine hopper loads. The result of these counts can then be evaluated against the original slot hopper loads. Any significant differences should then be considered an adjustment to slot income.

A similar situation occurs, but with somewhat less financial impact, with table loads. The table load or table tray inventory represents the dealer's working fund. The fluctuations in this inventory are accounted for either in the game opening or closing inventory procedures or by end-of-shift fills or credits. These inventory fluctuations or end-of-shift fills are included in the determination of game win during the count procedures.

Fluctuations in table inventories, other than normal gaming activity, often take place. For example, table tray amounts may be increased for high-stakes players or during periods of increased gaming activity such as holidays or when special junket groups are in the casino. These special increases or decreases in table loads must be accounted for as capital transactions, just as with slot loads, with appropriate offsets to cash on hand. Current practice, which is concerned with the proper determination of casino revenues, requires that these changes in table inventory should not enter the revenue stream of the casino. If regular fill and credit slips are used to increase the amount on the table, then the inclusion of these fills or credit slips in the drop box results in the erroneous recording of casino table win for one period, with a second offsetting error occurring when the table inventory is reduced.

Casino Liabilities

Progressive Slot Liability

Progressive slot machines commonly used in a casino have a series of meters located immediately above the machine. These meters increase or progress jackpot amounts at a fixed rate based on the number of plays of the machine. For example, a $1.00 machine may increase its jackpot amount $1.00 for every $5.00 played on the machine. As the meter reading amounts increase, the amount of jackpot to be paid increases.

As the amounts in these progressive meter readings increase over time with a corresponding increase in unpaid jackpots, it is common practice in casinos to provide for a liability equal to the amount of the unpaid jackpots. This reserve is then increased or decreased as appropriate. The amount of the increase or decrease in liability is accompanied by an offsetting entry to be reported as slot income. This most commonly results in a reduction of the revenue, which in turn reduces the taxable income.[7]

Casinos treat the total amount of progressive slot liability at year end as a fixed liability directly related to current income. Therefore, it may be accrued and deducted in determining net income for income tax purposes. Although a single machine may have only a modest progressive slot adjustment from year to year, the introduction of new machines with larger denominations and larger payoff rates has created a very significant tax issue.

It is the position of the Internal Revenue Service, and the subject of pending appeal, that the payment of the progressive jackpots is contingent on a number of factors and that all events may or may not have occurred to establish the liability properly. The IRS feels that the accrual is an improper reserve and that the expenses associated with the unpaid progressive slot jackpots are not applicable in determining taxable income. The taxpayer's position is that the liability is indeed determinable and, by state regulations, required to be paid.

The deductibility of this type of accrual in the future has been severely limited under the premature accrual rules contained in the 1984 Tax Reform Act. It is suggested, nevertheless, that the progressive slot liability should be allowable for income tax purposes.

Chip and Token Liability

Another type of unique casino liability arises from the existence and nature of chip or token liability. Virtually all casinos have issued various denominations of gaming chips for use in their casino operations. More recently, various casinos have sought and secured permission from the U.S. treasury to issue their own gaming tokens for use in slot machines and in gaming operations to avoid the cost of refitting the $1.00 slot machines.

From an operational standpoint, the chips and tokens that a casino has outstanding must be redeemed by the casino upon presentation by a patron or other casino. At any time, the amount of liability or chip float is the difference between the total amount of chips and tokens issued and in use by the casino and the total amount of chips and tokens actually on hand. Over a period of years, the amount of chip liability has generally tended to increase, as the casino has more and more of its chips and tokens in circulation.

The primary reason for this increase over time is not merely the float in the immediate casino trading area, but also the propensity to keep chips and tokens for souvenirs. The new $1.00 tokens are difficult to separate and identify in counting procedures and are not widely redeemed between casinos. There are currently a very large number of $1.00 gaming tokens outstanding in Nevada casinos.

The basic income taxation issue is how much income should be recognized that is derived from the exchange of chips and tokens for cash. Of the total number of chips outstanding, it is not clear how many represent sales as souvenirs and how many may ultimately be redeemed. The souvenir sales portion would then be taxable income. The amount of income would be the face value of the chip or token minus the cost of the chip or token. In most cases, the cost of the chips or tokens has been written off as an expense of casino operation, so the entire face value of the chip or token is profit.

The IRS maintains that some portion of the chip float is permanent and that some portion of the total chip liability should be considered as sales income and the chips permanently retired.

Current practice indicates that only at specific times, such as during the change of ownership of the club or at the introduction of a new series of gaming tokens, can a casino's actual liability for chips be determined. Upon redemption of all old chips and tokens, the actual amount of liability is therefore reduced to zero. Exceptions exist, however, and Harolds Club in Reno prides itself on honoring old gaming tokens discovered in obscure hiding places and redeemed at the club—as much as fifty years later. This seems to indicate an informal policy of unlimited redemption.

Under these circumstances, the casino clearly has a continuing liability for the redemption of all gaming chips and tokens. For income taxation purposes, this liability is clear and distinct. The accrued chip liability and the related expenses are clearly properly allowable items.

Other Casino Expense Items

The last area of discussion concerns more traditional issues of income taxation as they are specifically applied to casino operations. These areas are depreciation, repair and maintenance expenses, pre-opening expenses, and investment tax credits.

Depreciation of Casino Assets

The principal taxation issues in depreciation deal with the estimated useful lives, salvage values, and methods of depreciation used. These areas have been substantially simplified following the enactment of the 1981 Economic Recovery Tax Act (ERTA), which removed much of the debate from the depreciation expense area by adopting the new Accelerated Cost Recovery System (ACRS).

Ranges of useful lives of common gaming equipment are indicated below:

	ACRS	Pre-ERTA New	Used
Slot Machines	5 years	5 to 8 years	3 to 4 years
Pit Tables	5 years	4 to 6 years	3 to 5 years
Keno Equipment	5 years	8 to 10 years	3 to 5 years

One of the most critical decisions in depreciation policy is the selection of an appropriate useful life. For most casino equipment, there are factors of both technical and competitive obsolescence, as well as traditional wear and tear.

Equipment used in pit games, such as 21, craps, and roulette tables, are all considered much the same and are generally depreciated over a fairly long time period. A major difference exists in the areas of slot machines and keno equipment. In both these cases, the recent advent of electronic games and components has resulted in rapid technological obsolescence. The rate of replacement of slot machines is considerably higher, however, than the replacement rate for keno equipment. In addition, slot machines have very high rates of wear and tear. Depreciation lives as short as five years have been allowed for slot machines. The general furniture and fixtures in casino public areas are subjected to extremely rough use and are generally worn out from a structural or appearance standpoint in about three to four years. For business reasons, keeping a casino looking clean and neat is of vital importance, so these items are frequently replaced or renewed. This tends to lead to very short depreciation lives.

A final issue of useful lives concerns the use of component depreciation methods for the various elements of a casino building. Although eliminated in the 1984 Tax Reform Act, this method is still in use in many casinos. Under the old component depreciation procedures, the heating and air-conditioning equipment was subject to a life of about ten years, while the structure itself might have an estimated useful life of thirty years or more. Component depreciation has been widely discussed in other areas and has been used in large hotel-casino operations. The rules applied to casinos indicate that component depreciation is acceptable if the overall reduction of the estimated useful life of the entire casino is not more than 10–15% of the building life.

Salvage Values   The issue of salvage values is a highly subjective one, and there are generally no reliable estimates. Again, the changes in the ACRS system have eliminated many issues. The salvage values of game tables generally tend to be fairly high, assuming that there is a regular program of repair and maintenance. In this area, salvage values of 10–20% seem to be appropriate. For slot machines or keno equipment, there tends to be very little salvage value. The value, if any, is certainly not in the used machine market but only as parts to maintain other older machines. It has been estimated that the salvage value of most slot machines should not exceed 10%. This is especially true when most new machines are entirely electronic. The Internal Revenue Service has from time to time proposed salvage values in the range of 25% to 30%, but as this discussion has suggested, lower salvage values appear to be fully justified.

Depreciation Methods The casino industry frequently uses a very conservative approach to depreciation in the adoption of the straight-line methods. The use of accelerated methods of depreciation is very infrequent. The application of bonus depreciation is also infrequent. There are also very few applications of the class-life system for casino assets. There seems to be no valid tax reason for the popularity of the straight-line depreciation methods used for tax purposes, other than their simplicity of application. This simplicity argument is expected to result in virtually uniform acceptance of the ACRS system for all new casino property acquisitions.

Maintenance and Repair Expenses

The decision to capitalize or expense various maintenance and repair costs is the same in the casino industry as it is in other businesses. The principal difference is that casinos operate on a 24-hour basis, with intense public usage of their facilities. This factor, coupled with the need for the casino to present a pleasant appearance to attract and retain customers, makes casino operations a high-maintenance business. As previously mentioned, this maintenance is particularly high in the areas of slot machines and public area furnishings. Repair and maintenance expenses are generally high and are almost always deducted currently from income, rather than being capitalized as substantial improvements. This represents a proper treatment of these expenses for income taxation purposes.

Pre-Opening and Pre-Production Expenses

The pre-opening expenses of a casino can be very significant. First, there is a very long lead time associated with building or acquiring a casino due to the licensing, investigation, and background checking that must be completed prior to issuing a gaming license. Second, the pre-opening advertising and promotion are extensive. They are necessary to build a new customer base for the casino. Rules that allow the amortization of start-up costs over a period of 60 months after the business is begun are applicable to the casino industry; yet, under financial accounting guidelines, they may be immediately deducted. This creates an item of timing difference between the book and tax profits.

A second area of expense that is currently deductible is pre-production expenses for a stage or production show intended to run for a considerable period in a showroom. The expenses for financial accounting purposes are capitalized and written off over the estimated run of the show. In this case, a second but offsetting timing difference is created.

Expenses attributable to the expansion of an existing casino continue to be currently deductible. The current treatments of organization and pre-production costs appear to be a proper and realistic approach to the expenses of a casino operation.

Investment Tax Credits

Investment tax credits are widely utilized in the casino industry. The principal reason for the importance of this type of tax credit is that most casinos have a very large amount of qualified Section 38 property in the casino, particularly slot machines. The qualification of casino gaming devices or equipment is not often challenged by the IRS. The frequent replacement of slot machines has, however, created a substantial problem of investment credit recapture accounting for casino accountants.

Other Taxation Issues

Entertainment Facilities

Many hotel and casinos maintain off-premise facilities to entertain important customers and entertainers who appear in their showrooms. The general crackdown on "entertainment facilities" appears to have caught these premises in the net. The examinations have resulted in questioning whether these facilities meet the definitions of an entertainment facility, which threatens the disallowance of the expense. In general, the expense has been accepted by the IRS after proper verification of substantial customer and entertainer use. The deduction appears to be allowable if documented.

Withholding, Reporting, and Information Returns

There is a complex set of rules regarding the supplying of several levels of information to the IRS about customer winnings. In general, the lowest level of information is the use of a W-2G information return where the keno winnings exceed $1,500 and slot or bingo winnings exceed $1,200 (IRC 3402[g][5]). No withholding is presently required, although the IRS recommends that a withholding program be implemented on certain transactions.

Withholding rates of 30% for nonresident aliens and 30% for Canadian residents on winnings are still in place. These withholding rules are applied to keno, slot, and bingo payoffs. In general, table game winnings are ignored by the casinos, although this type of winning appears to be covered by the existing rules.

Recently introduced rules also require casinos to report all cash transactions (those in excess of $10,000) to the IRS as a part of controlling the so-called underground economy and to prevent laundering of illegally acquired funds.

Tax Status of Complimentary Services

Although originally challenged under various bases, such as income to the recipient, a gift exceeding $25, and information reporting (Form 1099) requirements for amounts received in excess of $600, this entire issue seems to have died. Complimentaries are, and will continue to be, considered an ordinary and necessary cost of business. Future challenges to extraordinary complimentaries beyond the normal food, beverages, and lodging may cause them to become taxable.

Conclusions

The expansion of legalized casino gaming from what was once a highly localized industry into the newest emerging national industry has focused attention on many issues relating to income taxation of casino operations.

The issues of casino revenues subject to taxation currently rest on the foundation of widespread industry practice. Casinos expect to continue as they have in the past. No dramatic challenges appear to be forming from either the IRS or state taxation authorities for change. However, as tax reform is implemented, the adoption of a corporate minimum tax may affect casino corporations. Changes in partnership taxation may have an impact on the classification or deductibility of certain types of revenues and expenses passed through to partners by operating casino partnerships.

The issues of casino liabilities are far less certain. The uncertain foundation of progressive slot and chip/token liabilities is under active attack by the IRS. In spite of cogent argument on both sides, both types of liabilities appear to be fully justified and proper for inclusion in the computation of current income.

As the casino industry grows, the taxation issues will undoubtedly proliferate. However, it is fairly certain that these future issues will only expand on the fundamentals of casino revenue and casino liabilities and expenses.

CHAPTER 12

Managerial Accounting in Casinos

Introduction

The unique objectives of casino accounting could be described as focusing on three main areas of concern:

1. Internal controls to assure prevention of theft of assets.

2. Controls to ensure the accurate reporting of all revenue transactions.

3. Accounting information to provide analysis of data for managerial decision making.

In addition to these three unique areas, the traditional financial reporting aspects of asset, liability, revenue, and expense accounting are also of significant interest.

Theft Prevention

The first concern of casino accounting is the necessity of constructing controls over the operations that assure the maximum amount of control over the assets of the casino. Since the casino operates in a highly liquid environment, with virtually all transactions consisting of cash or chips, the control over these assets is the first and foremost concern of any accounting system.

Accurate Revenue Reporting

The second concern of casino accounting is to assure that the revenue transactions of the casino are properly reported. This accuracy of reporting is necessitated by the fact that most, if not all, of the revenue transactions such as slot machine play and table game play are accomplished without any recording of the transactions at that time and are only recorded once a day during the

335

counting process. The accounting problems associated with this delayed recording are akin to operating a large department store without any cash registers or inventory to relate to and being able to tally the sales transactions only once a day.

Managerial Accounting

The final area of concern in casino accounting is the maintenance of various accounting records to provide information of use to management. These uses include measurement of economic benefits as appropriate to any expenditure. This gives rise to various accounting and record-keeping systems that, while not a formal part of the revenue or expense transactions, are nonetheless necessary. An example in this area is a marker control system that not only records the amount of credit issued but also determines the extent and quality of the play (including amount wagered, duration of play, and so on) of the various marker customers. Another example is the record-keeping of the total costs incurred by a particular complimentary customer or the total costs of a junket or bus tour when related to the amounts wagered by those junket or bus tour customers.

The issues of managerial accounting in the casino industry are considerably less understood than in many other industries or businesses. The lack of a traditional manufacturing environment and, perhaps, the unique aspects of its services rendered have contributed to the lack of good managerial accounting practice in the industry.

Very little information is available regarding the various managerial accounting practices of the industry, and few, if any, applications have been considered, let alone implemented. In spite of this present low level of use of managerial and cost accounting procedures in the casino industry, many of the concepts of managerial and cost accounting are perfectly applicable.

Some basic concepts of managerial accounting that could be applicable to casino operations are:

1. Use of break-even analysis and cost volume profit calculations, leading to a better understanding of casino cost behavior.

2. Cost-finding analysis for new games; assessing the cost impacts of revised operating procedures for the casino games; and analysis of profitability of junkets, bus programs, or complimentaries.

3. Development of standards for employee performance, together with analysis of variances.

In addition to these traditional managerial accounting areas, the use of various forms of departmental income statements is very important to hotel-casino operation. In many cases, the food and beverage and hotel departments exist to support the primary revenue generation of the casino. In such cases, a policy develops of expecting to lose money in the food and beverage area or in the rooms operation, largely due to the high level of complimentary services rendered. In the absence of a distinct profit motive, the process of controlling costs in these support areas can be very important. The objective is no longer generation of profits but cost containment. Another major attitude change is not focusing on inordinately complex allocation costs in the calculation of departmental profits, but rather using the contribution margin approach, with the recognition that certain costs are controlled at the top management level and should not be charged against the department.[1]

A final area of key management accounting is the development and use of budgeting for the casino operations.[2] Casinos that have used a comprehensive budget process have experienced significantly improved operations in terms of operating efficiency and lower costs as well as better revenues, adding to improved overall profitability.

The worth of a budget system lies in several factors. The first is that the process of construction of the budget forces the casino managers and supervisors to take a close look at the cost and revenue behavior. This may be the first time that many casino managers have even tried to understand what their costs really are, and how the various factors such as season, conventions, mix of customers, advertising, and promotion may affect the number of customers in the casino and the amount of gaming activity. In addition, focusing the manager's attention on the costs of operation may lead to realization for the first time of the extent of the costs, their nature, and what steps can or cannot be taken to control them. For example, the two largest costs in the casino department are labor costs and gaming taxes. The latter cannot be controlled in the short run, while the former can be carefully controlled within a fairly short time horizon. This labor control can be easily increased by more careful attention to the process of assignment of staff and, where casino activity justifies it, cutting the number of staff on hand.

The second key element in the budget system is the necessity of having a system set up to control the costs, to record them, and to report the results of the operation compared to the budget on a frequent basis. This feedback element allows the manager again to understand how costs behave and ultimately to improve the process of future cost estimation and budgeting.

Attention Directing

The attention-directing issues of accounting for a casino operation lie in three areas that are distinct from the areas previously examined. These are:

1. Specific detailed cost analysis of a particular part of the casino (for example, the keno department) or of a specific activity (such as the profitability of a junket or bus program).[3]

2. The use of financial forecasts in order to justify capital expansion programs or to secure funding from lenders or the public capital markets.

3. The comparative analysis of activities such as mergers or acquisitions, where different candidates are evaluated and selected, based largely upon their anticipated financial performance.

Complementary Nature of Management Accounting

Although they are often felt to be two separate and distinct aspects of accounting, the use of management accounting techniques can contribute tremendously to the maintenance of a good system of internal control in the casino. This fostering of better control is achieved in the following ways:

1. Accountants are often involved in the design of internal control systems for the casino. This involvement, whether by internal accounting personnel or by external accounting consultants, has the effect of increasing the level of understanding of the control system by the accountants and leads to a higher level of reassurance about the controls on the part of the accountants. Also, there is a higher level of confidence in the casino controls on the part of independent accountants if they are both familiar and comfortable with the operating procedures.

2. In addition to familiarity and reassurance, the use of managerial accounting analysis can provide an excellent ongoing source of information by which the effectiveness of the various fi-

nancial and accounting controls can be monitored. For example, a monthly analysis of the profitability of a junket, complimentary, or bus program can be performed. Any unusual declines or inordinate increases in the profitability may be indicative of a problem with the program that should be investigated. In any case, the casino knows immediately that something is wrong and that action must be taken to correct a problem. This is substantially better than waiting for a quarterly or annual audit review of the profitability of the overall casino.

3. Another area where managerial accounting can contribute to the control of casino operations is in its focus, which typically is directed toward small elements in the accounting system, rather than the whole financial reporting entity. In this way, the managerial accounting interest has the same focus as the internal control interest—that is, the smaller operating units, which are responsible for implementing the key internal controls. Managerial accounting deals with smaller units and is in a better position to evaluate the effectiveness of these controls that might be overlooked in the larger audit focus.

4. Finally, the use of managerial accounting techniques to perform the analysis of various statistical information, or perhaps even to perform statistical analysis on accounting information, often leads the accountants to a better understanding of the dynamics of casino operation and thereby to a better job of overall financial audit and control evaluation.

Specific Managerial Accounting Applications in Casinos

Cost Allocations

The topic of cost allocations is one that has generated an inordinate amount of concern in the literature of cost and managerial accounting. There are rational arguments both for and against the use of these allocations.

Complimentary Costs The primary concern in a casino environment is the allocation of the various costs of complimentary services rendered to customers by the divisions other than the casino. As previously mentioned, the food and beverage and rooms departments often incur substantial costs without any revenue in the pursuit of good casino gaming customers. The accepted industry procedure is to allocate the costs to the casino in an administrative cost category with the rooms being charged at a standard rate and the food and beverage at menu prices. These are reflected in the revenue of the rendering department, while the expenses are charged to the casino department. This allocation procedure results in more accurate results in terms of the revenue of these service departments, when compared to their costs. However, the allocation to the casino could be somewhat arbitrary and result in charges that could be excessive.

Another method of accounting for complimentaries is to grant the allocated revenue benefit to the service department, but, instead of charging the costs to the casino department, to charge them to overall administration. The rationale behind this procedure is to recognize that the overall complimentary expenditure is usually a top-level management policy decision, and the casino manager is only charged with the implementation of the complimentary service program. Also, there are aspects of the complimentary programs, such as free drinks, that could be expressed more accurately as relating to the overall casino advertising policy. Therefore, it is more reasonable that these costs be recognized for what they really are—advertising and promotion costs—and included with those overall administrative costs in that category.

A major debate rages throughout the industry regarding the basis for these cost allocations. In general, a set standard is used for the various service departments. This allows the casino to use a standard cost over a long period of time and saves the executive time that is inevitably consumed in the process of agreeing on these costs. In most circumstances, the following types of costs are used:

1. For hotel rooms charged to the casino complimentary account, the cost basis is usually a discount of 20–25% from the published room rack rate for the type of room, season, and other factors. This lower rate recognizes two factors. First is the slightly reduced cost of rendering the service, due to a lower level of billing and accounting. Second is a recognition of the market realities that complimentary rooms are usually used most extensively during slow periods and might have to be discounted anyway in the open market to keep them occupied during these slower periods. The room rate is sometimes justified based on a perceived minimum cost for the room, including variable costs associated with the front desk, the reservation office, the maid and room service, and a por-

tion of the debt service. It represents a no-profit point for the room rental.

2. For food rendered to the casino customer on a complimentary basis, it is customary to use the menu price for allocation. This is based on the fact that most food operations in the casino are not designed to provide an operating profit, but rather merely to provide food at a minimum cost. Again, free or very cheap food is used as an advertising ploy by many casinos. Given the assumption that the menu must achieve at least a break-even point in its operation, the menu prices are a close approximation of the no-profit point for the food operation and thus are used as the key allocation price.

3. For beverage and bar service, a slightly different policy is used, again recognizing the basic costs of the materials in the drinks. For drinks that accompany food service, which include wine and mixed drinks, the menu or list prices are used much in the same manner as for the food operation. For beverages served directly at bars, as well as for drinks delivered to slot machine or table game players, the cost used for the allocation is the estimated cost of the drink. In these cases, the cost may be substantially below the selling price. In general, the allocated cost is approximately 50% of the menu or selling price of the drink.

In no circumstances is casino gaming allowed on a complimentary basis, so the valuation issues in this area simply do not exist.

Other Administrative Cost Allocations   Some additional cost allocations are used in order to determine financial results in bars or restaurants. These financial results, after allocation, could be compared to industry standards. These comparisons are more accurate since all costs, including support activities, are now included in the restaurant and bar costs. In these cases, there may be common restaurant or bar support activities that have to be allocated to many different restaurants in the casino or to many different bars.

In addition, other allocations take place in the general and administrative area. Examples include allocated costs of corporate communications—telephone, executive expenses, and other items. For some casino operations with sales offices in various locations, there may also be some allocation of home office expenses to the costs of operation of these branch offices. Also, fully integrated operations, which operate in more than one location or in more than one gaming jurisdiction, may use certain cost allocations more accurately to reflect the actual operating results.

Responsibility Accounting and Departmental Statements

Another area of managerial accounting that is widely used in the casino industry is departmental profit and loss statements. The recognition of these statements as an integral part of the managerial control system in the casino may seem almost trivial to many more mature industries. However their use in the casino industry is relatively recent and their importance in managerial decision making in the casino quite critical.

Most departmental profit and loss statements are divided into the principal operating units of a hotel-casino. These main divisions are then further divided into individual bars, restaurants, or other food and beverage areas such as convention or banquet food functions. In the casino operation, the highest level of the division is the overall casino financial statement, which is the responsibility of the casino manager. Immediately below that responsibility level would be the departments of the slots, the pit, and support areas, including the cage and credit department. In the slots as well as the pit for larger casinos, there may be separate pit areas that have a mixture of games; in some casinos, there may be a suborganizational unit consisting just of crap games in a certain pit area or just of baccarat in another. Each of these subunits has a departmental profit and loss statement.

For most smaller clubs, the division among pit, slots, and overall casino operation (which would encompass the support cage and credit areas) is all the detail that is presented in the departmental financial statements.

Departmental Reporting Elements   In the use of departmental profit and loss statements, the number of items of financial interest that are reported can vary considerably from casino to casino. Some casinos have attempted to include virtually every cost element incurred in the operation of a department or subdepartment and have tried to report all of these costs with all applicable revenues for the department. This approach has been taken in an attempt to report virtually all of the costs in the overall casino-wide financial statements on a departmental basis.

The primary problem with this approach is that many of the costs may be arbitrarily allocated or the ability of the responsible manager to control the costs may be very low. Therefore, the reporting of those costs at the department level may have an adverse effect on the manager's motivation. The problem of overallocation of costs and the frustration based on the uncontrollability of the reported costs are the most common criticisms leveled at these departmental profit and loss statements.

A proposed solution to this dilemma is to construct not departmental profit and loss statements, but rather departmental contribution statements. In these statements, only the costs directly attributable and controllable by the department are charged to that department. In this way, the costs that are reported at each responsible level are those costs that the manager should and can be concerned about. For example, charging the slot machine manager with a portion of the advertising budget based on the percentage of revenues may be a rational allocation basis, but unless the slot manager has some say in how the advertising dollars are spent and how many dollars are spent, it is unreasonable to expect the departmental financial statements to reflect advertising cost. However, if the slot manager is empowered to grant complimentary privileges or free drinks to players, then it may be reasonable to include these costs in the slot department costs of operation.

The adoption of this contribution margin approach eliminates many of the behavioral problems associated with current full presentation departmental financial statements. It does require a substantial amount of education of both department managers and higher-level managers in order to work effectively in the casino environment.

Suboptimization Problems One of the serious organizational problems that has developed in the casino business in the last few years has been a growing suboptimization of the overall hotel-casino performance. There have been many reasons advanced for this situation. One of the most significant is that the importance of overall profit performance has become a widely recognized ideal within various training programs as well as traditional educational institutions over the past five to ten years. The result of this "profit focus" is that new managers, usually trained in traditional areas of hotel management such as food and beverage operations, tend to focus on the profitability of their individual departments and fail to recognize the complex interplay between the service or support functions of the hotel and the primary revenue-generating function of the casino.

The use of complex departmental profit and loss statements may have accelerated this process by improperly focusing the attention on the bottom line of the departmental unit rather than the overall hotel-casino operation. Thus, the unfortunate situation arises where decisions are made to maximize the departmental profit—or perhaps contribution—while the overall quality of casino customers is slipping, casino revenues are decreasing, or costs are being increased in the casino area.

The problem of suboptimization cannot be avoided simply by the use of one form of financial statement or another, but the use of some types of financial statements that create the illusion of "bottom line responsibility" may have contributed to some undesirable trends in hotel-casino management.

Statistical Analysis

The impetus for the recording of statistical data in the casino originally was the Nevada laws that required detailed information regarding the gaming activity, including the financial performance of each of the various games and slot machines used in a casino.

The focus of the early statistical reports was on the aspect of control over the honesty of the gaming operation and, to a lesser degree, on assuring against any mechanical malfunction that might adversely affect the play of a slot machine. The controls over the games were oriented toward ensuring consistent performance in terms of win in relation to drop and that any fluctuations were thoroughly investigated and fully accounted for.

In recent years, the traditional controls over the slot operations and table games have evolved into larger-scale statistical data gathering and analysis. These projects soon became the base for managerial planning and control activities and replaced the traditional focus with a new concern for management performance and efficiency in operation. This has only been accomplished in the last few years when advances in data collection methods, database programs, and microcomputer technology allowed casinos to collect and analyze the data in an efficient manner for the first time.

The use of statistical analysis is a very new technique for casinos. The principal thrusts have occurred in two primary areas.

The first is the collection of aggregate statistics, which can be used to predict the estimated future performance of a casino. Examples of this type are:

1. Traffic counts of visitors to a city.
2. Airline passenger counts into and out of a city.
3. Visitor hotel room inventory.
4. Hotel occupancy statistics.
5. Average expenditures per visitor.

Most of the above information has been routinely collected by various governmental or community service agencies for a number of years. Significant new strides in understanding the business of casinos came from the analysis of these statistics. The statistics were not new, merely their use.

The initial step in the analysis was an attempt to determine if there were relationships between various gross indicators of economic activity and the financial and operating results of a particular casino. Eventually, it was found that certain indicators were very good at predicting hotel activity and that hotel reservations and occupancy rates were very good indicators of the activity that could be expected in the casino. Thus, staffing for the casino was related to the number of reservations in the hotel and the estimates of the hotel occupancy.

In some areas, there was a fairly close relationship between the amount of food and beverage sales and the gaming revenue. This relationship proved to be amazingly stable over time and over the various seasons of activity. Using this relationship, plans could be made for ordering of food and beverage supplies based on the estimated gaming activity, which in turn could be estimated by hotel occupancies. Many of the old-time casino managers asked, "What's new?"—and they were certainly correct: they had been using these intuitive rules for years. However, the decision rules and relationships were brought to light by the application of various concepts of statistical analysis by management accountants.

Another analysis that proved of some significance, although it did not have much predictive capacity, was the use of various traffic statistics to correlate with an individual casino activity. If the number of visitors to a city was high, then the casino was fairly sure—unless there was some problem or disruption—of having a high number of customers. If after-the-fact analysis indicated that the traffic was indeed high, yet the casino had only a modest level of activity, steps could be taken to find out the reasons for the deviation from the expected results and action could be taken before any problem was allowed to get out of hand.

Slot Control Systems Another application of statistical analysis is in the use of the raw data required for regulatory reporting of casino results linked to a more comprehensive program to evaluate performance of the various slot machines in the casino.

There are several computer-controlled slot machine systems in use in the casino industry today. They are briefly discussed in chapter 5. The key to their operation is the use of the data collected, either on a real-time basis by direct linkage from the slot machine to the computer, or on a batch basis, with the data entered from the manual meter readings into the computer. These data are then analyzed to determine if any significant deviations from the expected ratios of win (as determined by the mechanical or electronic setting of the machine) are occurring. This control information is presented in a formal report that indicates both significant winners and losers. Another use of the analysis is to segregate the slot machines by profitability, and to use this information in relation to the physical location and denomination of the slot machine to identify the most profitable locations within the casino for various types of machines. The use of this type of statistical analysis thus moves beyond the mere recording and presentation of data to become a dynamic tool for planning and controlling the slot activity.

Detailed performance reports allow the casino manager to develop performance conclusions on the effectiveness of specific games, of specific personnel, of various areas within the casino, of different time periods, and of specific advertising activities.

Traditional statistical evaluations have been used to determine the anticipated win of new games that are being introduced into a casino. Statistics are also used for control reports of existing games and slot machines where the odds are consistently in a predictable range. Other applications of statistics might be to verify the randomness of various games such as keno or bingo.

Limitations of Statistical Analysis There are three severe limitations of statistical analysis that must be recognized by managers. If these limitations are kept in mind, then the statistical results can be used with care. Without a knowledge of these limitations, the statistical results can be badly misused.

1. There must be a consistent definition of terms, units of measurement, and items that make up various data elements that are being analyzed. This applies across time and across units that are being compared. For example, the definition of game drop cannot be changed without resulting in the distortion of statistical analysis of the expected normal drop in a casino. In addition, if different definitions of a measure such as drop are used by two different casinos, their performance is not comparable, and statistical comparisons of the results of their operation should not be made.

2. The stability of the underlying process is assumed in all statistical analysis. If the process is changed or disturbed, then the accuracy of the statistical analysis and the conclusions drawn from it are in question. For example, if the payoff structure on a keno game is changed, the results in terms of win to the casino will change dramatically. Analyzing data on profitability before and after the change, without recognizing the underlying change in assumption, leads to invalid results.

3. The development of statistical measures has largely been limited to the explanation of past performance based on historically developed information. This can lead to three significant problems. The first is that care must be taken in making a general statement about the future performance of a gaming factor while relying solely on past data. The second problem is that the existence of a statistical relationship does not prove any causality of the factors; the lack of causality may mean that the analysis is treated with a "so-what?" attitude and has little significance in planning the future management activity in the casino.

Finally, there may be changes in the underlying factors that create the statistical results. For example, the introduction of large-denomination slot machines in the late 1970s was a major market shift that prior data could not have discovered. Thus, there can be significant changes in the underlying behavior that limit the applicability of the statistical conclusions or results.

Even with these significant limitations, the use of statistical analysis has led to an increased understanding within the casino of the interrelated nature of casino financial performance.

The Human Factor Statistical analysis is formidable and impressive, particularly to those with little or no formal education in the techniques. Good data results from analysis usually end with the confirmation of management practices that have been proven over the years by successful casino operations. However, good statistical results can often lead to bad judgment if various aspects of the human factor are not considered. An example of this type of factor occurred when a casino snack bar was eliminated due to its heavy financial losses (when determined by a department-by-department analysis of profitability). However, a factor not considered in the analysis was the impact that the drop in trade to the snack bar had on the play of closely adjacent casino tables and slot machines. During the first month of the discontinued snack bar operation, revenues in that section of the casino fell by 35% (even after consideration of the additional machines placed in the former snack bar floor space). The management reinstalled the snack bar and saw the casino revenues recover to exceed former levels. Clearly, the snack bar operation was tied in some obscure manner to the casino activity. People dropped in for a quick snack and left a few dollars on the tables or in the slot machines. This aspect—the so-called human factor—was not adequately considered in the first decision to close the snack bar.

Fixed and Variable Expense Analysis

Another aspect of managerial accounting in a casino is the pedestrian topic of cost analysis. This type of cost analysis focuses on two primary cost characteristics. The first is the division between the fixed and variable costs that are incurred in the casino. The second is the determination of the aspects of cost controllability at the hands of the casino management and the impact that these two factors together may have on casino profitability.

The discipline of having the responsible casino managers perform the analysis of categorizing all costs as fixed or variable usually is a major contribution to their understanding of the costs of operation. This in turn leads to an understanding of those areas where costs can be trimmed, controlled, or otherwise merely understood.

Most casinos have a very substantial amount of fixed overhead costs, and the understanding of the necessity of maximum utilization of the facilities leads the casino managers to be much more mindful of the volume of customers in the casino. They begin to understand why the off-season promotions are so important to build a level of activity necessary to cover the fixed costs of operations during those slow times.

The analysis of how casino costs change with volume of customers or other measures of activity is usually the first step. The second step is attempting to build a realization of the controllability of each of the costs, both fixed and variable. The issue of controllability of the costs usually leads to a greater concern for making additional fixed cost commitments. After study of cost behavior and cost controllability, casino managers invariably are much more conservative in requesting additional projects or improvements that tend to increase the fixed cost burden in the casino.

One cost analysis area that is unique to the casino business is the nature of labor costs. Labor in different areas can have vastly different behavior patterns. For example, labor cost in a keno game is largely a fixed cost, with a minimum of three or four persons required merely to keep the game open. This means that during periods of slow keno play, the game could actually be losing money. For the slot machine area, the minimum labor requirement is fairly low, and the costs of labor change in fairly direct proportion to the total number of customers playing the machines and the volume of business. For table games, the labor costs are really semivariable, due to physical arrangement of the table games, with one dealer playing against anywhere from one to seven customers on a table. Given the work rules, once a dealer has begun a shift, the costs of labor are fixed for that shift since the dealer has to be paid for a minimum of half a shift, and the decision to open a table in the casino requires making a minimum fixed cost commitment for a short duration.

Cost controllability is a key area where casino managers may not be able to make too many decisions involving fixed costs on a short-term basis, but their increasing sensitivity to the costs results in some overall reductions over the longer period. Thus, costs of support personnel in the casino cage, which are largely fixed, are trimmed to a bare minimum during periods of slow activity.

Rational Cost Control   Again, as in the case of many businesses, the cost control concepts must have a rational limit. The costs in a casino can be minimized to the point where the customers are faced with degradation of service and, in a service industry such as a casino, will undoubtedly express their dissatisfaction by taking their business elsewhere. Thus, cost control must be balanced with the need to provide adequate levels of customer service. The perception of what constitutes an adequate level of service must be a top-level decision made by casino executives who have a clear understanding of the needs and desires of their customers. For example, Caesars Palace cannot expect to have staffing levels like the Nevada Club, since each casino has its own style and intensity of service to customers.

Budget Planning and Forecasting

One of the key contributions of managerial accounting to the casino industry in the past ten years has been the increasingly widespread use of budgets and budgeting techniques in all areas of the casino. The use of these budgets has led to a deeper understanding of the factors that drive the casino industry, the ways in which revenues are earned, and the manner in which all of the costs are incurred.

Compared to other businesses of equivalent size, the use of budgets is still very limited in the casino business. However, the increasing number of large, corporate-owned and -operated casinos has resulted in increasingly formal financial evaluations. An effective budgeting system is an integral part of that process of financial evaluation.

The use of financial budgeting in casinos has a significant behavioral impact on management. There are several important dimensions. First, the operating personnel ideally are involved in the analysis and preparation and finally become responsible for the implementation of the budget. In this way, they are sensitive to the operating problems and the cost structure of their departments. This process alone is a major benefit to the casino operation. Second, the involvement of the operating personnel in the budget cycle adds to their dedication to achieving the results that were planned. There tend to be fewer excuses made and a higher level of commitment to making the plan work.

Casino Budgets

In a 1980 survey of Las Vegas casinos, it was found that 20 of a group of 28 large casinos actually did some form of financial budgeting.[4] The survey reported on the budgetary procedures for those 20 casinos. It is significant to note that slightly less than one-third of the largest casinos did not do any budgeting during this period. Also, the period under survey, 1978–1980, was a time of significant operating problems for the Las Vegas casino industry as a result of national economic downturns as well as competition from the newly opened New Jersey casinos.

Budget Organization   Most of the casinos budgeted according to the main operating departments and divisions within their operation. For a hotel-casino, the budgeting process included all the support functions, such as food and beverage and rooms departments, in addition to the traditional casino areas.

Within the casino department, the principal budget division was the pit games, with subdivisions for different games, such as 21, craps, baccarat, and roulette. The second division was the slot department, where all slot machine operations are budgeted. A customary third division involved the so-called side games, which typically include keno, bingo, and card rooms. Following these principal casino departments, the budgets were organized to report the costs of the support departments, including the casino cage, credit, vault, and count rooms. Other miscellaneous casino revenue functions were usually included only under a minor miscellaneous department category.

Budget Development Guidelines   The casinos surveyed varied widely in the degree of budget development and the apparent effectiveness of those budgets. The overall budget procedures tended to be poorly defined, and only a few of the casinos had detailed budget manuals. The absence of clearly defined guidelines for budget development resulted in poor coordination during the budget preparation process.

The budgets were developed and organized according to each individual department or profit center as described above. The apparent degree of integration was not very high. The budget documents were typically prepared for an annual operating cycle, and only one casino prepared a budget that included a longer-range portion covering more than one year. The budgeting process typically occurred during the 3–5-month period immediately preceding the fiscal year for which the budget was prepared. There did not appear to be any circumstances where a rolling budget horizon was used for the budgeted casino operations.

The budget organization process was most frequently a bottom-up process, with department heads contributing the key budget figures. In other cases, the budget process could be described as a mixture, with some figures being assigned by the top management, controller, or financial vice-president, and other budget items coming from various department heads. The budgets seemed to have a fairly high level of involvement, sufficient to assure that they would be accepted by the operating personnel.

In approximately one-half of the casinos studied, the budget, once set, tended to become static, with no deviations from the stated objectives allowed. The remaining casinos made frequent alterations to the budget on a monthly or quarterly basis to reflect changes. This budget update process resulted in considerably more effort, but the identification of budgetary variances was more accurate and tended to result in better acceptance of the budgetary information.

The budget development cycle has the following key components:

1. Historical data for each department's revenues and costs are prepared by the accounting department.

2. Significant plans and goals for the budget year are set by the executive management and communicated to department heads in budget planning meetings.

3. The initial budgets are prepared by the operating departments. This step may involve more than one repetition, since the various factors with an impact on revenues and expenses are analyzed and decisions made regarding major operating items.

4. The budgets are reviewed by a budget committee or senior management personnel and with the general manager.

5. The budgets are refined, and, if required, changes are made in the goals, revenues, or expenses for the operating departments.

6. The budget is compiled by accounting, and final approval is given by the top-level management.

7. The budget system is updated in data processing, and the budget figures form the basis for the subsequent reporting system.

8. In each monthly reporting period, the actual to budget comparisons are reported on each department's operating statement.

9. Department managers follow up significant budget variances and take corrective action where necessary.

10. Information is collected for the next budget cycle.

The use of historical data for the budget preparation is occasionally cited as a weak point since this system tends to perpetuate inefficiencies of the past. However, it is crucial to have good historic data on which to plan the budget. Given the attention to financial detail that the gaming regulatory authorities have traditionally required, virtually all casinos have excellent databases from which to develop comprehensive management information. The only possible limitation of these data is that the most detailed reporting is in the area of revenues generated, and the overall quality of the cost or expense information is not as good as for revenues.

In addition to this historical information, the budget process should also include consideration of the major internal or external changes planned for the budget period: significant casino expansions, major new marketing efforts, or changes in the competitive environment or economic factors.

Other Budget Considerations   Another area of concern in the budget process is the degree of sophistication of the budget analysis and preparation process. In general, the process is quite simple. The information taken from the past is intuitively analyzed by the department manager and presented in the next budget. Some innovative changes have taken place, including the development of casino department performance standards, merely as a result of the department manager taking a close look at the costs in the department. Performance and budget standards are much more common in the area of food and beverage accounting where cost standards have been a part of management literature for a long time. In the area of casino operations, however, standards are emerging regarding service levels, number of personnel needed for a given level of activity, and the extent of other costs such as complimentaries, based on the number of persons in the casino and the level of wagering activity.

The quantitative tools used in budgeting can vary widely. One of the most productive is the use of regression analysis to develop an understanding, as previously discussed, of some of the interrelated costs or performance factors in the casino. Also, econometric forecasting techniques, such as time series analysis to predict aggregate levels of casino activity, are also helpful in guiding the overall direction of the casino budget.

Flexible budgets, which give consideration to changes in various fixed operating costs depending upon the overall volume of activity, can also be of considerable use in the casino budgeting process. The consideration of changes in business volume, particularly during periods of high or low activity, can help to make the budgeting process more realistic. It can also make the reporting of differences between the budget and the actual performance results more creditable to the responsible department.

Living with the Budget   An integral part of the success of any casino budgeting system is the ability of the reporting system to provide timely and accurate follow-up and comparison of the budgeted figures and the actual performance figures. The casino accounting system is set up to provide almost daily information on the revenue flows into the casino, and the typical casino can provide very good monthly information on the costs. It is important that the system have some method to report only the responsible costs to the department manager. For example, it is counterproductive to charge the casino pit with its share of the annual property and casualty insurance premium, thereby creating large budget differences, when the casino pit manager does not have any control over the timing, amount, or payment of that expense. Again, the use of contribution margin budget statements, as previously discussed, might be the most positive type of budgetary reporting system.

Beyond the accuracy and integrity of the reporting system, there must also be a commitment of top management to the use of the system and a program of follow-up of significant budget variances and, if necessary, investigation of the differences between the budget and actual figures.

Analysis of Variances

Another traditional managerial accounting technique that has considerable validity as an application in the casino industry is the analysis of variances in costs.

For the casino operation, the product is a service with virtually no material component, yet it has an extremely high labor and overhead cost component. For this reason, limited analysis of variance can be a productive tool for assuring proper management of a casino.

In the area of labor cost analysis, including the use of variance analysis, the principal focus should be on the cost and usage of the labor. Traditionally, the casino industry provides a fairly low level of direct compensation for the dealers and other casino personnel.

This low level of compensation is augmented by the tip earnings of the dealers. This structure has resulted in the focus of the management being primarily on minimum-wage employment or at least on wage levels substantially below comparable worth in other industries. The overall compensation to the employees is, however, roughly equivalent to employment in other industries. Thus, in most analytic circumstances, the labor rate variances tend to be very low or nonexistent. The primary reason for variation tends to be the usage of different amounts of labor than may have been originally anticipated.

In the area of overhead variances, there are three major factors to consider. The first is the overriding importance of the consideration of varying levels of operation of the casino. This is particularly significant in places with wide seasonal fluctuations, such as Reno and Lake Tahoe. Here the levels of activity in the casino can swing as much as 60–80% between the high and low season. Analysis of what are largely fixed overhead costs in this environment cannot be done meaningfully without a flexible overhead budget. The second factor to consider is that there are often unforeseen circumstances that can disrupt the budget. The best example here is the impact that a big snowstorm that closes mountain roads has on the level of economic activity in Reno. Gaming virtually comes to a stop in Reno if Donner Pass is closed for more than a day or so. These events, although unplanned, have to be at least anticipated and included in some way in the consideration of changes in the level of activity. The third factor to consider in the analysis of the overhead variances is the very significant size of the overhead in a typical casino. The overhead expenses are a very close second to the labor expenses and must be understood and controlled very carefully.

Managerial Accounting and Consulting Activity

There are several areas of managerial accounting that form the basis for various consulting activities that individuals typically conduct for casinos. These consulting activities are briefly outlined below, with some examples of the application of various managerial accounting and analysis techniques.

New Casino Feasibility   An important consulting function is the examination of various plans of action for proposed new casino operations. Other activities include the preparation of financial projections when new stock is issued or when the purchase or sale of a casino occurs. These types of casino consulting activities involve several steps.

Financial Projections   Financial projections are based on the design of the casino, including some of the earliest spreadsheet models used on microcomputers. These financial projections involve preparing lists of key assumptions to be used, including the detailed discussion of the revenue assumptions used in the casinos, as well as a full and complete disclosure of the amounts of costs expected to be incurred. The comprehensiveness of this review is the key to achieving a reasonable result and, more importantly, a result that is creditable to the reader of the projection. In some circumstances, the process of financial projection discovers serious design faults in the casino or the supporting facilities and results in the physical redesign of the facility before completion. These financial projections also frequently find that the level of earnings anticipated for the casino would be insufficient to meet the anticipated debt service. In these circumstances, the casino project is terminated, largely based upon the strength of the financial projections.

The accounting technique used in these financial projections is quite simple and involves projecting forward the profit and loss statements of the casino. For situations where the casino is not currently being built, the projections usually use a contribution margin approach and specify, not the profit to be generated, but the amount of funds available to meet anticipated debt service needs or to meet other administrative and overhead costs. A second important distinction is that, with the exception of an expansion of an existing casino, the only projected financial statements that are prepared are profit and loss statements; projected balance sheets and statements of changes in financial position customarily are not prepared.

The format of the projected financial statement usually parallels the traditional departmental financial statements with separate schedules for each of the major operating departments. There usually is also a separate schedule for the general and administrative costs that are considered only a cost department for purposes of these projections.

Casino Systems Consulting   A second major area of casino consulting activity on the part of accountants has been in assistance with the design of various systems of internal control for the casino. Examples of these types of system design projects include a slot machine revenue reporting system; development of new cage and vault accounting procedures, documents, and systems, including providing documentation of the procedures; design and implementation of new marker control systems for a casino; and, perhaps the most important, the development of internal control documentation for new casinos in accordance with the various regulatory requirements.

Accountants and consultants are often called upon to perform these system consulting activities for several reasons. The first and most important is that they may have experience in another casino with a similar problem, and this knowledge can be easily and cost-effectively transferred to the new consulting engagement. Second, the accountants' experience in the areas of financial controls is probably second to none, and the casino is buying the best experience available in the design of internal control systems.

Finally, by employing the accountant or firm that eventually may be required to issue an opinion on the adequacy of the system of internal control, the casino is placing the responsibility squarely on the shoulders of the accountants. The accountants will design the best possible system because they will take a considerable degree of responsibility for the same system in later annual financial audits.

Notes

Chapter 1

1. For an excellent discussion of the historical development of gambling, see Alan Wykes, *The Complete Illustrated Guide to Gambling* (London: Aldus Books Limited, 1964), especially chapter 2, "Gambling through the Ages." See also Henry Chafetz, *Play the Devil, A History of Gambling in the United States, 1592 to 1955* (New York: Clarkson N. Porter, Inc., 1960), p. 3.

2. Arline Fisher, "Power and Magic," in *Nevada Magazine* 41/2 (March/April 1981): 34.

3. Wykes, *Complete Illustrated Guide to Gambling*, p. 152.

4. As discussed by William R. Eadington, "The Evolution of Corporate Gambling in Nevada," Bureau of Business and Economic Research, Working Paper 80-20, University of Nevada, Reno, p. 35; and Wykes, *Complete Illustrated Guide to Gambling*, p. 27.

5. Wykes, *Complete Illustrated Guide to Gambling*, p. 41.

6. As described in John C. Deane, "Financing the Casino Gaming Industry" (thesis for Stonier Graduate School of Banking, American Bankers Association, Rutgers University, June 1978), pp. 8–10; and Wykes, *Complete Illustrated Guide to Gambling*, p. 44.

7. *Gambling in America: Final Report of Commission on the Review of the National Policy Toward Gambling* (Washington, D.C.: GPO, 1976), pp. 144–155.

8. Wykes, *Complete Illustrated Guide to Gambling*, appendix 2, "Gambling around the World," p. 330.

9. "1984, A Year of Peaks and Valleys in Gaming," *Gaming and Wagering Business* 6/5 (May 1985): 1.

10. Deane, "Financing the Casino Gaming Industry," p. 8.

11. Ibid., p. 9; and Gary L. Cunningham, "Chance, Culture and Compulsion, The Gambling Games of the Kansas Cattle Towns," *Nevada Historical Society Quarterly* 26/4 (Winter 1983): 255–271.

12. Deane, "Financing the Casino Gaming Industry," p. 9; and Wykes, *Complete Illustrated Guide to Gambling*, p. 299.

13. Caroline J. Hadley, "America's Doxy Grows Up," *Nevada Magazine* 41/2 (March/April 1981): 6.

14. Susan Horton, "The Party Begins," *Nevada Magazine* 41/2 (March/

April 1981): 90; and Ron Tillotson, "Just a Winnemucca Cowboy," *Nevada Magazine* 41/2 (March/April 1981): 87.

15. Thomas C. Wilson, "Nevada or Bust," *Nevada Magazine* 41/2 (March/April 1981): 109; and Sheila Caudle, "Turn of the Cards," *Nevada Magazine* 37/4 (October/November/December 1977): 13; and *Sierra Magazine* (September 1960): 19.

16. Leon Mandel, "Arrival in Gomorrah," *Nevada Magazine* 41/2 (March/April 1981): 36.

17. "City in Orbit," *Nevada Magazine* 41/2 (March/April 1981): 22.

18. State of Nevada, Employment Security Department, *Annual Report*, 1983; and discussions with Jay Cornmeyer, Manager of National Gaming Accounts, First Interstate Bank of Nevada.

19. State of New Jersey, Casino Control Act (P.L. 1977, c. 110).

20. "Atlantic City II—A Trend Analysis," *Gaming Business* 3/6 (August 1982): 4.

21. State of New Jersey, Casino Control Act, Article 6, specifies that in order for a casino to be considered for a license in Atlantic City, it must offer a minimum of 500 hotel rooms, 30,000 square feet of casino space, and 25,000 square feet of convention space.

22. Governor Robert List, "The State of Gaming," *Nevada Magazine* 41/2 (March/April 1981): 8.

23. "1984, A Year of Peaks and Valleys in Gaming," *Gaming and Wagering Business* 6/5 (May 1985): 1, indicated that the gross win for all Nevada casinos was $2,941.4 million dollars. This represented a 14.5% increase over fiscal 1983 operating results.

24. Thomas F. Cargill, "Is the Nevada Economy Recession Proof?" *Nevada Review of Business and Economics* 3 (Summer 1979): 9.

25. "Atlantic City II," *Gaming Business* 3/6 (August 1982): 4–7.

26. Information from published Annual Reports of Resorts International and Harrah's, 1977.

27. Information from the Nevada Gaming Control Board, *Gaming Abstract*, and Atlantic City Casino Association, "Fact Sheet."

28. "Jersey Shifts Emphasis on Casino Building," *Nevada State Journal* (May 10, 1979): 18.

29. "Casino Gambling Isn't a Game of Chance," *Fortune Magazine* (March 12, 1979): 132.

30. Gaming Control Board, State of Nevada, *Nevada Gaming Abstract*, 1984.

31. For an excellent discussion of the development of corporate gaming, see William R. Eadington, "The Evolution of Corporate Gambling in Nevada," *Nevada Review of Business and Economics* (Spring 1982): 19, as well as various discussions regarding Howard Hughes and his activities in Nevada. For example, see Guy Shipler, "The Shadow Emperor," *Nevada Magazine* 37/4 (April 1977): 4.

32. It is generally accepted that premium players more commonly frequent the Las Vegas Strip casinos and, to a lesser degree, South Lake Tahoe, Reno, and Downtown Las Vegas. A premium player is generally

regarded as a patron who gambles larger amounts of money on a consistent basis. Each casino has standards and guidelines for qualification as a "high roller." Average gambling patrons are called "grind" customers.

33. "Atlantic City II," *Gaming Business* 3/6 (August 1982): 4.

34. Virtually all major brokerage houses in New York City now have an individual responsible for tracking the casino industry as a viable investment segment. In addition, major conferences regarding the casino industry and financing are now held on a regular basis.

35. Deane, "Financing the Casino Gaming Industry," p. 102; and Malcolm S. Ercanbrack, "The Growth in the Reno Gaming Industry and Its Impact on Commercial Banks" (thesis, Pacific Coast Banking School, Western States Bankers Association, University of Washington, 1979).

36. John Scarne, *Scarne's Complete Guide to Gambling* (New York: Simon and Schuster, 1961), p. 223.

37. Eadington, "The Evolution of Corporate Gambling in Nevada," *Nevada Review of Business and Economics* (Spring 1982): 19. Eadington discusses in considerable detail the problems of the Las Vegas casinos during the early 1960s, including the widespread development of the perception of organized crime infiltration into casino management.

38. "The Shy and the Mighty," *Nevada Magazine* 41/2 (March/April 1981): 38.

39. Stuart E. Curtis, "The History of Going Public in Nevada," *Gaming Business* 4/2 (February 1983): 30.

Chapter 2

1. Jerome H. Skolnick, *House of Cards* (Boston: Little, Brown & Co., 1978).

2. *Gambling in America*, p. 195.

3. Ibid., p. 199.

4. NRS Chapter 463.

5. NRS Chapter 463.390.

6. Guy Shipler, "How the White Hats Won the West," *Nevada Magazine* 41/2 (March/April 1981): 114; and Guy Shipler, "The Gaming Czar," *Nevada Magazine* 41/2 (March/April 1981): 115.

7. William R. Eadington and James S. Hattori, "A Legislative History of Gaming in Nevada," *Nevada Review of Business and Economics* (Spring 1978): 13–17.

8. Nevada Gaming Commission and State Gaming Control Board, "Gaming, Nevada Style," Carson City, Nevada, April 1984, p. 12.

9. Ibid., p. 12.

10. Ibid., p. 14.

11. Ibid., p. 13.

12. NRS 463.690 and Gaming Control Board Regulation 3.060.

13. Edward Olsen, as quoted in *Nevada State Journal* (August 28, 1981) and *Wall Street Journal* (January 9, 1980): 28, discussing Mr. Sinatra's reapplication for a gaming license in New Jersey and his application in Nevada, February 12, 1981.

14. Edward Olsen, "The Black Book Episode: An Exercise in Muscle," in Eleanor Bushnell (ed.), *Sagebrush and Neon* (Reno: University of Nevada Press, 1973), p. 21. See also NRS 463.151 et seq.

15. 86 Nevada 374 (1970).

16. 93 Nev 36 (1977) cert. denied 434 U.S. 803.

17. Civil No. LV 75-31BRT (Dist Ct. for District of Nevada, 1977); 96 Nev Adv. Op. 251 (1980).

18. *State of Nevada* v. *Glusman*, Nevada S. Ct. #12946; and *Glusman* v. *State of Nevada*, S. Ct. #13217.

19. *Nevada State Journal* (June 26, 1979) and *Wall Street Journal* (May 31, 1979): 3, which outline the temporary licensing status given to Caesars Boardwalk Regency Hotel. Also *Wall Street Journal* (April 10, 1980): 5, describing the temporary 5-month license extension for Bally's Park Place, Inc.

20. The ABSCAM problems were chronicled in both the national and local press in Nevada and New Jersey. For example, "Nevada View of ABSCAM," *Gaming Business* 1/3 (March 1980): 11.

21. *Wall Street Journal* (October 31, 1980): 31.

22. For a comparison of the gaming regulation procedures in New Jersey and Nevada, refer to a special report prepared by the State of Nevada, Gaming Control Board, "Report on New Jersey Gaming Controls," Carson City, Nevada, 1977.

23. "Gaming, Nevada Style," p. 17.

24. These duties and responsibilities are outlined in NRS 463.030–NRS 463.144.

25. NRS 463.160 and Gaming Control Board Regulation #3.

26. NRS 463.482 et seq.

27. NRS 463.165 and 463.530 and Regulations 3.020 and 15.3503 require the licensing of lenders if determined to be significant by the Gaming Control Board.

28. NRS 463.175 exempts national banks and trust companies from licensing requirements where they are lenders to casinos. Nevada's Gaming Control Board refused two financing packages, a savings and loan and a Texas bank, as not being acceptable unless they were licensed. Both declined licensing, and their financing was not allowed.

29. NRS 463A requires the licensing of employee labor organizations, while NRS 463B provides for the state to take over and administer a casino after revocation of the casino license.

Chapter 3

1. For a discussion of the taxation of casinos, and its impact on the economy of the state of Nevada, see William R. Eadington, "Economic Trends in Nevada's Casino Gaming Industry," *National Tax Association Proceedings*, 1978.

2. Gaming Control Board, State of Nevada, *Nevada Gaming Abstract*, 1985, pp. 1–45.

3. *Nevada State Journal* (October 10, 1979): 37.

4. Governor's Office, *Nevada Statistical Abstract, 1984* (Carson City, Nevada: State Printing Office, 1984), p. 98.

5. The gaming tax collections in New Jersey are specifically delegated to identified funds for redevelopment and control purposes and do not flow into the state general fund. Estimates prepared by the New Jersey Casino Control Commission indicate gaming tax revenues constitute only 4–5% of the state's general fund revenue.

6. Assembly Bill 134, 1981 Legislative Session.

7. See Gaming Control Board Regulation 6.080.

8. Senate Bill 320, 1981 Legislative Session, which amends NRS 463.0114 to broaden the meaning of "gross gaming revenue" to include poker rake-off.

9. Senate Bill 320 specifies seven criteria for disallowing the writeoff of markers: 1. if the marker is improperly executed; 2. if the licensee does not have the patron's address; 3. if the licensee has not made a reasonable effort to collect the marker; 4. if the licensee failed to check the patron's credit prior to granting credit; 5. if the licensee cannot produce the marker, with some identified exceptions; 6. if the signature is forged and the licensee has not made a report to the police; 7. if the licensee asks the Control Board not to confirm with the patron and there is no other way to confirm the debt.

10. NRS 463.375.

11. NRS 463.373.

12. For a definition of *entertainment status*, see Gaming Control Board Regulation 13.020.

13. NRS 463.660.

14. For an excellent discussion of the new casino reinvestment tax in New Jersey, see Nicholas Casiello, Jr., and Harry Levin, "The Last Word On: The Casino Reinvestment Act," *Gaming Business* 5/5 (May 1985): 50.

15. See, for example, the Nevada Society of CPAs, Report of the Accounting Principles Committee, Nevada Quarterly State Gaming License Fee, draft report, October 21, 1980.

Chapter 4

1. For a discussion of internal administrative controls, see *AICPA Professional Standards, Volume A* (New York: American Institute of Certified Public Accountants 1984), SAS #1, Sections 320.26–29.

2. A good working definition of *win* is the same as the statutory definition of *gross gaming revenue,* as contained in NRS 463.0114 and Gaming Control Board Regulation 6.080.

3. Excellent theoretical discussions of hold percentages appear in unpublished research papers by Gerald Stroup, "Determinants of Table Game Hold Percentage," and Shawn McGhie, "Hold Percentage on Table Games." Both papers describe a simplified model of computing table hold percentage based on buy-in, average bet, house advantage (true odds), hands per hour, and duration of play. The importance of casino profitability based on hands per hour has been recognized by various experiments

aimed at speeding up the pace of play. See, for example, University of Nevada, Las Vegas, College of Hotel Administration and Department of Mathematics, "Casino Card Shuffling Report," 1975.

4. Bill Friedman, *Casino Management* (Secaucus, N.J.: Lyle Stuart, 1974), p. 16.

Chapter 5

1. Private conversation with Bally Manufacturing, Reno, Nevada.

2. The use of privately minted tokens is allowed under NRS 463.080 and Gaming Control Board Regulation 12.

3. All slot machines manufactured after 1965 and in use in Nevada casinos must have in and out meters installed.

4. Nevada Gaming Control Board, *1984 Gaming Abstract Supplement*, Carson City, Nevada.

5. Friedman, *Casino Management*, pp. 233–234.

6. For a discussion of various slot machine marketing strategies, see Gary Selesner, "Slot Machines Undergoing a Metamorphosis, Part I," and "Slot Strategies in the Casino, Part II," *Gaming Business* 1/3 (March/April 1980).

7. Mary Jurica, "Buy the Slot Machines the Public Wants to Play," *Gaming Business* 2/3 (March 1981): 22.

8. See, for example, William R. Eadington, "The Economics of Gambling Behavior," Bureau of Business and Economic Research, University of Nevada, Reno, 1973, for a detailed discussion of the various social and economic motives for casino games. Robert Herman, "Gambling as Work, A Sociological Study of the Race Track," in Herman (ed), *Gambling* (New York: Harper and Row, 1967), explains that small, frequent rewards tend to be preferred by some types of gaming patrons.

9. This requirement is spelled out in Gaming Control Board Regulation 5.012.

10. Basic minimum accounting and control procedures over the slot drop processes are contained in NRS 463.156 to 463.1594 and Gaming Control Board Regulation 6.230.

11. "Nevada Gaming Officials Say Millions Vanished from Argent's Slots," *Wall Street Journal* (September 10, 1979): 1.

12. For a complete description of this type of slot machine arrangement, see John R. Mills, "Innovations in the Gaming Industry: The Case of 'Megabucks,'" *Nevada Review of Business and Economics* 10/3 (Fall 1986).

13. Examples of slot machine management and reporting systems include Slot Machine Management and Maintenance System (SMMS) by Kafoury, Armstrong & Co., Reno, Nevada; Slot Data System (SDS) by Bally Manufacturing, Chicago, Illinois; and Dacom 1000 Slot Analysis System by Aristocrat, Inc., Reno, Nevada.

Chapter 6

1. For example, see Brian G. McNiven, "The World's Best New Casino Games," Sydney, Australia, undated.

2. The procedure for new game licensing in Nevada is outlined in Gaming Control Board Regulation 14.070.

3. Scarne, *Scarne's Complete Guide to Gambling*.

4. See Gaming Control Board Regulation 6.010.

Chapter 7

1. The dramatic growth of the sports book segment of the casino industry is discussed in "1984, A Year of Peaks and Valleys in Gaming," *Gaming and Wagering Business* 6/5 (May 1985): 1, as well as in the 1984 and 1985 *Nevada Gaming Abstract*.

2. For an excellent discussion of the game of keno, see Scarne, *Scarne's Complete Guide to Gambling*, chapter 17, p. 432.

3. Mark Sampson, "Costing a Keno Game" (unpublished research paper, University of Nevada, Reno).

4. According to John Scarne (*Scarne's Complete Guide to Gambling*, p. 182), bingo is a $2-billion-a-year national "pastime," expressed in 1960 dollars!

5. Mandatory regulatory rules for the control of card room accounting and operations are found in Gaming Control Board Regulation #23.

6. Gaming Control Board Regulation #2 covers the operations of race books, sports pools, and other wire-service-oriented businesses. Regulation #26 covers the operation of pari-mutuel wagering, while Regulation #27 covers games such as jai alai.

7. Kirk Gardner, "Procedures of a Race and Sports Book" (unpublished research paper, University of Nevada, Reno).

Chapter 8

1. A general presentation of casino accounting, including a summary of the counting procedures, is found in Virginia Bakay and Steven Michel, "Jackpot," *Management Accounting* (May 1984): 27.

2. "Nevada Gaming Officials Say Millions Vanished from Argent's Slots," *Wall Street Journal* (September 10, 1979): 1.

Chapter 9

1. Mandatory requirements for the accounting and handling of casino markers are contained in Gaming Control Board Regulations 6.220 and NRS 463.156. Mandatory New Jersey rules are found in New Jersey Regulations 19:45.24–28.

2. An excellent discussion of credit evaluation is presented in Friedman, *Casino Management*, chapters 4–7.

3. New Jersey Regulation 19:45.27 spells out the hold periods for various instruments, depending upon their form and amount. The maximum hold period is 90 banking days for counter checks of $2,500 or more.

4. For a description of the role of casino hosts in credit granting, see "Gambler's Pals—Casino Hosts Pamper High Rolling Bettors to Keep Them Rolling," *Wall Street Journal* (September 3, 1980): 1.

5. For a discussion of special problems related to junkets, see Paul Blu-

stein, "For a Special Breed of Recruiter: Cultivating Casino's High Rollers," *Wall Street Journal* (December 8, 1980): 31; also Debra J. Hancock, "The Accounting and Controlling of Junket Transactions" (unpublished research paper, University of Nevada, Reno).

Chapter 10

1. *Auditing and Accounting Guide—Audits of Casinos* (New York: American Institute of Certified Public Accountants, 1984).

2. The bulk of the mandatory audit and financial reporting requirements under regulatory law are found in NRS 463.156 and Gaming Control Board Regulation #6. New Jersey requirements are found in New Jersey Regulations 19:45.6–7.

3. Gary Royer, "The Audit Function of the Gaming Control Board," presentation to the State Bar of Nevada, First Annual Gaming Seminar, February 28, 1980, p. 17.

4. NRS 463.159 and New Jersey Regulation 19:45.6.

5. The Foreign and Corrupt Practices Act amends the Securities Exchange Act of 1933, and its requirements are enforced by the SEC, together with other accounting, auditing, and financial reporting requirements.

6. *Auditing and Accounting Guide—Audits of Casinos*, p. 19.

7. *AICPA Professional Standards, Volume A—Auditing Standards,* Section AU 509.45–47, regarding opinion qualifications due to scope limitations.

8. Gaming Control Board Regulation 6.030 and New Jersey Regulation 19:45.6.

9. Gaming Control Board Regulation 6.050 and New Jersey Regulation 19:45.7.

10. Gaming Control Board Regulation 6.040-4.

11. New Jersey Regulation 19:45.7(e).

12. Gaming Control Board Regulation 6.040-4.

13. Gaming Control Board Regulation 6.040-4 and New Jersey Regulation 19:45.7(h).

14. Gaming Control Board Regulation 6.050-1a.

15. *Internal Control for Casinos: Report of a Study* (Reno: Nevada Society of Certified Public Accountants, Gaming Industry Committee, 1972).

16. The accounting firm of Arthur Young & Co. has developed an evaluation questionnaire for New Jersey Internal Control compliance evaluations: *Casino Internal Control Questionnaire, Regulation 19:45, Volume III* (Philadelphia: Arthur Young & Co., 1979).

17. *AICPA Professional Standards, Statement of Auditing Standards #23, Analytic Review Procedures* (New York: AICPA, 1976).

18. Chapter 5 of the *Auditing and Accounting Guide—Audits of Casinos* describes some of the suggested analytic review procedures that should be followed in a casino audit engagement.

19. Ned Day, "Nevada Gambling Debts, To Collect or Not to Collect," *Gaming Business* 1/3 (March 1980): 4; also Larry D. Strate, "The Double-Edged Sword of the Statute of Anne in Nevada—Where Do the Casinos Stand?" (unpublished research paper, University of Nevada, Las Vegas).

20. For an excellent discussion of the accounting issues surrounding progressive slot machines, see B. J. Fuller, "Money in Progressive Slot Machines: Revenue or Liability," *Nevada Review of Business and Economics* (Spring 1979): 23.

21. Some of the research relating to complimentaries is presented in Kafoury, Armstrong & Co., "A Position Report on Accounting for Complimentary Services" (unpublished memorandum, Reno, Nevada, 1981).

22. Arthur Young & Co., "Compilation of Casino Financial Accounting Disclosures" (unpublished memorandum, Philadelphia, 1980).

Chapter 11

1. The material in this chapter is based on E. Malcolm Greenlees, "Income Taxation of Casino Operations," *Public Gaming* (October 1981): 39.

2. Larry D. Strate, "The Double-Edged Sword of the Statute of Anne in Nevada," p. 1.

3. Day, "Nevada Gambling Debts," p. 4; and "The House Always Wins in Taxing Matters," *Forbes Magazine* (July 5, 1982), p. 155.

4. "Controversy over Gambling Markers in Court," *Nevada State Journal* (March 21, 1980), discussing *Summa Corp (dba) Desert Inn* v. *Nevada Gaming Commission*, 8th District of Nevada, December 29, 1980.

5. "Accrual of Gambling Debts under Internal Revenue Code Section 451," *Michigan Law Review* 80/2 (December 1981): 334–349.

6. Nevada Gaming Control Board Regulation 6.220 and New Jersey Regulation 19:45 (28)(h).

7. Fuller, "Money in Progressive Slot Machines: Revenue or Liability," *Nevada Review of Business and Economics* (Spring 1979): 23.

Chapter 12

1. Conversation with Donald E. McGhie, CPA, Kafoury, Armstrong & Co., Reno, Nevada.

2. James H. Bullock and Virginia H. Bakay, "How Las Vegas Casinos Budget," *Management Accounting* (July 1980): 35.

3. For examples of applications of cost and managerial accounting in noncasino areas of hotels, see Clifford T. Fay, Jr., Richard C. Rhoads, and Robert L. Rosenblatt, *Accounting for the Hospitality Service Industries* (2nd ed.; Dubuque, Iowa: Wm. C. Brown Company, 1971).

4. Bullock and Bakay, "How Las Vegas Casinos Budget," p. 35.

♠ ♡ ♣ ◇

Selected Bibliography

AICPA. *Auditing and Accounting Guide—Audits of Casinos.* New York: American Institute of Certified Public Accountants, 1984.

———. *AICPA Professional Standards, Statement of Auditing Standards #23, Analytic Review Procedures* New York: American Institute of Certified Public Accountants, 1976.

———. *AICPA Professional Standards, Volume A* New York: American Institute of Certified Public Accountants, 1984

Arthur Young & Co. "Compilation of Casino Financial Accounting Disclosures." Unpublished memorandum, Philadelphia, 1980.

"Atlantic City II—A Trend Analysis." *Gaming Business* 3/6 (August 1982).

Bakay, Virginia, and Steven Michel. "Jackpot." *Management Accounting* (May 1984).

Bullock, James H., and Virginia H. Bakay. "How Las Vegas Casinos Budget." *Management Accounting* (July 1980).

Cargill, Thomas F. "Is the Nevada Economy Recession Proof?" *Nevada Review of Business and Economics* 3 (Summer 1979).

Casiello, Nicholas Jr., and Harry Levin. "The Last Word On: The Casino Reinvestment Act." *Gaming Business* 5/5 (May 1985).

Caudle, Sheila. "Turn of the Cards." *Nevada Magazine* 41/2 (March/April 1981).

Chafetz, Harry. *Play the Devil, A History of Gambling in the United States, 1592 to 1955.* New York: Clarkson N. Porter, Inc., 1960.

Cunningham, Gary L. "Chance, Culture and Compulsion, The Gambling Games of the Kansas Cattle Towns." *Nevada Historical Society Quarterly* 26/4 (Winter 1983).

Curtis, Stuart E. "The History of Going Public in Nevada." *Gaming Business* 4/2 (February 1983).

Day, Ned. "Nevada Gambling Debts, To Collect or Not to Collect." *Gambling Business* 1/3 (March 1980).

Deane, John C. "Financing the Casino Gaming Industry." Thesis for Stonier Graduate School of Banking, American Bankers Association, Rutgers University, June 1978.

Eadington, William R. "The Evolution of Corporate Gambling in Nevada." *Nevada Review of Business and Economics* (Spring 1982).

———. "Economic Trends in Nevada's Casino Gaming Industry." *National Tax Association Proceedings,* 1978.

————. "The Economics of Gambling Behavior." Bureau of Business and Economic Research, University of Nevada, Reno, 1973.

————, and James S. Hattori. "A Legislative History of Gaming in Nevada." *Nevada Review of Business and Economics* (Spring 1978).

Ercanbrack, Malcolm S. "The Growth in the Reno Gaming Industry and Its Impact on Commercial Banks." Thesis, Pacific Coast Banking School, Western States Bankers Association, University of Washington, 1979.

Fay, Clifford T. Jr., Richard C. Rhoads, and Robert L. Rosenblatt. *Accounting for the Hospitality Service Industries* 2nd ed.; Dubuque, Iowa: Wm. C. Brown Company, 1971.

Fisher, Arline. "Power and Magic." *Nevada Magazine* 41/2 (March/April 1981).

Friedman, Bill. *Casino Management*. Secaucus, N.J.: Lyle Stuart, 1974.

Fuller, B. J. "Money in Progressive Slot Machines: Revenue or Liability." *Nevada Review of Business and Economics* (Spring 1979).

Gardner, Kirk. "Procedures of a Race and Sports Book." Unpublished research paper, University of Nevada, Reno.

Governor's Office. *Nevada Statistical Abstract, 1984*. Carson City: State Printing Office, 1984.

Greenlees, E. Malcolm. "Income Taxation of Casino Operations." *Public Gaming* (October 1981).

Hadley, Caroline J. "America's Doxy Grows Up." *Nevada Magazine* 41/2 (March/April 1981).

Hancock, Debra J. "The Accounting and Controlling of Junket Transactions. Unpublished research paper, University of Nevada, Reno.

Herman, Robert. "Gambling As Work, A Sociological Study of the Race Track." In Herman (ed.), *Gambling*. New York: Harper and Row, 1967.

Horton, Susan. "The Party Begins." *Nevada Magazine* 41/2 (March/April 1981).

Jurica, Mary. "Buy the Slot Machines the Public Wants to Play." *Gaming Business* 2/3 (March 1981).

Kafoury, Armstrong & Co. "A Position Report on Accounting for Complimentary Services." Unpublished memorandum, Reno, Nev., 1981.

List, Robert. "The State of Gaming." *Nevada Magazine* 41/2 (March/April 1981).

Mandel, Leon. "Arrival in Gomorrah." *Nevada Magazine* 41/2 (March/April 1981).

McGhie, Shawn. "Hold Percentage on Table Games." Unpublished research paper.

Mills, John R. "Innovations in the Gaming Industry: The case of 'Megabucks'." *Nevada Review of Business and Economics* 10/3 (Fall 1986).

————. Employment Security Department. *Annual Report, 1983*. Carson City, Nev.

Nevada. *Nevada Revised Statutes*. Chapter 463, Licensing and Control of Gaming. Carson City, Nev.

————. *Regulations of the Nevada Gaming Commission and State Gaming Control Board.* Carson City, Nev.

Nevada Gaming Commission and State Gaming Control Board. "Gaming, Nevada Style." Carson City, Nev., April 1984.

Nevada Gaming Control Board. *Gaming Abstract.* Various years. Carson City, Nev.

————. "Report on New Jersey Gaming Controls." Carson City, Nev.

Nevada Society of CPAs. "Report of the Accounting Principles Committee, Nevada Quarterly State Gaming License Fee." Draft report, October 21, 1980.

"Nevada View of ABSCAM," *Gaming Business* 1/3 (March, 1980).

"1984, A Year of Peaks and Valleys in Gaming." *Gaming and Wagering Business* 6/5 (May 1985).

New Jersey. Casino Control Act (P.L. 1977, C. 110).

————. Gaming Regulations. Section 19:45.

Olsen, Edward. "The Black Book Episode: An Exercise in Muscle." In Eleanor Bushnell (ed.), *Sagebrush and Neon* Reno: University of Nevada, 1973.

Powell, Stephen. *A Gambling Bibliography.* University of Nevada, Las Vegas, Special Collections Department, 1972.

Sampson, Mark. "Costing a Keno Game." Unpublished research paper, University of Nevada, Reno.

Scarne, John. *Scarne's Complete Guide to Gambling.* New York: Simon and Schuster, 1961.

Selesner, Gary. "Slot Machines Undergoing a Metamorphosis, Part I." *Gaming Business* 1/3 (March 1980).

Shipler, Guy. "The Shadow Emperor." *Nevada Magazine* 37/4 (April 1977).

————. "The Gaming Czar." *Nevada Magazine* 41/2 (March/April 1981).

————. "How the White Hats Won the West." *Nevada Magazine* 41/2 (March/April 1981).

Skolnick, Jerome H. *House of Cards.* Boston: Little, Brown & Co., 1978.

Strate, Larry D. "The Double-Edged Sword of the Statute of Anne in Nevada—Where Do the Casinos Stand." Unpublished research paper, University of Nevada, Las Vegas.

Stroup, Gerald. "Determinants of Table Game Hold Percentage." Unpublished research paper.

Tillotson, Ron. "Just a Winnemucca Cowboy." *Nevada Magazine* 41/2 (March/April 1981).

U.S. Government Printing Office. *Gambling in America: Final Report of Commission on the Review of the National Policy Toward Gambling.* Washington, D.C., 1976.

University of Nevada, Las Vegas. College of Hotel Administration and Department of Mathematics. "Casino Card Shuffling Report." 1975.

Washoe County Library. *Gambling Bibliography, Chapter 7, Industry.* Reno, Nev., undated.

Wilson, Thomas C. "Nevada or Bust." *Nevada Magazine* 41/2 (March/April 1981).

Wykes, Alan. *The Complete Illustrated Guide to Gambling* London: Aldus Books Limited, 1964.

―――. "The Shy and the Mighty." *Nevada Magazine* 41/2 (March/April 1981).

―――. "Accrual of Gambling Debts under Internal Revenue Code Section 451." *Michigan Law Review* 80/2 (December 1981).

―――. "The House Always Wins in Taxing Matters." *Forbes Magazine* (July 5, 1982).

―――. "Slot Strategies in the Casino, Part II." *Gaming Business* 1/4 (April 1980).

―――. *Internal Controls for Casinos: Report of a Study* Reno: Nevada Society of Certified Public Accountants, Gaming Industry Committee, 1972.

―――. *Casino Internal Control Questionnaire, Regulation 19:45. Volume III.* Philadelphia: Arthur Young & Co., 1979.

―――. *Sierra Magazine* (September, 1960).

―――. "Casino Gambling Isn't a Game of Chance." *Fortune Magazine* (March 12, 1979).

―――. "City in Orbit." *Nevada Magazine* 41/2 (March/April 1981).

―――. *Proceedings of the National Conferences on Gambling and Risk Taking* Bureau of Business and Economic Research, University of Nevada, Reno. Six conferences have been held since 1972, and each conference has a compilation of abstracts of papers delivered.

―――. *Proceedings of the Laventhol and Horwath Conference on Gaming.* Philadelphia: Laventhol and Horwath. This national gaming business industry conference is held once a year.

―――. *Proceedings of Annual Gaming Conferences: Nevada CPA Society and the Nevada State Bar Association.* Reno: Nevada CPA Foundation for Education and Research. These conferences are held annually, with proceeding and workshop notes on technical subjects presented.

♠ ♡ ♣ ◇

Index